AL~~ONE~~

with

a

PC

Alan Bradley

SIGMA PRESS
Wilmslow, England

Typeset and Designed by Sigma Press

Cover Design by Design House, Marple Bridge.

First published in 1993
Sigma Press, 1 South Oak Lane, Wilmslow, Cheshire SK9 6AR, UK

First printed 1993

ISBN: 1-85058-323-4

British Library Cataloguing in Publication Data
A CIP catalogue record for this book is available from the British Library

Printed and Bound by
Manchester Free Press, Unit E3, Longford Trading Estate, Thomas Street, Stretford, Manchester M32 0JT. Telephone 061 864 4540

Acknowledgement of copyright names and trademarks

General disclaimer

Foreword

Small businesses are the seed-corn of the economy. From the acorn of the self-employed and the small company will grow the major employers and wealth generators of tomorrow.

The number of small businesses has grown by more than a third since 1979, and the self-employed now account for over 12 per cent of the workforce.

Too many small businesses are strangled by paper-work, red tape and bureaucracy. Government has pledged itself to reduce this burden, but the technological revolution which has swept the developed world means that personal computers are, almost literally, eating paper-work, and making manageable the problems of the modern office.

But personal computers are not only administrators, coping with the requests of others for information, they are a valuable tool in forward planning, in strategy development, and taking a business forward into the 21st century.

From factory floor to desk top, the computer has revolutionised our work environment and increased almost exponentially the productivity of our economy. I hope that this book will assist those who are perhaps, like me, slightly Luddite in their instincts, to understand the benefits and potential of the technological revolution.

Nicholas R Winterton MP

Preface

Small Businesses are in fashion, and supporting them is big business today. Junk mail from suppliers, advisers, and finance companies pours through the letter-box, and the bookstalls are full of business magazines and books.

But what if the small business is just you on your own? Does all that advice and information meet your needs? Of course your business is a small business; but it is one with characteristics and problems of its own. You are an expert in your own line. Now you must learn also to be bookkeeper, marketer, salesman, secretary, filing clerk, and telephone operator, not to mention manager and planner. And the amount of money you can play with is in scale with the size of the business. Every purchase – not least office equipment – must be looked at critically. So must every demand on your time.

Thus the spate of 'Small Business' publications seems to pass the one-person concern by. That was my experience when I set up on my own, as a technical consultant and writer, a few years ago. I bought books and journals in quantity, no doubt more than my turnover justified. But I looked in vain for advice on those matters where the needs of my one-man business differed from those of the 'typical' small business which all the writers were trying to help.

In these few years I've learnt a lot, the hard way. So, I suspect, have thousands of other sole traders and one-person limited companies. But how much time and precious cash we would have saved if there had been books on the market aimed directly at the one-person business! Surely it's high time the gap was filled. I am not qualified to write on finance, or accounting, or marketing – though I know a lot more about these than I did when I first went solo. But my career has made me very much aware of computers, and my one-man business would have been impossible without one. So I've written down what I would have liked to know about computing when I first went into business on my own, and what I believe others want to know. I hope it will help those who are now taking that exciting step themselves.

This book is intended mainly for those with no prior knowledge of computers. Its first aim is to help you to decide if a computer would be of value in your business, by describing some of the things it can do for you and the costs in money and time to set against this. In the next few chapters I run through the various types of software and hardware, to help you to make a choice. I do not describe specific products because these change so quickly, but I show you where to get advice and information.

Next I give you some advice on how to get your new system up and running. This is meant to help you arrange the various parts of the system in the way you want them, not to replace the instructions which you get with each separate part. In particular, it is not my purpose to explain how to use each piece of software. This is covered in detail both by the manuals which come with the software and by a wealth of books which cover much the same ground in a more readable way. These books and manuals add up to a lot of reading. If you haven't the time for that, Phil Croucher's 'Computing under Protest: the new user's PC book' (from the same publisher) will tell you enough about the popular software packages to get you started.

Finally I give you some advice on how to get help when you need it, and how to keep in touch with developments and to tell if and when you need to enhance your system.

You may decide to choose the hardware and software for yourself. More probably you will discuss your needs with a dealer or a consultant, or perhaps with a friend in a similar line of business. You will only get the best from any of these if you have prepared yourself by finding out what a personal computer and its software can do, and assessing the needs of your business in the light of the hardware and software that is available. When you have read this book you should be able to do that, and so help your dealer or consultant to help you.

Something of a mystique has grown up around computers. The businessman or woman may feel less at home with a computer than the youngster still at school. I do not assume that you have any knowledge of computers, and I hope to show that you need very little. If you learnt to drive a car you can certainly learn to drive a computer. Like a car or any other tool, the more familiar you are with your computer, the more it can do in your hands. But also, to take the metaphor further, carelessness can lead to disaster. The best precaution is to take good advice. I try to give it.

Many of the illustrations in this book are captured from the screen of my PC. For technical reasons, the proportions and details differ slightly from what I saw on my screen, and what you may see on yours. Where the image is one that was supplied by a software publisher, the copyright remains with that company. The software illustrated is a selection from the programs I happen to own, and does not necessarily represent the latest or best programs of each type.

Nicholas Winterton MP, whose support for small businesses is well known, has contributed a Foreword to this book. I am very grateful to him for doing so. I trust my readers will not read any political message into it; the Foreword, and the book, are completely non-political.

I have used a number of trade names in this book. I hereby acknowledge all the rights of the owners of these names. These include Microsoft Corporation ('MS-DOS' and 'Windows'); Digital Research Corporation ('DOS-Plus', 'DR-DOS' and 'Gem'); Apple Corporation ('Macintosh'); Wordstar International ('Wordstar'); Word Perfect UK Ltd. ('Word Perfect'); Buttonware Incorporated ('PC-File'); Arnor Ltd. ('Protext'); Tomorrow's Designs Ltd. ('Trees'); Sorcim Corporation ('Supercalc'); Grafox Ltd. ('Logistix'); GST Software Products Ltd. ('Timeworks' and 'Deskpress'); JP Software Inc. ('4-DOS'); Scandinavian PC Systems AB ('Readability'); Editor Software Pty. Ltd. ('Stylewriter'); Pedigree software ('Pedigree'); Connect Software Ltd. ('Money Manager'); Trius Inc. ('Draft Choice'); Zortech Ltd. ('Zortech C'); Mix Software Inc. ('Power C'); Executive Systems Inc. ('XTree'); Travelling Software Ltd. ('Laplink'); Amstrad Consumer Electronics plc.; Dan Technology Systems Ltd.; Ricoh Company Ltd.; Star Micronics Co. Ltd.; Oki Electric Industry Co. Ltd. ('Okimate'); and of course IBM Corporation, who own the trade names 'PS/2' and 'OS/2' and probably also 'PC', 'XT' and 'AT', although these have become general currency. To any firms that I have inadvertently left out of this list, my apologies and my assurance that nevertheless I do recognise their rights.

Alan Bradley

CONTENTS

Introduction

Why is the one-person business different?

If you look in any good bookshop you will find many books on running a small business. But very few of these are aimed at the one-person business. Does this matter? Is there any real difference between the firm consisting of a single person, and that with three, or six, or a dozen? I believe there is, and that is why I have written this book. Would you have picked it up unless you thought so too?

What, then, are the problems that we loners do not share with larger firms? First and foremost, each of us has to be a Jack-of-all-trades (or a Jill, of course). In a larger company, each person can specialise. One may deal with marketing, another with the financial side, others with the actual manufacture or service that is the company's reason for existence. Typing (or word processing) may be left to a secretary, accounting to a bookkeeper. It is different for us. We are all specialists in our own lines – plumbing, programming or psychoanalysis – but we still have to do **everything** that is needed to keep the business running. So we look for ways of doing each job that do not call for too much expertise, or training, or background knowledge. In other words, in all but one of our many functions we are non-experts, and likely to remain so. We need advice from people, or books, which recognise this.

The second problem is one of money. Of course, money is everyone's problem, but for us the scale is different. Where a larger company can afford to think in thousands of pounds for office equipment, we may have to think in hundreds. But we have to do much the same tasks as the larger business. If they need photocopiers, telephones, typewriters or word processors, so do we, although in our business they may be less intensively used. So, far more than the larger firm, we must make sure that we spend no more than we need on equipment. The larger firm can afford to play safe by buying the 'best' of everything. We aim to spend no more than we must.

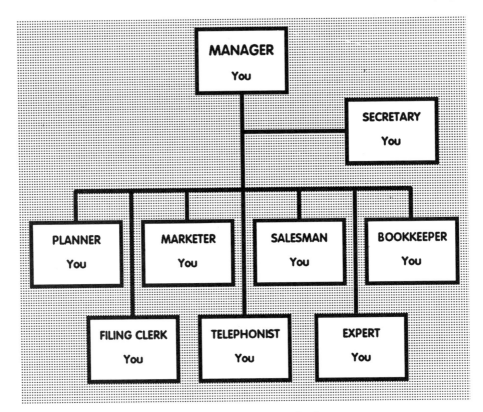

Figure 1.1 The one-person business.

The third problem is that of time. Everyone working alone finds that there are not enough hours in the day. Every hour that we spend working out accounts or writing letters is an hour lost from making widgets or cleaning windows or whatever. So we need a quick and simple way to do each task; one which concentrates on the problems we have in our own particular businesses. Larger firms have a wider range of problems: many of them we can happily ignore.

Yes, there are problems which the one-person business does not have. In particular, people problems. Small business books may have chapters on payroll and personnel management; we do not need them. We need not worry about how to make sure that one member of the company remembers to pass on information to another, or about the risk that one may use terms that another does not understand. We need not fear that someone will leave at short notice, so that a newcomer has to be trained to do the job. And there will be no arguments about how the company is to be run!

So although this book has much in common with the typical 'small business' book, its emphasis is different. It looks at many of the same problems, but from a different angle. It assumes that time, money, and experience are all limited, and shows how to choose and use a computer to make the least demand on these resources. That is, of course, if you need a computer at all. Computers can create problems as well as solve them, and I shall help you to decide whether you need a computer or whether the traditional way of doing things would suit your business better. I couldn't run my one-man business without a computer, but that doesn't mean that no one else can.

Why use a computer?

Benefits

How would you benefit from using a computer in your business? Only you can tell, because every business is different. But first you need to know what problems computers can solve, at what cost in time, money, and mental exercise. I hope that by the time you've read this book you will be ready to decide whether you need a computer. If you do, you should have a good idea about what sort of computer, and what sort of programs, will suit you best. I shall not recommend particular products or particular suppliers. I could never claim to have looked at all the contenders. Even if I had, the market changes so fast that my suggestions would be out of date before you read them. But I shall show you what features to look for, so that you yourself can make an informed choice. Of course, you may well decide to employ a consultant to recommend a system for you, or put yourself in the hands of a trustworthy dealer. You will be far more likely to get the best from either if you know what you can hope for, and what sort of system is likely to meet your needs.

The first benefit you will expect from a computer is a saving in time. A computer can add up your accounts and present you with a VAT account, or a balance sheet, in seconds whereas it might take you hours with pen and paper. But you must balance this against the extra time you will spend in setting the computer up for the job, and then entering data with the keyboard. So do not take it for granted that the overall time for a job will be less if you use a computer. If there is a lot of processing to be done, the computer will save you time. Jobs like arithmetic, or sorting and selecting, are more natural to a computer than to a human. On the other hand, some tasks involve very little processing – writing a letter, for example, where what comes out of the computer should be exactly what goes in. For such tasks, you may gain time only if there is repetition involved. For example, to write a letter to one customer by hand may well be quicker than typing it. But if you have to write a similar letter to fifty customers, changing only the name and address, then the computer can save you hours. You need to look at each task separately, but in general the computer will save you time on complex or repetitive tasks, while you can probably do the simple one-off job faster on your own.

Next, money. Your computer is going to cost you hundreds – possibly thousands – of pounds. But it will save money if you can do jobs, without spending too much time on them, that you would otherwise farm out to someone else. Typing is an obvious example. Authors used to hand-write their manuscripts, and pay (or persuade) someone to type them – often several successive drafts of each work. Now most writers use computers, as word processors. It saves us money, and it makes revision easier too. Another example is bookkeeping. This varies from one business to another, but many one-person firms pay a bookkeeper to keep their financial records in order because they have not the time to do it themselves, or because they lack the training they think is necessary. For businesses with simple finances like mine, this task becomes easy with the help of a computer – though I would certainly not want to be without guidance from my accountant. You may put work out to a printer when you want your publicity material to have a professional look. Maybe this is something you could do yourself with the aid of a computer. Or maybe not; you will need to look at each potential computer application in the light of your own needs.

A third way in which a computer may be worth money to you is in improving the image of your company. Whether image matters will depend on your line of business, but certainly a cleanly typed letter or report produced with the help of a word processor looks better than a typed one with as many corrections as typing like mine makes necessary. If you have to submit estimates or accounts, a computer will help you to achieve a neat and standard presentation. And for some kinds of paperwork, image can be taken further by using desktop publishing to enhance the work with varying type sizes and fonts.

Accuracy is something which is easier to achieve with a computer than by manual methods. Of course, computers can make spectacular mistakes. We all know of the friend-of-a-friend who had a gas bill for ten thousand pounds – or perhaps for zero. In fact computers very rarely make mistakes – their users do – but the point here is that these **are** spectacular mistakes, and easily recognised. The common sort of human error, like adding a column of figures incorrectly, or misplacing a decimal point, is less easy to find; and computers do not make that sort of mistake. Getting things right is important to your image, of course, but it can be much more important than that – whether you are designing a structure or just submitting a VAT return.

Costs

Against the benefits that a computer may bring you, you must set its costs in money and time. Some are obvious. Once you have decided what hardware and software you need, it is easy to find its price. But you must allow for other costs as well. You may need extra furniture, more power points; even more office space. You will certainly spend money on computer supplies, such as floppy disks and printer ribbons. And, in spite of what you may have read about the 'paperless office', the chances are that you will find yourself buying more paper than you expected. Computers do go wrong, unfortunately, so you will have to pay for servicing – either as and when required, or through a maintenance contract. You will want to insure your computer, and you may think it worthwhile to join a user group, and perhaps to subscribe to a computer magazine. And if it all gets too much for you, perhaps you will pay a consultant to choose your system for you, or to sort out some problem in its use.

The computer will demand some of your time, besides that spent in actually doing the jobs you bought it for. To start with, a few days choosing the machine and its software, buying it, and setting it up. Then you have to learn to use the system as a whole, and each individual program. You could put aside time to go on a training course, if you feel you learn faster that way than by sitting down with the computer and the instruction manual. All this is 'front-end' time – when you've done these things once you shouldn't need to repeat them, except for learning your way round any further programs that you buy. But the computer will also make continuing, if smaller, demands on your time. I shall have something to say later about the importance of backing-up data. Regular cleaning will be needed to keep your machine running smoothly, and there are other maintenance tasks we shall be looking at. And inevitably you will have to spend some of your time solving problems – finding why you have failed to get some result you wanted, or making arrangements to deal with a hardware failure. Perhaps this list is daunting: in fact it would be unusual if it added up to an hour a week. But it must be one of the factors in your decision for or against a computer.

Remember that, sooner or later, you will have to replace your computer. As with a car, you must allow for depreciation. In fact the computer itself is not likely to wear out (though keyboards, disk drives and printers may do). But the amount of computing power and memory that your money can buy is steadily increasing; and as it does, so does the amount that is needed to run the newer programs. So long as you are satisfied with the programs you started with, you can resist this pressure to upgrade. But probably, sooner or later, you will realise that there are more tasks that you could usefully put onto the computer, and at this point you may need a new computer to keep up. It is also likely, if you have a maintenance contract, that the cost will go up as the machine gets older. Eventually it may seem more attractive to upgrade than to soldier on. It is difficult to suggest how soon you will want to replace your machine, but accountants often suggest writing off the capital cost of a computer over four years. I had my first for five, and it would have been good for a few more – though I had spent some money on improvements. But there were things I wanted to do that really needed a more powerful machine, and it was that rather than age that led to the retirement of my old faithful.

Risks

Nearly everything you do in business involves some risk, and using a computer is no exception. However, common sense and reasonable attention to detail are all you need to keep the risks within reason.

The most serious risk for most businesses is that of losing data. If you make much use of a computer you may have vital information stored within it and nowhere else: your accounts, for example, or your customers' names and addresses, or the nearly complete text of your latest book. If you lose the lot, you may be in real trouble. In the worst case it could be the end of your business. Yes, it is perfectly possible to lose all your information in this way – easier than it would be if everything was on paper. But it's not difficult to manage your computer to make the risk very small. After all, banks are all computer-based these days, and no one would accuse them of taking risks without making sure that they were covered. (Or would they ...?)

The other big risk is that of a breakdown which leaves you without the use of the computer for a while. For some businesses, a few days without the computer matters very little. For many, your time may be less efficiently used, but the work still gets done. In other cases, however, the computer may be an essential part of your system and its failure may mean you let down customers and lose business for good. Again, if you plan for this eventuality you can overcome it; for example by keeping a spare machine, or arranging to use someone else's, or at worst by insuring against loss from this cause.

There are lesser risks; for example the possibility of damage or injury through some fault in the computer. With modern computers this risk is very small; common sense and insurance are the answers. See Chapter 8 for a discussion of radiation and other possible health risks.

So do you really need a computer?

I put the question to emphasise that not every business needs a computer. Your business is unique, and you are the only one who can make decisions about it. In the last few pages I have pointed out, in very general terms, the advantages and disadvantages of using a computer. In the rest of this book I shall put flesh onto those bones. As you read each chapter, consider how it relates to your own problems. When you reach the end of the book you should be ready to assess how much a computer could do for your own business, and whether the benefits justify the time and cost involved.

One point should be stressed. Don't suppose that, if your business gets in a muddle, a computer will sort it out for you. If you are the sort of person who can get in a mess without a computer, then you can certainly get into a much worse mess with one. Success with a computer does require a systematic approach. If your present approach is not systematic, sort it out first and **then** consider whether you need a computer. Quite a few people have sorted out their methods so that they could use a computer, and then found that this brought all the benefits they wanted – there was no need to go on and actually get a computer.

What kind of computer?

The title of this book begs the question – it is about the Personal Computer, not any other type. I make no apology for this. The number of one-person businesses that could benefit from any other type of computer must be very small, and their owners will know better than I do what it is that they need.

But we had better look more closely at the term 'Personal Computer'. What it really means is a computer which is designed for the use of a single person, without any provision for sharing its use with others, and this definition suits the purpose of this book very well. However, the term is usually used with a narrower meaning, limited to those computers which are compatible with the series of PCs introduced by IBM from about 1980 onwards. By compatible we mean that they will all run the same software, and can be used with the same peripheral devices – screens, printers, and other less common devices. Most one-person businesses will be best suited by such a machine, but there is one alternative which may be better for some types of business, and that is the Apple Macintosh range. The IBM PS/2 and Amstrad PCW machines also deserve mention.

The Macintosh (its friends always call it the 'Mac') was introduced at about the same time as the IBM PC, but in their earlier days the two machines were very different. The first vital difference is that IBM chose to make their design 'open', in the sense that competitors were free to make machines which were compatible with IBM's own and could run the same software. This policy succeeded beyond IBM's wildest dreams, in that the number of firms making IBM 'clones' now runs to several hundred, and IBM has a relatively small share of the business. We need not feel sorry for IBM. The PC has become far more popular than they had expected, so their share of the market represents a lot of business. However, the real significance of the open design policy is that it made this PC design the world standard, and the one which every software company found it profitable to support. The result is a vast choice of software for the IBM-clone user. In contrast, the Apple Macintosh is a closed system – no one but Apple is permitted to make machines of this design. In consequence there is no direct competition and these machines are more expensive than IBM clones of equivalent power. More important, the market for Apple-compatible software is relatively small and so such software is more expensive and scarcer. There is, of course, software for all the standard business operations, but if your requirements are less usual the Mac may not be able to meet them.

The other basic difference between the two approaches is that the Apple was a graphics-based machine from the start, while the IBM was initially character-based. While graphics facilities have since been added to the IBM design, the fact that they are something of an afterthought has obviously been a handicap. The significance of the difference between graphic and character-based designs will be discussed later, but the practical consequence is that Apple machines developed an early start in graphics-based applications, especially desktop publishing, and are still regarded by many as the best for such applications.

I shall not be saying much more about the Apple Macintosh, partly because I have never used one and partly because this is intended to be a book about

IBM-compatible PCs. However, I shall remind readers of its existence when I discuss those applications for which the Apple machine appears best suited. If you feel that a Macintosh might indeed be the best choice for you, you will find a number of books including a couple from the same publisher as this book (see Appendix 2). You would also be wise to talk to a few Mac users, most of whom seem to be very enthusiastic about their machines.

IBM's flagship range of personal computers goes under the name 'PS/2'. IBM's intention was that this should supersede the original PC family, but this seems not to be happening in practice. The PS/2 machines, except the smallest, can run a new operating system (see Chapter 3) called 'OS/2' which is, in many ways, an improvement over the established system MS-DOS. But it needs more powerful – and more expensive – hardware to run well, and there is relatively little software written that takes full advantage of OS/2. The PS/2 may have advantages for corporate users, but the one-person business will be better off with the 'standard' PC.

A machine which has been used almost exclusively by one-person concerns is the Amstrad PCW. This has been sold primarily as a word processor, although in fact it is a general-purpose PC and so can be used for any of the usual PC applications, which are discussed in the next chapter. Its virtues are its very low price and the fact that it comes as a package complete with printer and word-processing software, so the new user can start work with the minimum of trouble. The chief drawback is that it is not compatible with the IBM design, and consequently little software exists for it; what software there is, apart from the excellent word processor, tends to be dated and rather slow. The nature of the design also means that the user can only use the printer supplied with it. For these reasons this machine is becoming less popular, though it is still on the market at the time of writing. It is a reasonable choice only for those who have no requirements beyond word processing and need a minimum cost machine.

How much do you need to know about computers?

In two words – not much. Modern schoolchildren become familiar with computers in a way which an older generation did not. But you don't have to be technically minded to make use of a computer. After all, you can drive a car without knowing what goes on under the bonnet; and if you started to worry about the dynamics of cycling, you'd probably fall off!

Modern computer programs are designed to be easy to use. They come with instruction manuals, often excellent though their sheer size can be off-putting. But there's no need to learn, or even read, everything that's in the manual. Nor are training courses essential, though some find them useful. It usually pays to work through the simple introductory exercises that you find in most manuals, and then just sit down and play with the program. Try various things you'd like to do with it. Look at the manual, or at the built-in 'help' advice, when you get stuck. In half an hour you'll be ready to do simple work, and you can learn how to use further features of the program as you need them.

This assumes that the system has already been made ready for use. A dealer will do this for you, if you want, and leave you all set up and ready to go. But even if you prefer to set up your own system, it is only a matter of following instructions. It is as well to know where to go if you do need help – to the dealer, perhaps, or a friend, or a user group or advice service. But you shouldn't need to depend on them. If you can drive a car, you can certainly drive a computer – it's a good deal less dangerous, and you can always stop to think!

I'm not suggesting that it's a bad thing to have some idea of what goes on inside your computer. Again, compare it with a car. If you know something about how a car works, you can drive it more economically and probably make it last longer. You will understand its limitations better, and if it does not do just what you want you can perhaps see why, and find a way round the problem. You will save money by doing minor maintenance work yourself. And you will be able to deal with minor breakdowns, and know who to call for major ones – the garage or the scrap merchant. It is much the same with computers. It is when things don't turn out as you expected that a little knowledge may help you to solve a problem, or see a way round it. Or you may spot a better way of doing your own particular task. But this isn't essential. A little reading and rather more practice will teach you all that you must know to make good use of a computer in your business.

Some computer jargon

Jargon has a bad reputation. Jargon users are suspected of trying to hide their meaning, or perhaps just conceal their own ignorance. One dictionary definition of jargon is 'gibberish'. But besides this meaning for the word, the dictionary gives 'words or expressions used by a particular group or profession'. And in this sense jargon is valuable, because it is a concise way of conveying a meaning between two people who are familiar with it. How much time a doctor would waste if he had to say 'the inner of the two bones extending from the knee to the ankle' every time, when his colleague would know just what he meant if he said 'tibia'. It's the same with computer jargon. Manuals could be written without it, but they would be so long-winded that by the time you reached the end of a sentence you would forget how it started. Using a few technical words makes the instructions far more concise. Once you're used to these words, you will wonder how you managed without them – provided, of course, that they are clearly explained when you first meet them. I shall use some computer jargon in this book, to save having to repeat long phrases many times. Some words will be explained as we come to them, but an introduction to some of the most common will be useful here.

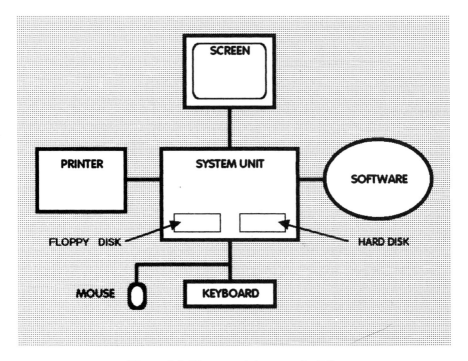

Figure 1.2 The essential parts of a PC.

I hope I don't need to explain what a **computer** is, but its two major components –
hardware and software – may be new to you. **Hardware** describes the physical part
of the computer itself, the part you can see and touch; the keyboard, screen, disk
drive, printer and so on, as well as things which are not actually part of the system
but associated with it, such as disks and printer ribbons. **Software** is the intangible
part of the system: the **programs** that tell the hardware how to carry out each
particular task. Software is information, in the most general sense of the word. Of
course software has to be carried on some physical medium. This could be a listing
held in the computer's memory, or displayed on the screen or printed on paper.
However, the form that will become familiar to all personal computer users is the
floppy disk (or **flexidisk**), a disk of flexible plastic with a magnetic coating on which
signals are recorded, much as music is recorded on the magnetic tape in an audio
cassette.

The term **personal computer**, or its abbreviation **PC**, will be very widely used. Until
the 1980s, most computers were large and expensive. These machines, called
mainframes, were fast and powerful, and therefore each of them served many users
so that it could be kept busy all the time. Only when technology advanced and
computers became smaller and much cheaper was it practicable for workers to have
their own individual computers, even though each machine would spend much of its
time idle. The world's biggest computer company, IBM, introduced the term

'Personal Computer', although it was not the first to put such a machine on the market. Most of the PCs now on sale are designed to be **IBM compatible** – that is, they will run programs written for the IBM PC. They are sometimes described as **IBM clones**. In fact the term 'PC' is very often understood to mean 'IBM compatible PC'. There are other PCs, but they are usually referred to by their own brand names. **'Workstation'** started as a general term which could apply to any PC, but is now used mainly to refer to more powerful machines than those I deal with in this book.

The **processor** is the heart of the PC. It is an insignificant-looking black box, about an inch square and a tenth of an inch thick, inside the system unit. This is the bit that actually does the computing. Everything else is concerned simply with storing information or with moving it to and from the outside world.

That part of the computer hardware which displays information on a screen is properly called a **visual display unit**, or **VDU**. However, the term **screen**, or sometimes **display**, is widely used for the whole unit.

The term **data** (the computer world treats the word as either singular or plural regardless of the rules of grammar) describes information of any kind that may be handled or stored by a computer. There is some ambiguity in the use of the term; sometimes it excludes programs, sometimes it includes them. The distinction can be difficult to make because, in some circumstances, a computer does not distinguish between the two. I shall usually use 'data' to exclude programs, and 'information' to cover both. Incidentally, note the spelling of the word 'program'. This spelling is due to American influence, but is nevertheless useful to distinguish a computer program from the more general use of the word.

The function of a computer is to process data, which implies altering it, rearranging it or combining it in some way. In doing this the computer has to **store** both data and programs. In fact they are stored in exactly the same way, and the computer's storage space may be divided at random between the two. There are of course ways in which the computer can distinguish between them. There are two forms of storage which concern us: disk and memory. **Disk** (spelt this way in the computer world, unlike the entertainment world) is a non-volatile form of storage; in other words, when information has been written it stays put until deliberately changed. The most familiar example is the floppy disk described above. Also important in computers is the **hard disk**. This is similar in principle to the floppy disk, but the magnetic coating is put on a hard (i.e. inflexible) substrate, usually of metal. A hard disk is normally embedded in the computer and cannot easily be removed. Hard disks can hold far more information than floppy disks, and can deliver it much faster.

The other essential form of storage is called **memory**, or occasionally 'main store'. It is built into the computer and made from the same sort of semiconductor devices as those which do the processing and control the computer. Memory is very much faster than disk, and so the programs and data in use at any moment are held in memory, being copied there from disk when they are needed. But memory is expensive in comparison to disk, and so the amount of memory in any PC is very limited. Also it is volatile, so any information stored in it is lost when the machine is switched off. So data is **saved**, or copied to the disk, when it has been processed. Programs need not be saved, because they are not altered when they are used and the original copy remains on the disk. A process similar to 'save' is **backup**, but here the data is copied from one disk to another; usually from a hard disk to a floppy disk. This is done as a safety precaution, so that if for any reason the original data is lost, it can be recovered from the backup copy.

The unit of data which you will most often meet is the **file**. This is a collection of data grouped for your convenience; it could represent for example a letter, a table, or a drawing. A file can be of any size (and there is no need for the user to know its size). Each file is identified by a **file name**, which is given by the user. Newcomers to computing sometimes find the idea of a file name difficult to grasp. Imagine that you put all your documents into identical envelopes. Rather than open all the envelopes when you wanted to find a document, you would write a title or brief description – perhaps a serial number – on the outside of each envelope. That is what the file name is. Of course you can call your files 'One', Two', 'Three' and so forth, but you will soon learn that it is easier to remember what they are if you give them meaningful names. You may have a very large number of files – I have over a thousand stored in my computer – so you need some system of **file management** to make sure you can find files easily when you want them. This is discussed in Chapter 8, 'Starting work'.

The term '**program**' is a little elastic. It describes, in general, the set of instructions which the computer follows to perform a specific task or set of tasks. Strictly speaking a program occupies a single file, but the term is often used of a group of files which contain a set of related programs and perhaps also instructions or examples of data. Such a group may alternatively be called an **application package**, or just an **application**. In fact certain groups of programs are not applications but **operating systems**; I shall explain the distinction in Chapter 3.

So much for software and data, for the time being. Returning to hardware, the term **peripheral** refers to any hardware which is part of the computer other than the 'processor' itself – i.e. everything but the main store and the electronics that does the actual processing. However, in the PC world the keyboard and screen are so closely associated with the processor that they are often not regarded as peripherals, and the same may apply to disk drives if they are mounted in the same boxes as the processor and store. But printers are definitely peripherals, and so are some other devices such as scanners and modems which we shall meet later.

Finally, **a mouse** is a device which you can use to control the position of a 'pointer', or marker, on the PC screen. It is a little plastic box with a ball in its base. This turns as you move the mouse about your desk, and its movement is measured and conveyed to the computer. The movement of the pointer on the screen corresponds to the movement of the mouse across your desk. A mouse is not essential – you can use the keyboard to move the pointer – but it makes many tasks easier. Nowadays a mouse is supplied with most PCs. For some reason the trade press does not like to repeat the word 'mouse' and often talks about 'furry little rodents' instead!

2

What a computer can do for you

The computer differs from most office equipment in that it is not designed for a single task, like a copier or a fax machine. Indeed, it is probably the most versatile device that exists other than the human body. Of course it has limitations, and the most important of these are to do with the way it communicates with the outside world. For most office applications this means the keyboard (and perhaps a mouse), the screen and a printer. In the office we use the computer for data processing. There are other uses for computers, most notably in 'process control'; for example, the largest chemical processing plants today are controlled by computers, and so at the other end of the scale are many domestic washing machines. However we are not concerned with these uses in this book; we want to see how a personal computer can help you to run your one-person business.

There are two areas in which you may find a computer useful. The first covers the general administrative tasks which are much the same for all businesses: correspondence, accounting, keeping track of lists of customers or stock or whatever. There is a wide choice of standard software packages for these tasks, and the first part of this chapter discusses what such packages can do for you. The second area covers tasks which are specific to your business. If you are a designer you will want to produce drawings; if you are a builder you will want software to help you produce quotations and plan the best use of your time and equipment; if you are a car mechanic you may want to use your computer to get information on spare parts. Because this field is so diverse I cannot cover every trade, but I shall give a general idea of what can be done. Finally, even a sole business person finishes the day's work some time, so I shall say just a little about leisure uses of the PC.

In this chapter I shall show what kind of tasks a computer can tackle, and what type of software you need for each. I shall discuss each type of software more fully in the chapters on 'Application Software'.

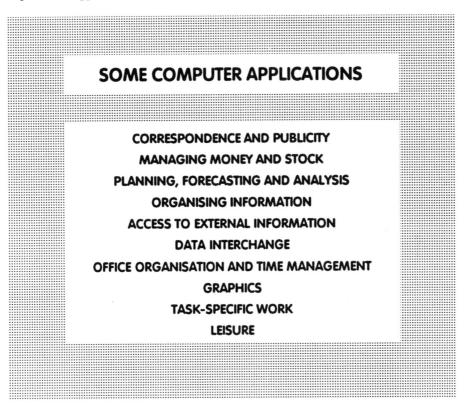

SOME COMPUTER APPLICATIONS

CORRESPONDENCE AND PUBLICITY
MANAGING MONEY AND STOCK
PLANNING, FORECASTING AND ANALYSIS
ORGANISING INFORMATION
ACCESS TO EXTERNAL INFORMATION
DATA INTERCHANGE
OFFICE ORGANISATION AND TIME MANAGEMENT
GRAPHICS
TASK-SPECIFIC WORK
LEISURE

Figure 2.1 Some tasks a computer may help you with.

Correspondence and publicity

Every business, however small, has to deal with correspondence, and this is probably the widest and most profitable use of the PC. Here we are using the machine as a **Word Processor**. A decade ago, computers were made which were designed for word processing and nothing else; they did the job very well, but of course lacked versatility. They have been superseded by standard PCs running software which gives them the same functions as the old dedicated word processor, and so 'Word Processor' now defines a piece of PC software rather than a complete machine.

The word processor is an alternative to the typewriter, though it can do many things that the typewriter cannot. The difference in principle is that a typewriter prints each character as soon as the corresponding key is pressed (although some modern machines will store one or two lines); the word processor does not print immediately, but instead displays the typed text on the PC screen and can also store it as a data file. This file is subsequently printed to paper as a separate operation, but also remains stored in the computer so that it can be used again and again. The virtue of this way of working is that you can type in your whole document and then check it on the screen, make any corrections you need, perhaps change the order of the paragraphs or insert a new one, and only print it to paper when you are sure it is right. You then have a 'clean' document with no evidence of the changes it has been through. Not only does this take the agony out of typing for those of us who hit the wrong key from time to time, it also makes it possible to think at the keyboard rather than copy-type from a draft, since it is easy to deal with afterthoughts.

Another virtue of the word processor is that it looks after the ends of the lines for you. You don't need to worry about whether a word will fit on the end of the line, or should be put at the beginning of the next one. You just go on typing regardless of the line length, and if a word will not fit on one line the computer moves the whole of it to the next line. This, together with the ability to correct and manipulate text, is in itself enough to make a computer worth while for many users; certainly, as a technical author, I could never go back to the old draft-and-copy-type methods.

The simplest word processors do little more than this, but most offer more features. One of the commonest is a spelling checker, which will detect many (though not all) of your typing errors. Another is 'mail merge', which allows you to produce 'personalised' letters by combining a basic letter with a list of features which vary from copy to copy; most obviously names and addresses, although you can do more than this, for example by varying the phrasing according to how long a bill has been unpaid.

You may want to produce paperwork which is more sophisticated than normal correspondence. For example you may need advertisements, price lists, or perhaps simple newsletters or journals, using 'display' typefaces or at least a wider range of type sizes and styles than you can get from a word processor. Traditionally you would have typed out the text and taken it to a printer, or possibly a graphic designer. However, you can do your own 'text enhancement' with a computer and a **Desktop Publisher** program. This may not necessarily be the answer to your problem; even if you have reasonable skill as a designer, the software and hardware needed are quite expensive and it may still be cheaper to take your work to a specialist. I shall discuss this in more detail later. Incidentally, the most sophisticated word processors will do many of the things that a desktop publisher will do – but with the same requirements for skill and money.

Managing money and stock

Money is another feature of every business. But while correspondence does not vary very much from one business to another, accounting methods do. At the one extreme, a technical author like myself may only have a few transactions a month, and need not be concerned with complications like VAT. At the other, a shop with a high turnover may make thousands of transactions a day, and a tradesman may have to manage invoices, discounts, part-payments and perhaps bad debts. There are **accounting programs** to suit both these cases and many more. However, far more than with word processing, it is vital that you choose the accounting method – whether manual or computerised – that suits your particular business. So I can only give limited advice; you should certainly discuss your needs with your accountant, and if necessary with a software consultant or a supplier who specialises in accounting.

Much the same applies to **stock control**, and here again there are packages to suit most needs. Some of them can be linked to your accounting package or are part of it. On the other hand, if your stock control requirements are simple you may not need a specialised (and therefore expensive) package; you may find that you can do the job with a database package of the kind discussed below under 'Organising information'.

Planning, forecasting and analysis

Planning ahead – especially budget planning – is important for many businesses, although formal planning may be difficult if you depend on unpredictable events (like getting a contract to write a book). Often planning is based on a 'worksheet', a chart on which for example you predict sales, material costs and labour costs for each month and then do repetitive calculations to see whether you are in line for cashflow problems, a reasonable profit, or whatever else the figures may predict. Of course the calculations may be a good deal more complicated than this. If you don't like the answer you may want to change some of the original figures and calculate it all again. This can be very tedious, and naturally enough the computer has been enlisted to help. The computer equivalent of the manual worksheet is the **Spreadsheet** program. Spreadsheets were among the first practical programs for the PC and were responsible for much of its early popularity, and there are many now on the market. In principle they are all much the same, although some have become very sophisticated; the calculations are not limited to the simple arithmetic operations but cover things like compound interest, discounted cash flow, and even more specialised matters. Nearly all these packages can also display figures from the spreadsheet in the form of graphs or pie charts, which can be a great help in understanding the significance of a mass of figures.

Spreadsheets are not limited to forecasts and to financial predictions. They are useful wherever data can usefully be calculated or analysed by repetitive calculations. For example, the computers used for weather forecasts are in effect calculating gigantic spreadsheets – although this is hardly a job that could be done on a PC!

Organising information

Many businesses need to keep a large amount of data of one sort or another, and to organise it in such a way that they can extract the information they want quickly and in a convenient form. This often involves sorting or selecting from the data, a job for which the computer is well suited. For example, in my days as a consultant I aimed to keep detailed data on all the computer peripherals on the market, within a certain class. Once I had fed this information into the computer, I could get instant answers to questions like 'list, in order of price, all the tape drives which will store 600 megabytes or more and fit into a 5.25 inch computer slot'. This would have been a long and tedious process by hand.

An organised collection of data like this is called a database, and the software which organises and gives access to it is called a **Database manager**. Here the manual equivalent is the card index, and where we are storing information with a regular structure we can imagine each card (or **record**, in computer jargon) as being pre-printed with a number of headings defining different items of information, or **fields**. For example, if each record represents one of the magnetic tape drives on the market, one field may hold the maker's name, another the type number, and others the price, size, storage capacity and so on. We have in effect a table of information. In this respect a database is very like a spreadsheet. The difference is in the facilities provided for relating items of data and producing the 'reports' which give you the information you want to extract from the database. However, there is indeed a good deal of overlap between the two types of software; many spreadsheets can carry out the simpler functions of a database manager, and some database managers can do much of what a spreadsheet can. Possibly in a few years the distinction will disappear.

Although most databases are designed to handle well-structured data, and in particular expect the data in each field to have a fixed maximum length, there are also **free-text database managers** which, as the name implies, can handle text which is not limited in this way; for example, abstracts from scientific publications. Often there will also be fixed-length fields as well, in this case to store the author's name and the source and date. Data is located in the free-form fields by asking the program to find particular words or phrases; for example, to find all records in which the phrase 'monosodium glutamate' appears.

Within these two classes, most database managers vary little in principle (although when we discuss them in more detail in a later chapter we shall see that some of them have very powerful features); they are virtually independent of the type of data that is stored in them. However, there are packages which are more specialised. We have already mentioned accounting and stock control packages. These are basically database managers, since data must be entered and stored systematically; but they are specialised to make it easy for the user to insert and extract data in the most suitable form. Another example is the range of packages designed for those interested in family history. Again these are database managers, but with additional features to bring out the relationships between the records representing individuals. Many of the more powerful general-purpose database managers could be set up by their users to do these tasks, but buying a more specialised package saves the user the work that this would involve.

Access to external information

Much of the information you use in your business will have come from outside; price lists, catalogues, dictionaries and so forth. Often it would be convenient for this information to be available to your computer. For example, if you are using a spreadsheet to track the performance of your investments, you don't want to have to type in the price of each share on each day; you would prefer the computer to find this information for itself. This it can do, if you can acquire the information in 'machine readable' form.

There are two ways in which you can do this, which we distinguish as **offline** and **online** (or **realtime**). In the first case the information comes to you in tangible form – on a floppy disk or a CD-ROM. This implies that you buy a complete set of information, from which you select what you need as and when you want it. 'Online' information comes to you down a telephone wire from a 'host' computer, and you need to have extra equipment (a 'modem') attached to your computer and also software (a 'communications package') to control it. You can again import a complete set of information, but because this tends to be expensive you are more likely to pick out just the bits you want from the set held on the remote computer.

All sorts of information are accessible in this way. For example, catalogues, stock market results, bibliographies, encyclopaedias, abstracts of legal and scientific information, and also a wide range of software. Some of this is in a form in which it can be processed by a computer – such as the stock market results, which could be read straight into a database. Other types of information, such as abstracts, are intended only to be read by a person (although you could copy them into a document you were creating on a word processor). The benefit of having them in machine-readable form rather than on paper is that you can use the computer to search for the information you want, rather than picking it out yourself. When you consider that one CD-ROM disk will hold the contents of a large encyclopaedia, you can see that this sort of help is useful.

There is a large overlap between information that is available in online and offline forms. In general, if the information remains valid for some time (say a month or more), and you are likely to make a lot of use of it, then the offline form is suitable: if it must be right up to date, or you only consult it occasionally, online may be better.

Data interchange

You may also want to exchange information with other computer users. Obviously this is related to the last topic, but here we are thinking of a one-to-one interchange of data relating specifically to your business, whereas before we were considering information which was available to many users. Data interchange is widely used within companies, but obviously that does not apply to us. However there are cases where correspondence between companies, whatever their size, is conveniently done in machine-readable form. An example is the transmission of orders and invoices. These are often generated by the sender's computer and have to be entered into that of the recipient, so it makes sense to avoid the need to re-key the information. Indeed, the purchasing departments of some companies will only deal with suppliers who will work in this way.

Again there is a choice between online and offline communication, but in this case online is much more common. It is possible for the computers concerned to be linked directly by telephone line while they communicate. However, an alternative is **Electronic mail** (or **E-Mail**). There are several companies offering this service, and each has computers in which messages are stored. The sender's PC sends the message via the telephone link to this computer, complete with an address (the same message can be sent to several addresses if required). All messages for a particular recipient are stored in a 'mailbox' in the service computer, and the recipient can then (via his own computer) extract the messages from his mailbox at a time convenient to him.

It is also possible to use the PC as a fax machine, in which case documents written with a word processor can be transmitted directly without first printing them on paper. There are several ways of doing this, which will be discussed in a later chapter.

Office organisation and time management

The Filofax has become the mark of the modern businessman, and it is not surprising that the computer has also been enlisted to serve as a **personal organiser** and to help with time management. The advantage over a manual system is that information can readily be amended, sorted and selected, and presented in the most convenient way. Most PCs have a real-time clock, so they can remind the user when an appointment is nearly due – provided, of course, that the machine is switched on and the user is there to hear or see the reminder. The big drawback of the computerised organiser is that the user cannot slip the PC in his pocket (though he might put a portable PC in his briefcase). So it is important that the program can print out an address list, appointment diary and so on in a form that will fit a pocket personal organiser. Most will do this very neatly, although it may involve putting special paper in the printer.

All organisers have the basic functions of address list and appointments book. Most also include a telephone dialler, associated with the address list. If the PC is fitted with a modem to connect it to the telephone line, the user need only indicate the entry in the list and the dialler will dial the number.

Many organisers have other features, which vary from one program to another. Some allow data extracted from word processor or database files to be printed out in personal organiser format. Others allow the organiser data to be accessed remotely via the modem and telephone line; this can be useful if you also have a portable computer and are working away from your desk machine.

If your business involves much long-distance road travel you may find a **Route Planner** package useful. These are based on road maps and will show you the best route between start point and destination, usually in both text and map form. The best of these programs will take into account your preferences (such as motorways, main roads or scenic routes) and allow for specified calls en route, and will estimate journey time. Some can be advised of road works or other delays to be avoided.

Graphics

For most business purposes you will work with letters and figures, but there may be times when you want to produce pictures of one sort or another; perhaps to liven up an advertising leaflet or to illustrate a book or a magazine article. We use the term **Graphics** to describe everything that can be shown on a computer screen, including both drawings you create yourself with the aid of the computer and photographs or drawings that you import from elsewhere, as well as text. This distinguishes graphics from the text-only mode of work.

Early PCs (other than the Macintosh) had screens which could not cope with graphics, but these are now obsolete and all current PCs can make use of graphics programs. Whether you can print out the results depends on the type of printer you have. Most modern printers are suitable, but the obsolescent daisywheel type is not. However, you should be aware that graphics programs are not always easy to use and the results may disappoint, especially if you use a dot-matrix printer. So this is an area in which computer and manual methods are very much in competition, and the computer approach may not be the best for your business.

Task-specific work

There is a very wide variety of software available to help with tasks which are associated with specific types of business. Some of these packages do a job which the more general packages cannot do. More often they are in effect 'customised' versions of the standard packages; the user could set up, say, a standard database package to do the job for him, but the specialised package saves him the effort, besides embodying the experience of someone who knows that line of business well. I shall give a few examples of applications for which there are task-specific packages, but I can only scratch the field. The best way to find if there is a package that would suit your business is through the trade press or trade shows or associations which deal with your kind of business, or from others already in the business, rather than through computer industry channels or dealers. These packages sell to a narrower market than the general-purpose ones, so they tend to be more expensive, though sometimes they can be bought more reasonably through trade associations or other groups.

Retailers are well served with specialised packages. Some of these serve to turn the PC into a cash register; most of them provide links between database and accounting packages, and perhaps others, to save the user having to transfer data or even to re-key it. Some of these packages are so specialised as to be aimed at a particular class of goods.

Various kinds of tradesmen are served by specialised packages. These usually link together facilities for estimating, time management, invoicing and accounting. Consultants have similar packages, although in this case scheduling and time management get more emphasis and there are packages for specific calculations, such as engineering design.

There are several packages designed for the catering trade, in particular for hotel and guest-house billing systems and for recording orders in restaurants. The later often use a special peripheral device which is in effect a list of the items on offer with a button associated with each item.

Finally I should mention my own trade, writing, which is catered for by such packages as the 'writer's shelf' which contains the text of various specialised dictionaries and guides to English usage, with means for rapid access to any entry. There is also a range of **style checkers** and **grammar checkers**, apart from the **thesaurus** which is included in many of the better word processors.

Leisure!

I don't propose to say much about computer games. New games appear, and old ones disappear, so rapidly that this month's favourite will probably be forgotten by the time you read this book. Games are widely available in every sort of computer shop and high street entertainment store. There are several magazines dedicated to computer games, and many of the more serious computer magazines have a games section. However, there are also some games which have a longer life: particularly those based on traditional board games such as Backgammon, Chess, and Go. These packages are often very well designed, if less spectacular than the arcade games. In most cases you can either play against a real opponent or against the program itself, and you can select the level of skill that the program will use; at the highest level you may find it very hard to win. Sometimes you can also set the program to play against itself, which can be quite educational.

However, computer games are only a means of killing time, and the sole businessman or woman will have little need for this – unless business is very bad! You are much more likely to use the computer to help with existing free time activities or hobbies. For many of these you will find the standard computer applications useful, especially database managers, word processors, desktop publishers and graphics programs of various kinds. There are also programs designed to help with specific activities. Many of these are in fact specialised databases, and there is a very wide range; to name but a few there are programs for cataloguing photographs, books, and recordings; programs for organising church or club membership lists; programs to help with various organised sports, such as sailing; programs for those interested in family history, astronomy, and amateur radio; programs to help manage your wine cellar and your garden; and a wide range of help with cooking and diet control.

Moving away a little from database management to straight data, you can buy on disk the complete text of the old and new testaments and the works of Shakespeare and a few other writers, and also a certain amount of music. The PC on its own is not a great machine for music, but for those who are interested and have cash to spare, various kinds of sound equipment can be added to it. There are also programs which allow the PC to be used to produce printed music, although these are rather specialised – at least one university team is at work in this area. For more information on PCs and music, see the book mentioned in Appendix 2.

Somewhere in between games and hobbies comes a large range of simulation programs. At one end of the range these are little more than arcade games; you can control the players in simulations of football, skiing or water polo, but the skills you use have more in common with computer games than with sport. More realistic simulations are available for games like golf – often based on particular courses – and snooker, and here some of the skill of the real game can be used, though of course the way you control the 'player' has little to do with the game. Probably the most detailed and realistic simulation programs are those which put the user in the position of the driver of a car or the pilot of an aircraft. Some of the flight simulators, in particular, have very realistic displays of control panels and scenery, and their response to the controls corresponds closely to that of the real machines. Most programs offer a choice, from a family saloon to a racing car or from a basic trainer to an advanced fighter plane or a modern air liner. There is still a big difference between a computer keyboard and the controls of a car or plane, though the really keen can buy a 'flight harness' which is a miniaturised version of an aircraft joystick and some of the auxiliary controls. Of course, dedicated (and extremely expensive) flight trainers are widely used in aviation, but some of the simulator programs that run on PCs are realistic enough to have their place in flight training too.

Finally there are educational programs. For the adult, the most interesting of these are probably those which help you to learn a foreign language. Computer-based language teaching is a well-established technique. It is usually applied in 'language laboratories' where a tutor monitors and guides a number of pupils who can thus work individually rather than as a class. However, much of the benefit of this system is available to individuals working on their own, and the PC is ideal for learning the written language in this way. Its sound capabilities are barely adequate for demonstrating speech, and it is unable to recognise and criticise the speech of the pupil.

There are also many PC-based educational programs which can help with your children's education. They are rather outside the scope of this book, and in any case it is desirable that they should link in with the child's school work; if you want to use the PC in this way, I suggest that you discuss it with the school.

A book which covers games and simulations in more detail is listed in Appendix 2.

3

System software

Two levels of software

Software for the PC can be divided into two classes: **Application** software and **System** software. It is application software that equips the system for a particular task, or application, such as word processing. Most users will have several application packages to carry out different tasks, although it is possible to combine a number of applications into a single 'integrated' package as we shall see in the next chapter.

Application software must "talk the user's language" so that you can enter data, and control the system, to make it produce the results you want. But software has to talk to the hardware in a different language, and we call this 'machine language'. It is made up of very simple orders or 'instructions'. For example, one instruction may move a single character from the keyboard to memory, after which another instruction copies the character to the screen. At this level, many instructions are needed to carry out even a simple operation such as entering a sentence of text.

The earliest application programs talked directly to the hardware in machine language. This led to much duplication. For example, nearly every program needs a sequence of instructions, or 'subroutine', to copy a line of characters entered at the keyboard into the computer's memory and also onto the screen. It makes sense for application programs to share commonly used subroutines like this, rather than each to have its own copy. To allow this we arrange our software in two 'levels'. The 'application level' carries out specific tasks for the user: the 'system level' provides common support to all programs at the application level. So now an application program does not need to speak 'machine language' to the hardware. Instead it speaks to the system software, giving it commands at a higher level, such as 'copy a file from memory to the printer'. The system software, or **operating system**, translates this into the long sequence of simple instructions which is all that the hardware can understand.

So you need two kinds of software for your computer – one operating system and one or more application programs. The operating system must match the particular hardware. For that reason, when you buy your hardware you will normally find that an operating system comes with it.

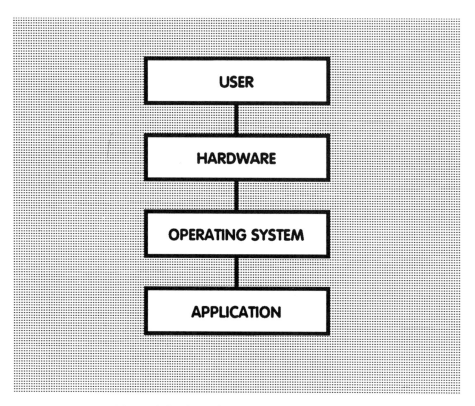

Figure 3.1 Where the operating system fits in.

The operating system is the link between the hardware (and through it you, the user) and the application program; see Figure 3.1. Despite this, you need to know very little about the operating system. Indeed, for most of the time you will not notice its existence. Instead, you will seem to be in direct contact with the application program. In computer terms, the operating system is 'transparent'. But you do have to talk to the operating system itself when you want to change from one application package to another. The best-known PC operating systems have a reputation for being unfriendly. For example you have to learn that when a message such as 'C>' appears on the screen, the operating system is saying 'I am waiting to be told what to do next'. In fact it is not difficult to learn how to control the operating system: but there are ways of making it more friendly, which we shall look at later.

Since system software deals with the 'machine language' communication between hardware and software, the application software need not be written to fit a particular machine. Instead it must suit a particular operating system. However, while there is a wide range of hardware on the market, there are only a few different operating systems. Indeed, there is at present one dominant PC operating system. This is called 'MS-DOS', or (when supplied with IBM personal computers) 'PC-DOS'. Thus any application program designed to run with MS-DOS will, in principle, run on any PC provided that MS-DOS is also present. Although the hardware may vary, the version of MS-DOS supplied with it will hide these variations. So any combination of hardware and MS-DOS looks exactly the same to the application program. At least, that is the theory; in practice, problems do occasionally arise as we shall see later. In technical jargon, the combination of any hardware with the right version of MS-DOS forms a standard **'virtual machine'**. Because of this standard, a vast amount of application software is available to every PC user. This is one of the reasons for the mushroom growth of the PC over the last decade. In contrast, larger computers often have different operating systems for each range of machines. So an application package has to be written for a specific machine; it thus has a much smaller potential market, and so a higher price. It is possible to adapt (or 'port') software to suit another machine, but that adds to the cost. The situation is gradually changing, as users press for interchangeability ('Open systems'), but the PC is still well ahead in this respect.

It should be said here that although MS-DOS is the dominant operating system in the PC area, it is not the only one. Perhaps one user in ten prefers to use 'DR-DOS'. This comes from a different supplier, but is very similar to MS-DOS. In particular, any application that runs with one of these operating systems should run equally well with the other. For this reason I shall not discuss DR-DOS further; anything I say about MS-DOS may be taken to apply to DR-DOS as well. Later in this chapter we shall discuss the use of 'Windows' and other 'graphic user interfaces' (GUIs) which are closely linked to operating systems. A more powerful operating system, OS/2, is suitable for more advanced PCs such as the IBM PS/2 range, but these are outside the scope of this book.

The user interface

As we have just seen, a major part of the task of the operating system is to handle the interface between you and the computer. Your commands to the computer will normally be given through either the keyboard or a mouse. You may also give commands through switches or buttons on other peripheral devices, such as a printer or scanner. You will expect a response from the computer, and nowadays you will nearly always see this on the screen.

Traditionally, the user uses the interface provided by the operating system when starting (or 'launching') application programs and for some other operations such as copying, backing-up or deleting files; but once a program is loaded, the user interface is provided by that program. This obviously has the disadvantage that the interface for each application program is separately designed, and may be completely different. For example, even when the same function (such as saving a file to disk) is provided in two application programs, you may have to call it in completely different ways.

Obviously this is not very satisfactory unless you only have one application package on your computer, and it is perhaps surprising that this situation is so common. Some half-hearted attempts have been made to overcome it, and if you happen to choose all your application packages from the same publisher you may find that they present something like a common interface. But this is by no means certain, and in any case there is no one publisher who produces the best package of every type. Some manufacturers sell 'integrated packages' in which several standard programs – usually a word processor, database manager, spreadsheet and sometimes a communications package – are bundled together. In this case you should find that the user interface is standard between the packages, though there may be lapses, and also that it is easy to transfer data between the packages. The various elements of such a package are often fairly simple, which may meet your needs, but you may wish that at least one of the elements was more powerful. And again, no one manufacturer produces the ideal integrated package.

The solution that is becoming popular is associated with the Microsoft **'Windows'** package, or with one or two packages from other sources which do a similar job. These packages are often described as **Graphical User Interfaces**, or **GUIs**. This is rather a misleading description. Although the packages do provide a graphical user interface, this is only a part of their function, and they are best looked upon as extensions to the operating system. For the moment the feature which interests us is that they provide a **common** user interface. In effect, they require that every designer who produces an application to be used with a particular GUI must follow a strict set of rules, which amongst other things ensure that all programs look alike to the user as far as their different functions allow this. Of course there could have been a common user interface without Windows, but the industry missed the opportunity to agree on one.

However, in the Windows context this system works well. There is a growing number of packages designed to run with Windows and their user interfaces are so alike that it is easy for a user to swap from one to another. The user interface is, as the term GUI implies, a graphical one. It depends very much on the use of a mouse to select 'icons' or symbols, representing application programs, from a screen display. This is claimed by the designers to be intuitive, and therefore easy to learn and use; not everyone agrees with this view, as we shall see later in this chapter. You may find the term **WIMP** used to describe the GUI approach; it is an acronym for 'Windows, icons, menus and pointers'.

Windows, and its alternatives, do a great deal more than this, as we shall see later. However, you never get something for nothing. There are two disadvantages to the use of a GUI. The first is that some of its advantages are only obtained if the application program is written specifically for that GUI (although you can still run any other program that suits your operating system). The second is to do with price and performance. If you add a GUI to an existing system you will find that applications running under it are much slower than those which do not use the GUI. In practice, you are strongly recommended to buy a more powerful PC if you intend to use Windows, and you should then find that applications run as fast as on a simpler machine without the GUI. However, you may have to pay up to twice as much for your system. Whether this price is justified by greater ease of use is something we shall discuss later in this chapter.

I have said that a GUI, such as Windows, is not itself an operating system. The GUI works in collaboration with the operating system and uses many of its facilities. The combination of the two is sometimes described as an **operating environment**. However, there is no practical reason why the two should remain separate, especially since the most popular operating system and GUI – MS-DOS and Windows – come from the same company, Microsoft. It is expected that a version of Windows which incorporates the operating system in a single unit will be released soon, although the first version will be aimed at users with more powerful machines than the one-person business is likely to use.

Operating system user interfaces

We have seen that one of the main advantages of Windows is that it imposes a common user interface on all application programs designed to work with it. It has also, of course, to provide a user interface to the operating environment itself, and naturally this interface is designed to be as similar as possible to the application program interface. Much the same applies to other GUIs. This means that the user no longer sees the original operating system interface.

GUIs are not the only alternative to the rather forbidding interface offered by the operating system. There are other choices, which can be divided into **shells** and **menu systems**. In the next few paragraphs I shall give a brief description of how the various operating system interfaces look to the user.

The MS-DOS user interface

All versions of the MS-DOS operating system (and the corresponding PC-DOS system used on IBM's own PCs) have essentially the same interface. The principle is very simple. The operating system displays on the screen a symbol, described as a **prompt**, to show you that it is ready to be told what to do. You can then, in your own time, type in a command which tells the operating system either to do something itself, or to start an application program. In the first case, there may be further dialogue. The operating system may ask you to put a particular floppy disk into the drive, or to give the name of a file which is to be processed in some way, or it may report a problem and give you a choice of ways to deal with it. Once the operation is complete a fresh prompt will be displayed on the screen.

```
C:\ > cd bk\text
C:\BK\TEXT > copy contract.1 a:
          1 file(s) copied
C:\BK\TEXT > a:
A:\ > print contract.1
Name of list device [PRN]:
Resident part of PRINT installed

  A:\CONTRACT.1 is currently being printed
A:\ > c:
C:\BK\TEXT > cd ..
C:\BK > cd\
C:\ >
```

Figure 3.2 The MS-DOS user interface. At the left of the screen, ending with the '>' symbol, are prompts. Following them on the same line are commands entered by the user. The remaining lines are messages from the computer to the user.

If an application is started, the user interface of the operating system will be replaced by that of the application program until the user decides to leave that application. The prompt will then be displayed again.

This is a simple and powerful system, but its disadvantage is that you have to know – or look up – every command you want to give to the operating system, and also the command which calls each application program. Also you have to know the name of each file you want to process. This isn't too bad where commonly used commands are concerned. There are probably only half a dozen that you need to learn, and the rest you can look up if you want them. All commands are short; eight letters at the most, and often only two or three. Whether you have too many file names to remember depends on your own situation. You may recall that I advised meaningful names rather than just numbers, but your scope is limited because the file name can have only eight characters, plus a three-character **extension**. (A useful tip when abbreviating filenames is to leave out vowels rather than consonants – the result is usually more suggestive of the full name).

However, a fly in the ointment is the fact that 'switches' can be added to many MS-DOS commands, to modify their action. A switch is usually a single letter. There may be several possible switches available for a command, and rules as to what combinations of them can be used together, so it becomes almost impossible to remember them all. For these and other reasons, if you use one of these operating systems you will need a good quick-reference guide, plus a list of your own files and application programs, and you will find yourself referring to them often. For example, the command 'DIR' will list your files, but 'DIR/p' lists them a screenful at a time. The '/p' is an example of a switch.

Things are not quite as bad as this suggests. There are various facilities built into the operating system to help you, such as the ability to display a list of file names, and if you use the system a lot you will find that you soon learn the commands and file names that you use often. For the first few years of the PC's history this was the only way it could be used, and it did not deter many thousands of users. However, nowadays the majority of PCs either use Windows or else use a shell or a menu system. These are in effect methods of hiding the operating system's own interface behind another more friendly one, and I shall describe them shortly.

The Windows user interface

Windows was introduced as a way of making things easier for the user, but paradoxically it is an extremely complex piece of software, several times the size of most operating systems, and with a bewildering range of facilities. I cannot attempt to describe it any detail; besides its own manual, which is an inch thick, there are dozens of books which aim to teach the user how to get the best out of it. All I shall do here is describe the principles underlying its user interface – which, as I have said, is effectively the same for the operating system as it is for application programs.

The basic idea of this interface is that you do not have to remember either commands and switches or programs or file names; they are displayed on the screen and all you have to do is to select from them. Well, not quite all; you still have to remember what they mean – though even here, much help is available. Commands, and the options which correspond to switches, are selected from **menus**, which are simply lists of possible choices. As there are so many commands and options they cannot all be displayed at once, so they are grouped into several levels. The first-level menu is displayed as a single line, or bar, across the top of the screen. Selecting one item from this menu causes a second-level menu to appear (or 'drop down') below the selected choice, and again an item can be selected from it. This may itself represent a command, but it may also lead to a further level of menu – perhaps giving a choice of options – and so on.

The usual way to select an item from a menu is 'point and click'. This assumes the use of a mouse. On the screen is a 'pointer', usually a bright square or an arrow, and as you move the mouse you will see a corresponding movement of the pointer. With very little practice you will find you can quickly move the pointer till it lies on the item you want to select from the menu, and then 'click' – which means pressing one of the buttons provided on the mouse. If you don't have a mouse, or prefer not to use it, you can move the pointer with the arrow keys on the keyboard, and press the

ENTER key instead of clicking; and for some of the menu choices a keyboard 'short cut' (generally holding down the ALT or CTRL key and pressing one other key) is provided. There is no doubt, however, that a mouse is the easiest way to use this menu system.

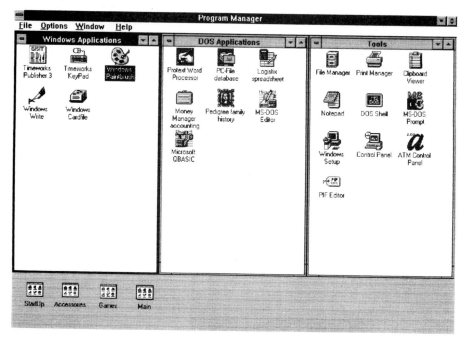

Figure 3.3 *The Windows user interface. Shown here is the 'desktop' from which you select the program or utility you want to run. You can arrange the number of windows and of icons to suit yourself.*

Application programs and files are selected in a slightly different way from commands. Instead of pull-down menus, the programs and files (which may be displayed mixed together, since a program is in fact just one sort of file) are represented by small symbols, called **icons**, which are displayed in a two-dimensional array on the screen. There are different icons to represent different kinds of files such as main program files, auxiliary files associated with programs, word processor data files, spreadsheet files and so forth. Beneath each icon appears the name of the corresponding file. Again, the file or program you want is selected by pointing and clicking with the mouse, or by moving the pointer with the keyboard arrow keys. You may have too many files and programs to display on one screen, and the displays are arranged in a hierarchy rather like that of the menus, which I shall not detail here although I shall have something to say about file management in Chapter 8. The number of files and their grouping is entirely under your control. There may still be more files in a group than the PC can show (as icons) on one screen. In that case the screen is treated as a 'window' allowing you to see part of a larger virtual display, and you can move the virtual display under the window until you see the part you want.

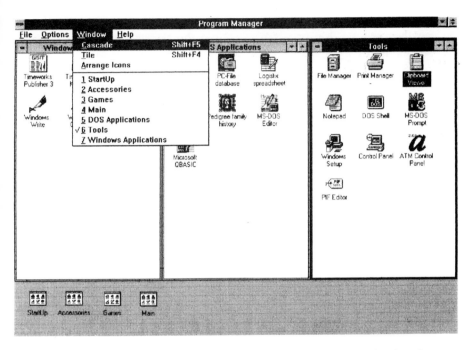

Figure 3.4 The Windows desktop with a 'drop-down' menu displayed.

This use of icons is one of the most controversial features of Windows. Many people are very happy with it; others hate it, and here I must admit my prejudices and say that I just don't get on with icons. I can never remember which is supposed to mean what, and the presence of the icons means that the file names have to be shown in smaller type than I like. I also find it much harder to find an item in a two-dimensional array than in a single list. However, all is not lost; for those who share my prejudices there are ways to display files in a list rather than as icons.

Shells and the user interface

A **Shell** is a program which provides the user interface of an operating system. Thus the interface I have described for MS-DOS is controlled by a shell which is part of MS-DOS (it is in fact a file called COMMAND.COM). However, MS-DOS allows you to replace this by a shell of your own choosing, and it is these substitute shells that I shall discuss here.

There are many such shells available. Some, such as the popular '4DOS', are designed to provide extra functions without altering the user interface. However, the shells that interest us here are those that provide a more friendly user interface. This is nearly always done by providing a screen display showing all the files (including programs) held on your computer's disk, grouped in whatever way you have chosen. You can then select a file or a program from this display, instead of having to remember its name. Such a shell is called a **file manager**. Windows can work in exactly this way – by using a shell which is actually called 'File Manager'. File managers can display files either as lists of names (usually structured so as to indicate the way you have grouped your files) or as icons. The file manager supplied with Windows uses icons, but you can replace it with one which does not. In either case, files are selected by moving a pointer or highlight bar to the file you want with either the cursor keys or a mouse. As with Windows, the display may not be able to show all your files at once, but it can be moved over a larger 'virtual display' till you see what you want.

The shell makes it easier to carry out the two types of function I have mentioned – starting a program, and internal operating system functions. To start a program you need only select the program file and press a single key. Other functions – such as copying, renaming or deleting files – are carried out in a similar way, and it is usually possible to mark a number of files so that a function can be carried out on all of them with a single command.

The advantage of a File Manager type of shell is that you never need to remember a file name, and that it can be installed very easily. Many shells also have extra functions which you may or may not find useful. For example, some will let you attach a description to each file if you find an eight-character name too cryptic. However, their disadvantage is that you need to remember the way in which you have chosen to group your files if you are to find the one you want quickly, and you need to remember what each of them does.

Version 5 of MS-DOS includes a shell which has adequate facilities, although less extensive than those in some shells that you can buy separately. It is slower than some of these.

Menu systems as user interfaces

The last type of user interface I shall discuss is the menu system. We have already seen the use of menus in Windows, but a menu can be used in any context and not only that of a GUI. In fact a menu is by far the simplest way to select one of a small number of actions – such as choosing whether to start a word processor, a spreadsheet, or a database manager. For most users, most of the time, this is how you want to use your computer. There is no need to see Windows, a shell, or the dreaded DOS prompt.

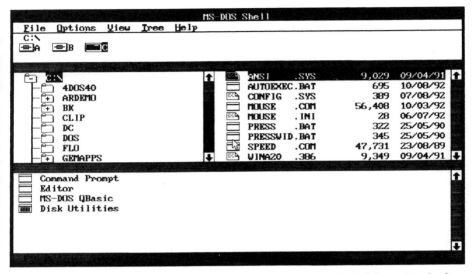

Figure 3.5 A shell. This one is 'Dosshell', which is provided with version 5 of MS-DOS although not with earlier versions.

The simplest menu system is usually the best, and in particular the number of choices on each menu should be kept small; ideally perhaps half a dozen, or at the most a dozen. If you need more choice than this you can use a hierarchy of menus. The first menu would then give you a choice of groups of applications, and any choice would then lead to another menu in which all the applications in that group were listed. Alternatively (and this is the method I use) the first menu can list the four or five applications you use most, with the last choice in the list being a supplementary menu listing the less popular programs. In this case, when you switch on the PC you will find a menu displayed, after the usual pause while the machine tests itself, such as that shown in figure 3.6.

In this example you select your choice by pressing a number key. If you prefer, you can set up the menu so that you press a key corresponding to the initial letter of your choice, or so that you move a highlight bar or pointer to your choice with the mouse or keyboard arrow keys. I find the use of numbers fastest; I can always find the number keys, whereas when I am not actually typing text I find it surprisingly hard to remember where a particular letter lives on the keyboard.

Such a menu system will take care of the operating system as far as starting programs is concerned. You can also make it carry out functions within the operating system itself, but this can get clumsy since there are so many such functions and so many options to each. You will probably find it best to set up the menu to cover those programs you use regularly, and possibly one or two of the most widely used operating system functions, but return to the operating system or Windows or the shell of your choice when you want to carry out other functions, or to start new or obscure programs.

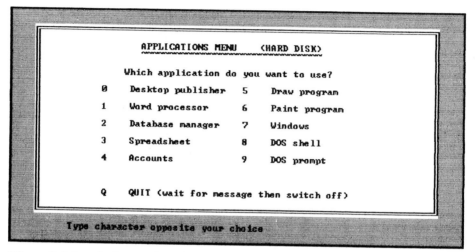

Figure 3.6 A typical menu for selecting applications. Note that in this case, unlike the Windows environment, all extraneous information is removed from the screen to avoid confusion.

Mention of new programs brings me to a disadvantage of menu systems. Unlike shells, or the bare operating system, you do have to do some work to set up a menu system. There are several menu generating programs on the market, some of which are quite easy to use, but as a minimum you will have to tell the program what text you want to appear on the menu display, and what program file is to be called for each choice. In fact there are menu generators which will look through your disk to see if it contains any programs they recognise, including many of the most popular. However this still leaves you to enter the rest, and may restrict your ability to list programs in the order you wish and to set up the menu hierarchy.

Some menu generators give you plenty of control over the appearance of your menu displays – box size, line spacing, colours and so forth – while others adopt a 'take it or leave it' attitude. The latter, of course, saves you the trouble of making decisions. If you want to have complete control over the appearance of your menus, and save the cost of a menu generator into the bargain, you can make your own menu system using **batch files**, which I shall discuss later. This is what I have done myself. It does take up quite a bit of time, and it is less easy to add additional choices to your menus than with the better of the menu generators.

Menu systems and Windows are not mutually exclusive, of course. You can include Windows as one of the choices on your initial menu (instead of DOS in the example I have shown). You can also call from the menu a program which you want to run in the Windows environment, and Windows will then be started and the program run automatically. Thus a menu system is very suitable if you have a mixture of programs which need to run under Windows and programs which are best run directly under MS-DOS (or DR-DOS). Many users will find themselves in this situation. Most menu generators can cope with calling Windows and starting an application in this way, but if yours can't there's no need to panic; it is easy to write a batch file which will fill the gap.

Typefaces and fonts

There are two ways in which information can be presented on screen or paper: character mode and graphics mode. In character mode the form and size of the characters depends entirely on the hardware – the video display and printer. Modern printers may offer some choice, but only within a limited range (we discuss this further in the chapter on hardware). If there is a choice, it is controlled by special characters embedded in the text sent to the printer. Since the text files are generated by application programs rather than the operating system, it follows that the latter is not involved in any way in the control of character form.

In graphics mode, however, the hardware does not determine the form of the characters. In this mode, all the screen or printer sees is a stream of data which forms a bit map, defining the brightness and colour of each dot on the screen or page. Therefore, if there are characters included in the image, their form must be determined by software.

At first, in the PC (though not in the Macintosh), each application had to make its own arrangements for defining character shapes. Later it was realised that common character designs, or **typefaces**, could be made available to a range of application programs in much the same way that other common services were provided by the operating system. To do this we need two components: **typeface definition** files, each of which defines the character shapes for a particular typeface, and a **typeface manager** which extracts information from these files and makes it available to the application program.

GUIs take this process a step further, by integrating the typeface manager into the GUI itself. Most GUI-based application programs now depend entirely on the GUI for the control of typeface in graphics mode, and consequently character design is standardised across all such programs and a single set of typefaces can be used by them all.

At this point we should distinguish between **typefaces** and **fonts**, although in practice there is still some confusion in the industry and the terms are often misused. A **typeface** is the basic design of a character set, which remains recognisable whatever the size of the characters and whether they are in normal, bold, or italic form. A **font** is a particular instance of a typeface in a single size and style. Thus, for example,

'Times Roman' is a typeface, but 'Times Roman 12 point bold' is a font. (A 'point' is a unit of measurement which originated in the printing industry; there are normally 72 points to the inch).

There are basically two ways of defining character forms in a typeface definition file. One is to define the form as a bit map, listing the state (black or white) of each element in a matrix which corresponds to the space allocated to a character. These elements are called 'pixels' or 'pels'. This is the same approach as is used in character mode for a screen or matrix printer. The alternative is to define it as a set of mathematical formulas representing the curves and straight lines which make up the outline of the character. A typeface defined in this way is described as an **outline typeface** (or more often, though less accurately, as an **outline font**).

In either case, the typeface definition file defines only one size of character, and usually only one style although sometimes the italic style is defined separately. However, it is easy to modify this single definition to produce fonts of whatever size and style you need. This is done by a program called a font generator, which is part of the typeface manager package. Sometimes this can be be done on the fly, so that only the original typeface definition need be stored. However this can be slow, since each character has to be scaled and modified every time it is used. So it is more usual for the user to decide beforehand what fonts will be needed, and to direct the font generator to generate them and store each in a separate font definition file. The application program, or the GUI, will display a list of available fonts and allow the user to choose from this list. 'Windows 3.1' has a fast typeface manager so individual font files need not be generated in advance.

It is usual for a few of the most useful typefaces to be supplied, in the form of typeface definition files, with a GUI or with an application program which does not depend on a GUI for its typefaces. Normally there will be at least a serif and a sans-serif typeface, and sometimes a 'script' (or pseudo-handwriting) typeface as well. However, you can always buy extra typeface definition files (usually described as 'font packages' or just 'fonts') and there is a wide range available, ranging from typefaces intended for use in continuous text, such as books, to 'display' typefaces for use in headlines, posters and the like. You must buy font packages in the form that suits your typeface manager. There are at present several of these, but as the 'TrueType' manager is now incorporated in Windows it is likely that font packages compatible with this will become the standard. These, incidentally, are outline rather than bit-mapped fonts.

Besides the typefaces supplied with your GUI, you can (at least with some Windows applications) use the hardware fonts built into your printer. Printing is faster with hardware fonts since graphics mode printing need not be used. These fonts may not be shown accurately on your screen. On matrix printers, hardware fonts often print better than others because each line of characters is printed at a single pass. This avoids any problem of registration between successive passes.

A variation on this system uses 'Postscript' fonts. This represents a useful compromise between graphics mode and character mode. Graphics mode gives complete flexibility but makes printing slow, because so much data has to be passed to the printer. Character mode is fast but is limited to the fonts built into the printer. However, a 'Postscript' printer incorporates its own processor with the equivalent of a typeface manager and a set of typeface definition files. Now the PC need only tell the printer what font to use, and then send data in character mode; the printer itself converts this into the precise character shapes that are needed. It is usually possible to add extra typefaces, although not as easily as if these were stored within the PC. There is more than than this to Postscript, of course. Postscript printers are rather more expensive than standard models.

It will be obvious that if a graphics-based program depends on a GUI to control its fonts, it cannot be run without that GUI. Consequently, some such programs are sold with the GUI itself included in the package. This applies particularly to desktop publishers based on 'GEM', which is a GUI that predates Windows by some years. GEM also uses a typeface manager, though in this case for bit-mapped typefaces. GEM was originally intended to be used as an operating system enhancement in the same way as Windows but is no longer being sold in this way, although it is still included with those graphics and DTP packages that depend on it.

Do you need Windows?

You are unlikely to have to make a choice of operating system. In nearly all cases an operating system will be supplied with the PC, and this will be either MS-DOS (or the IBM version, PC-DOS) or less commonly DR-DOS. It should be the latest version, or at least one that is no more than a few months out of date.

You do have to decide whether or not you want Windows, and this is an important decision because it affects your choice of both hardware and software. I mentioned earlier that the many advantages of Windows are balanced by the need to buy more expensive hardware unless you are ready to accept a drastic cut in performance. If you use Windows you really need to buy a '386' type of machine with at least 4 megabytes of memory (we shall see in Chapter 6 what this means). Without Windows you could probably get by with spending only half as much.

On the other hand, there are some application programs which you cannot run without Windows. I have mentioned that some graphics-based programs need a GUI installed. For many of these, this must be Windows. Others need GEM instead (or as well – installing GEM does not preclude installing Windows too), but in view of the decline in popularity of GEM it is likely that these will be replaced by Windows versions before long.

Many of the most popular applications, originally designed to be controlled by MS-DOS or its equivalent, are now available also in Windows versions. At the moment these versions tend to be more expensive, which is odd because Windows provides some of the facilities which otherwise have to be written into the program itself, but this premium is likely to disappear. They are often slower than the original versions. However, you may well feel that these disadvantages are outweighed by the advantages offered by Windows – which we shall review shortly.

In spite of the great amount of work going into Windows applications, and the spate of advertising that goes with them, it is worth remembering that something like three quarters of the PC software sold is still not Windows based. So if you choose not to use Windows there is little risk that you will not find programs to do what you want.

If you do want to run Windows-based programs you have no alternative but to install Windows; there are no compatible systems from other suppliers. However, the converse is not true. All programs that are designed to run with MS-DOS or its equivalents can be run with Windows. Whether this is a good idea is another matter; it may be better to run these programs directly from MS-DOS (there is no difficulty in doing this). They are likely to run faster without Windows but you will lose some of the facilities Windows offers even to these programs. These are fewer than the facilities available to Windows programs.

There are a number of advantages to using Windows, of which I have already mentioned one – that the user interface of all Windows application programs is the same, so that you do not need to learn a new set of keyboard codes for each. This makes it much easier to move from one application to another, or to find your way about a new application. Of course this only applies to programs specifically written for Windows. You can use Windows to run any application, but you will still see that application's own user interface. So you will not really benefit from this common user interface until you have at least two Windows applications. In time, all the best application programs may be available in Windows versions, but this is certainly not the case yet.

Another important advantage of Windows is that it lets you run several applications at a time (as do certain other shells). This is called **multiprogramming**. Of course, you have only one pair of hands, so you can only communicate with one program at a time; though you can receive information back from two or more by allocating part of the screen to each. These parts are described as windows – hence the name of the system. The advantages of this are firstly that you can swap from one application to another instantly, without waiting for one to unload and the other to load, and secondly that you can see information from one application on the screen while you are using another. A further advantage is that if one program is doing something that takes a long time – such as printing out graphics – you can be getting on with something else while you wait. Of course, if the PC can be used by more than one person at a time (for example if it is linked to another PC) multiprogramming is particularly useful, but this is unlikely to apply to a one-person business.

Multiprogramming works best with programs designed for Windows, although the latest version of Windows can multiprogram some other applications. Where multiprogramming is not possible, **context switching** may be. In this case only one program can actually run at a time, but other programs are 'frozen' so that you can return to them at the point where you left off instead of having to start them again at the beginning. You do not need Windows to do this, the latest version of MS-DOS will do it and so will some shells.

Associated with multiprogramming or context switching is another feature of Windows. This is the ease with which data can be transferred between one application and another. For example, if you have generated a table with a spreadsheet program and want to copy this into a word-processed letter, you can run both programs and a few keystrokes will transfer the data. If both are Windows programs you can do more than this; you can arrange things so that if you alter one of the figures you have copied into the letter, the spreadsheet will automatically accept the change and recalculate any other figures that depend on that one, and pass them back to the letter. Whether this linkage is of value in your own situation is for you to decide. You do need a clear head to get the results you want without altering data that you meant to leave as it was.

Another of the advertised advantages of Windows is the Graphical User Interface itself. The use of windows, pointers, and icons is intuitive, it is claimed, and much easier to learn than the alternatives. I have already declared my own view. I don't get on with icons, and I find a well-designed menu system much faster and easier to use. I also find the Windows approach of overlapping windows confusing, since so much irrelevant information can be on the screen at any moment. But this is very much a matter of opinion, and you must make up your own mind. In any event, as I said earlier in this chapter, you can if you wish use icons and mice without Windows, and you can, if you take the trouble, use Windows without the icons and overlapping windows.

So what is your choice? Only you can decide what is best for your own business. Don't let anyone talk you into using Windows because 'everyone else does' – under a third of PCs use Windows at present, and many never will, even though the software may be bundled with the PC. There is no doubt that Windows is attractive to the corporate market. Cost is not so important to bigger companies, and it is important to them to have a standard user interface so that staff can move easily from one PC or application to another. This hardly matters to the one-person business. So what does matter?

If you want to use any program which depends on Windows then there is no question about it, you must have Windows and a suitable PC to support it. This may come about because the only, or the best, application program for your job is only available in a Windows version. This is most likely to apply to some graphics and desktop publishing programs, and to word processors which work in true graphics mode (you will see in the next chapter that this is not necessarily the best type of word processor for you). You may want to use a Windows program for compatibility with some other organisation. For example, a friend of mine intends to write material for the Open University, and they have standardised on a Windows based word processor.

You may need the ability to run programs together, and to transfer data between applications. The ability to do this is not confined to Windows; some shells, and some integrated application packages, can do it too. But there is no doubt that the Windows way of doing it is now the standard way, and if you need this facility you would be best off with Windows and (preferably) with Windows based application programs.

You may not need Windows for either of these reasons at the moment, but anticipate that you will within the next two or three years. In this case you would be wise to buy a machine capable of running Windows; it will cost more, but the extra power will make things go faster in the meantime. Windows is often bundled with such a machine, but if not you may as well wait to see if there is a later version out by the time you need it.

And finally, you may want to use applications which are not Windows based but which need a powerful machine to give a reasonable performance. This is most likely to apply to graphics programs and especially desktop publishing. In this case you'd be wise to choose a machine which is capable of running Windows, but again don't buy Windows unless and until you feel you need it.

If none of these requirements apply to you, it comes down to a question of money and of personal feelings about the different user interfaces. If money is not a problem you may as well buy a top-end PC, you'll appreciate the extra power. And you may as well splash out on Windows while you are about it, to find out for yourself what it's like (though if you have a PC – or access to one – which does not have Windows installed, you can get a free demonstration disk from Microsoft). You can always stop using it if you feel the loss of performance outweighs its advantages. For the rest of us, in my opinion, it's not worth the substantial extra cost (especially in hardware) that's involved. There is plenty of non-Windows application software, and always will be. You can put some of your savings on hardware towards more, or better, software (or towards a good holiday!). If you like the WIMP interface, no problem; there are shells which will give you this with less performance penalty.

But, as I said before, ignore my prejudices and decide for yourself!

Utilities

Sooner or later you will come across a class of software which we call **utilities**. A utility is really a simple application program, and works in the same way – it is started by giving a command to your operating system, or from Windows or a shell or menu, and it interacts with the user just as any application program does. However, whereas you use an application program to get on with your business tasks, you use a utility to help you to manage the computer system itself. There is no clear dividing line between utilities and application programs. For our purposes we can think of a utility as providing a function which ought to be provided by the operating system itself, but may not be. That is why I have included utilities in this chapter rather than in Chapter 4 or 5.

Many utilities are concerned with handling files; copying them from one disk to another, changing their format so that files created by one application can be used by another, printing files or viewing them on the screen, renaming or deleting them, recovering them if they are deleted by mistake or are damaged by some accident, and so on.

But some of these facilities are already provided by the operating system, you may recall. Indeed so. In fact many of the functions of an operating system are not embedded in the core (or shell) of the system itself, but are carried out by separate utility programs which are supplied with the system. In use you cannot distinguish an operating system function which is embedded in the shell itself (an **internal** function) from one which is provided by a separate utility program (an **external** function). However, if you look at the list of files which make up the operating system you will see that some have names which are actually the commands you enter to carry out some of the operating system functions. Examples are FORMAT, PRINT, FIND, DISKCOPY, and BACKUP. These utility programs, although supplied with the operating system, work in exactly the same way as any independent utility program. You can delete them, replace them by other versions, or add more of them whenever you wish.

There is a vast choice of utilities which you can, if you choose, add to your system. Because they are usually simple (though there are exceptions), even an amateur programmer will create a new utility without hesitation if he wants a job done that his operating system will not do for him. Many of these utilities are put into the 'public domain', which means that the writer allows you to use them without charge. Others are available at a very low cost. Collections of utilities are often given away with computer magazines, or with printers or PCs. A few utilities, usually elaborate ones, are more expensive, and there are one or two well-known sets of utilities which are in the same price range as application programs. These aim to include all the utilities which you are ever likely to want. That is rather a tall order when the needs of each user are so different! Typically one of these collections will include a shell, a set of programs for recovering damaged files, a disk cache (a program which makes your hard disk appear to work faster), and some further functions intended for the experienced user.

Of course, operating system designers also aim to provide everything the user wants. Whenever an operating system is revised it is likely to have new utilities added to it. This makes some of the free-standing utilities redundant – though of course you may still prefer them to their bundled equivalents. Quite often the bundled utility is one which is already on the market, rather than one designed by the same people as the operating system.

Windows, in particular, includes a rich selection of utilities, and if you have Windows you may never need to buy another utility. However, because utilities are so cheap (and may land on your desk unbidden if you subscribe to a computer magazine), it is worth watching out for any of them which might make life a little easier, and trying them out to see how you get on with them. If you find after the initial enthusiasm that you never use them, they are easily ditched. I suppose I have had forty or fifty utilities on my system at one time or another, of which about twenty survive; I use four or five often, the rest occasionally.

I can only mention a few of the many types of utility, and I shall concentrate on the ones I find most useful. But of course they may not be useful to you; or you may not need them because something similar is already part of your operating system or shell or of Windows.

The utility I use most is one which simply displays the contents of a text file on the screen. Every operating system has a command that does this, of course, but often it is not done in a way I find convenient (for example the TYPE command in MS-DOS). So I use a utility which makes it easy for me to move backwards and forwards through the file, to find a particular word or phrase in it, and so on.

Next most useful is a utility which allows me to 'dump' the contents of the screen to the printer. Again, my operating system has this function, but in a simple form. The utility lets me select any portion of the screen to print, instead of just the whole screen.

Also in regular use till recently was a 'command line editor' utility. Often I want to repeat a command which I have used recently. This utility allows me to recall any of the last 20 commands, and amend it if I choose. It can save quite a lot of keying. However, I now have a later version of MS-DOS which includes this function, so I no longer need a separate utility.

If, as it is best to do, you leave your computer switched on when you are not using it, a 'screen blanking' utility will turn the screen black when no key has been touched for a set time, say five minutes. This prevents a standard picture (such as a menu) leaving a permanent shadow on the screen. This shadow effect is often seen on railway or airline destination displays; it is less likely to affect a computer screen, but it costs little to take the precaution. There are more elaborate screen blankers which display a message, or an image, which is constantly moving rather than always in the same place on the screen. Windows has a screen blanker built in.

A utility which I use only occasionally, but would not be without, is one which displays a chart of all the available colours on the screen. This allows me to set the brightness and contrast controls so as to give the best colour rendering.

Utilities which display on-screen clocks, calendars or calculators are popular. I have them, but I can't say I use them much. Maybe you would.

Other utilities, such as expanded memory managers and disk caches, are associated with particular pieces of hardware and are likely to be supplied with them or with your operating system, although you can buy alternative versions separately.

On the borderline between utilities and applications are some more elaborate programs, which are often supplied with operating systems but again can be had separately. One type is the 'text editor', which is really a rudimentary word processor. It is useful for writing and editing small simple files, such as batch files which I shall discuss in a later chapter. For such files it is often quicker and easier to use than your word processor. Most operating systems do include a text editor, but often it is so difficult to use (for example EDLIN, the editor supplied with all but the latest versions of MS-DOS) that a replacement is well worth having. The current version of MS-DOS does include a good text editor.

Other elaborate utilities include those which enable you to recover damaged files, and those which protect against viruses (I shall discuss these in a later chapter). These utilities tend to be more expensive, on a par with application programs. So far they have not usually been included in operating systems.

Most operating system packages include a 'BASIC interpreter', which is the software you need if you want to write and use programs in the simple programming language called 'BASIC'. This is quite a large piece of software, not just a utility, but it might be regarded as one because it comes as part of the operating system. I shall say more about programming languages in the next chapter.

Memory-resident programs (TSRs)

Sometimes you would like to make brief use of a utility, such as a calculator, without first closing down the current application and then re-starting it afterwards. If you happen to have Windows you can run the two programs together. If not, there needs to be some way in which you can 'pop up' a utility without leaving the main application. In fact MS-DOS does allow programs to be written so that they do this. We call them **memory-resident** programs, or **TSRs** (this stands for 'Terminate and Stay Resident', but don't let that worry you!). When you finish with a normal program, it is removed from the computer's memory to make room for the next program, so when you next want it the computer must fetch it again from disk. A TSR remains in memory even when you finish with it; or more often, a small part of it does. This part monitors the keyboard, and when it detects a particular sequence of key presses the program springs into action, displaying the calculator on the screen or whatever else it is designed to do. The key sequence, often called the **hot key**, is chosen to be one you would not normally use – for example, pressing the shift key and the space bar together. However, many TSRs allow you to change the 'hot key' to another of your choice, in case the original one does happen to mean something to an application or to another TSR you have already installed.

Before you first use the 'hot key' you must start the TSR program, just as any other program is started. However, if you want to have some TSRs available whenever you use the machine, you can arrange for them to be started automatically when you switch the machine on. This is done through the AUTOEXEC.BAT program, which we shall discuss in Chapter 7 (under 'Batch files').

There are a couple of possible snags. At least part of the TSR program must remain in memory, so that it can detect the 'hot key'. Some application programs need to use nearly all the computer's memory, which may be small, especially on the least expensive computers. It can happen that even the small amount of memory used by a TSR is enough to prevent that application running, and then all you can do is remove the TSR and try again. This is more likely to happen if you have several TSRs loaded, or if one of the TSRs takes up a lot of memory. The second problem is that sometimes two TSRs will interfere with each other, or occasionally with an application program. This comes about because TSRs were something of an afterthought in the MS-DOS operating system, and the rules they should follow were not well enough defined. Sometimes the problem disappears if the TSRs are loaded in a different order. If not, you just have to accept that you cannot use some combinations of TSRs.

There is another use for TSRs, and that is when you want a utility program to be started automatically rather than starting it itself. One example is the screen blanking program I have already mentioned, which is run when you have not touched the machine for a few minutes. In this case, instead of watching for a 'hot key' to be pressed, the resident part of the TSR watches the computer's internal clock.

Application Software 1:
the three classic applications

This chapter and the next one both deal with application software. In this chapter I shall look at application software in general, and then describe the three classic types of application packages which are found on nearly every PC. These are Word Processors, Spreadsheets and Database Managers. In Chapter 5 I shall look at some more specialised application packages, which you may or may not need, and at 'Integrated' packages which combine the functions of several types of package into one. Following this I shall look at the possibility of having software specially written for your business.

Matching application software to your needs

In Chapter 2 ('What a computer can do for you') we looked at the sort of problems that computers can solve for you. In principle you could have a computer system tailored precisely to your own set of problems – if, of course, you could define those problems precisely. In practice, most users choose from the range of software and hardware which is already available. You, or your consultant, will aim to select the combination which best suits your problems and your pocket. We looked at system software in Chapter 3, and we shall consider hardware in Chapter 6. Here and in the next chapter we shall look at the third part of your computer system: the application software.

You may choose application software yourself, or you may pay (or persuade) someone else to choose for you. Either way it is not just a matter of finding a software package labelled with your particular set of problems. Every business is different, and so its problems differ too. But developing software is expensive, and many copies of each package must be sold to keep the price within the range of the small user. So most software packages are designed to be able to handle a wide range of user's problems. For example, with a database management program you could keep stock records, or an address list, or even simple accounts. Such software packages are not labelled with the particular problems they solve, but with a more general description. Often this relates to the manual process they replace – such as an accounting package, or a spreadsheet. Other packages, such as a word processor or a database manager, do not have an exact manual equivalent. There are packages which have a closer relation to particular problems, such as stock control; but even these are designed to handle a range of such problems rather than the specific needs of one user.

This means that matching your problems to available software is your own task, or your adviser's, rather than that of the software designer. However, modern application packages have flexibility built in. They include options and parameters, which you can set to make the package fit your own needs. This is called **configuring** the package. How easy it is will depend on how much thought the designer gave to this aspect of the package, and how well the manual is written. The most expensive packages are not always the best in this respect. It also depends, of course, on the complexity of your needs. A good package will have 'default' settings for the options and parameters. In other words, they will be preset to suit a 'typical' user. These settings will suit some users with no change, or little change; you should find such a package easy to configure. More complex requirements, or a more complex (or less well designed and documented) package, may take a good deal more work. Beyond a certain point, you will find it worth getting expert help. This is most likely to happen if you need an elaborate database or accounting system.

Of course, if your problems are unusual, there may be no standard package on the market which will do what you want. Sometimes you can adapt your needs to fit something that exists, or do the job without a computer. If you still need a solution, you have two more options. You can pay someone to write software to meet your specific needs, or you can write it yourself. The first will be expensive: the second will take up a lot of your time. But if the need is pressing, either may be worth while. We shall look at these options in more detail in Chapter 5.

Word processors

Word processors are the most widely used of all PC application packages; it is a rare PC that is without one. Word processing was also one of the first applications to be available on a PC. Before this there were 'dedicated' word processors whose hardware was designed for this task and nothing else. These had some advantages compared with the PC, such as specially labelled keys for the operations most often needed in word processing. However, their specialisation prevented large sales and so made them expensive. They are now obsolescent. In contrast, word processing programs for the PC have flourished. There are now hundreds on the market, although only about half a dozen are widely used.

We saw in Chapter 2 that a word processor separates the keying and printing stages of document preparation, making correction and modification easier. Also it takes care of line and page ends automatically, and provides 'mail merge' functions to help you to produce variants of a standard document.

Most word processors will automatically 'justify' text, that is make the right margin as well as the left margin straight. This is done by putting extra spaces between some of the words on each line. Whether justification is desirable is for you to decide. Many people think it is out of place in correspondence, although it may be useful in more formal work. You can switch it off if you prefer. The more powerful word processors will also produce 'proportional spacing', if you have a printer that will support it – most will nowadays. This allows characters to have different widths (with 'i' and 'm' as the extreme cases), as in printed text, instead of the equal spacing used by most typewriters. Again, this is not needed for many applications, and it can cause difficulty in tables and sometimes with tabs. In many word processors you do not see proportional spacing on the screen, so the line length on the screen will vary. Some line ends may disappear off the end of the screen.

Most word processors now include a spelling checker, which is in effect an automated dictionary. When you have entered your text (or sometimes while you enter it) it is checked against the dictionary, and any words not found there are marked for your attention. All spelling checkers will let you change a marked word, or say that you do not want to change it. In the latter case, most let you add the word to the dictionary – either permanently, or just while you have this document in memory. The more powerful programs will suggest several possible words which may have been what you intended to type. These are occasionally more amusing than useful! Some word processors go a step further and include a thesaurus, so that if you are not happy with your choice of words you can pick another. Most of these programs are written in the USA, but have British-flavoured English versions of the spelling dictionary for UK buyers.

Another feature of the more powerful word processors is automatic hyphenation. If a long word over-runs the end of a line, these programs will automatically split it at a suitable point and insert a hyphen. If you later amend the text so that the word is no longer split, the hyphen disappears – in computer jargon, it is a **soft hyphen**.

Many other features are available in word processors. The most elaborate packages have a manual inches thick and may take up several megabytes of disk space. These powerful packages need a large memory too, although others will be happy with 512 or 640 kilobytes; a few with even less. The big packages are aimed at full-time users – secretaries and typists – who must be able to tackle a wide range of jobs. Users like these spend much of their time at the word processor, and learn by heart how to carry out complex operations. The great flexibility of these packages inevitably makes them harder to use, though usually you can simply ignore those features you do not need. However, in a one-person business you will probably be using a word processor for only a fraction of your time. A simpler program may suit you better, so long as it does have the features you need. Such a package may be easier to use, will take up less disk space, and may even be faster.

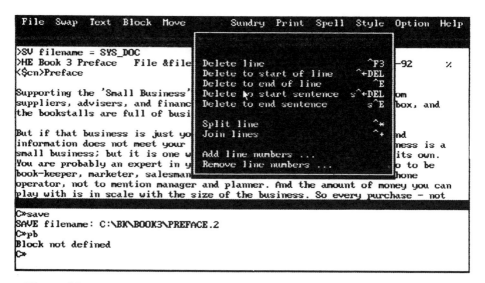

Figure 4.1 A character-based word processor ('Protext'), showing both menu and command-line control.

As far as straightforward text entry goes, all word processors are much the same. Differences appear when you want to carry out other operations: for example underlining or emboldening text, or moving text from one part of the document to another, or printing. In some programs you do these things with key codes, that is to say by pressing combinations of keys (usually 'Alt' or 'Ctrl' and a letter). In others you call up a menu and choose from it the operation you want. In others again you type the name of the operation, or a short code for it, on a 'command line', just as you would use the MS-DOS command line. Which of these is best is a matter of personal preference. For the beginner and occasional user, the menu approach is easiest because you do not need to remember key codes or commands. For the more experienced user, key codes and commands are faster, and using menus can become frustrating. The better packages give you the choice. You can use any key codes that you have learnt, which will be those that are most useful for your own work. And you can call up menus or 'help screens', or both, when you want to do something less familiar. If you have already learnt word processing, you may want to choose a word processor package that uses the key codes with which you are familiar, even though a beginner might find them difficult to learn. Some word processors deliberately use the same key codes as the market leaders, and others let the user choose the codes.

Word processors on the UK market will handle all the characters in the English alphabet and all the common punctuation marks. An exception is that the opening and closing quote marks, both single and double, are often not distinguished from each other. This is because some PC keyboards do not make the distinction, nor do many printers. If you want to use foreign characters, including those with accents, your choice of word processors is more restricted. The better packages will handle most foreign characters, although the absence of these from the standard keyboard means that you will have to use a reference table to tell you what keystrokes are needed. Often this table can be called up on the screen, and sometimes used as a menu from which you can select a character. Mathematical symbols are less readily available, and may be harder to use – especially those which are twice the height of normal characters. A few of the more expensive packages can handle them. There are also one or two word processors which are specially designed for mathematical and scientific work. These are not necessarily expensive. Your printer may restrict your use of these non-standard characters, although the better matrix and laser printers can handle all of them. A package designed especially for preparing mathematical and scientific papers, 'T_EX', is described later in this chapter.

Some word processors provide simple drawing facilities, for example to let you draw boxes and connecting lines round short pieces of text to produce organisation charts. The lines may be single or double. Again, not all printers can reproduce these, although most can.

Sooner or later you will meet the acronym **WYSIWYG**; 'What You See Is What You Get'. It is often used in connection with word processors, and sometimes other programs. The point here is that most programs which handle text (especially word processors, but not desktop publishing programs) use the 'character mode' of the screen. In this mode the screen can only display symbols from a fixed range. This includes all the letters and numbers and common punctuation marks. Most word processors also allow a range of special symbols. Characters can only be displayed in a single 'style', called Normal, or sometimes Roman. Bold or italic styles do not appear as such, nor can underlined characters be displayed on a colour screen, although they can on some mono screens. Also characters can only appear in a single size and in a fixed set of positions – typically 24 or 25 lines of 80 equally spaced characters, although this may vary with the hardware. If you enter italic or underlined or bold text, or specify proportional spacing, your printer will show these features (if it can) but your screen will not. So word processors provide some other method to indicate these features on the screen. For example, on a colour screen different colours may be used to identify bold, italic, underline and combinations of these. Another method is to insert special markers in the text where these styles start and end. Obviously, in none of these cases do you get in print what you see on the screen, although some manufacturers claim 'nearly WYSIWYG'!.

The alternative, and the only way to provide true WYSIWYG, is to use the 'graphic mode' of the screen. Word processors which use graphic mode do not treat the screen as a matrix of fixed positions in each of which one of a predetermined set of symbols can be displayed. Instead, they regard it simply as an array of dots. The number varies with the screen type; for example 200 rows of 320 dots, or 480 rows of 640 dots. This allows any image to be displayed within the limit of the screen resolution (which is less than the resolution of most printers), and thus a true WYSIWYG display is possible. However there is a penalty to be paid, and this is in speed. It takes longer to create an image on the screen in graphics mode than in character mode. On a powerful computer the delay in redrawing the screen is acceptable. On the simpler hardware that most one-person businesses can afford, it may not be. In either case, printing may be slower than in character mode, so unless you have powerful hardware, you should think carefully before choosing a word processor which works only in WYSIWYG mode. A few of the more expensive word processors give you the choice. They normally work in character mode but can produce a WYSIWYG image on demand. (I have to add that the publisher of this book disagrees with me: he claims to get excellent performance from a graphics-based word processor).

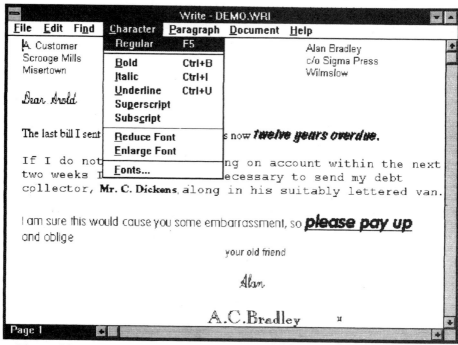

Figure 4.2 *A graphics-based word processor ('Windows Write'), showing how variations of character style and font are displayed accurately on the screen. The title and menu bars at the top of the screen, and the scroll bars at right and bottom edges, are typical of Windows programs.*

As we saw in the last chapter, in character mode you have no choice of screen font and only a very limited choice of printer fonts. Word processors working in graphic mode may have their own fonts, or use those supported by a Graphic User Interface. This gives a much greater choice of typefaces and styles, but, as we saw above, printing in graphics mode may be slower for some packages.

There is a wide range of word processors, and the choice is largely one of personal preference. If in doubt, you may as well start with one of the cheapest (or the one that happens to come free with Windows or some other software or hardware). Make a note of the features you don't like and those that you wish you had, and then go shopping again with these in mind before you have become too familiar with the program to want to make a change.

Spreadsheets

While the word processor introduced the PC to business at the secretarial level, it was the spreadsheet that brought computers to the desks of management. The first spreadsheet programs were designed for financial applications, such as expenditure analysis and cashflow forecasting. They gave managers the means to carry out these tasks quickly and easily by themselves, whereas previously a lot of time-consuming calculation was needed which would no doubt have been left to a junior. The management role of spreadsheets was reinforced when they became able to present data in the form of graphs.

A spreadsheet is basically a grid of **cells**, or individual spaces in which you can place data. Each cell is identified by the **row** and **column** in which it lies. Rows are always one character high, but a column can be as wide as you choose to make it. Columns are identified by letters, usually A to Z and then AA, AB etc. as far as needed. Rows are numbered. The cells are then identified by row and column, for example B33. Each cell can hold a single item of data. This is usually, but not necessarily, a number. You can put anything you like in any cell, but the spreadsheet becomes a useful tool only when you arrange data systematically in a table. The whole table is usually too large to show on the screen, so the screen forms a 'window' onto the spreadsheet and you can display any part you choose within the limit imposed by the size of the window.

To take a simple example, suppose you want to analyse last year's spending, in three groups – office supplies, software, and travel expenses. If you did this on paper, you would write 'Jan, Feb, Mar' and so on at the top of the columns, with a 'YEAR TOTAL' column after 'Dec'. Next you would enter the classes of expenditure down the left-hand side of the table, one class to each row (or line); say 'Paper, ink, blotting paper ...' and then a subtotal, 'OFFICE SUPPLIES'. You would continue down the page with the other classes, and finally label a row 'TOTAL'. Then you would then copy a figure from your accounts into each cell except those in the 'subtotal' and 'total' rows or the 'year total' column. Finally you would add up the subtotals and totals for each month, and the year totals.

On your computerised spreadsheet you do just the same. Thus you enter month names and 'YEAR TOTAL' in cells B1 to N1 and the labels for classes of expenditure in column A from cell A2 downwards. You can leave blank lines, or put in ruled lines, just as you would on paper. Likewise you enter the figures from your accounts in the appropriate cells. However, you no longer need to do your own addition. In the cell for your first subtotal, say A5, instead of a number you insert a **formula** which tells the computer how to calculate the number to be shown in this cell. In this case it would be something like 'SUM A2:A4'; the exact form depends on the particular program you are using. The program then adds up the figures in the cells A2, A3 and A4 and shows the result in cell A5, in place of the formula. You now want to put a corresponding formula in each of the cells B5 to N5, but you need not insert each one separately. Instead you give a command such as 'REPLICATE A5 into B5:N5' and the computer will automatically put the right formula in each cell, and use it to calculate a figure which then appears in that cell. You can then deal with the other subtotals, the column totals (for which the formula will be something like 'A5 + A9 + A14') and the year totals in the same way.

	A	B	C	D	E	F	
1	Household expenses: file HOUSEEXP.LGX						
2	Year	1969				1970	
3	Quarter	1	2	3	4	1	2
4	ELECTRICITY						
5	Standing charge						
6	Units	803	527	1100	743	818	576
7	Year total units				3173		
8	Total cost	7.57	5.66	9.74	7.14	7.57	5.92
9	Year total cost				30.11		
10	GAS						
11	Standing charge	3.25	3.25	3.25	3.25	3.25	3.25
12	Therms	643	502	62	205	581	519
13	Year total therm				1412		
14	Total cost	43.44	34.62	7.12	16.06	39.56	35.69
15	Year total cost				101.24		
16	Yr total gas+ele				131.35		
17	TELEPHONE						
18	Rental	4	4	4	4	4	
19	Total	4.85	5.15	4.78	5.05	4.57	4.68
20	Year total						

15% USED 11:32 am   G18(NMBR)=4   NUM
ENTER: Use arrow keys to move around, HELP(F1), or one of the following:
       +Expr "Text 'Rpt ,Graph <Time /Cmd =Goto !Recalc ;Jump

Figure 4.3 A typical spreadsheet ('Logistix').

There are of course many other ways in which you can use a spreadsheet, and for some of these it is useful to present the results as a graph. For example, if you were making a cashflow forecast you could assess the position instantly from a graph whereas a row of figures would take more time to absorb. Graphs are particularly useful when you want to convey information to others. This is less important in the one-person business than in the large corporation, where if you are to get a message over to your manager at all you may have to do it in thirty seconds. Nevertheless, graphical presentation may be useful when dealing with your customers or your bank manager. Every spreadsheet program worth having offers a range of graphical displays. There will certainly be line and bar charts and point graphs, and usually also pie charts. Some spreadsheets offer more elaborate displays such as maximum/minimum charts and Gantt or PERT diagrams, and some can insert a 'best fit' curve on a point graph. 'Three-dimensional' graphs are becoming particularly popular, especially for bar charts. Obviously the screen remains two-dimensional, but the use of perspective allows a third variable to be displayed.

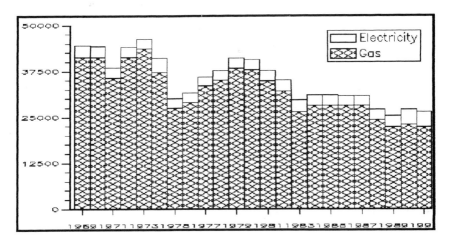

Figure 4.4 Graphical display of spreadsheet data ('Logistix').

We saw how a command is used to replicate a formula into a number of cells. A spreadsheet program offers a wide range of commands for various purposes; to name but a few, moving to a particular cell; saving or deleting the spreadsheet; adding or deleting rows or columns, or changing their order; and printing all or part of the spreadsheet. You may find that you repeat a particular sequence of commands often. In that case you can save that sequence as a **macro**. You then assign a particular set of keystrokes, for example 'shift' and 'F1', to that macro, and then whenever you press those keys together the whole sequence of commands will be carried out. Or you can give the macro a one-word name, and whenever you enter that name as though it were a single command the whole command sequence will be carried out. Quite elaborate macros can be created, and these save a great deal of time. The use of macros is not unique to spreadsheets. Many application programs allow them, but they are particularly useful in spreadsheet and database programs because these often call for long sequences of commands.

A spreadsheet is a general-purpose tool, so you can use it for whatever you want. We have already seen that financial management is one of the most popular uses. This includes forecasting, where the 'what-if' capability is of great use – for example, what will happen to your cash flow if interest rates fall, or if sales build up at a different rate from your first assumption. Once you have set up your spreadsheet with its formulas, you need only alter a few figures to see the results of each assumption. Some of the many other purposes for which spreadsheets are used include stock control, sales analysis, rent management, scientific and statistical work, tracking the performance of investments, and project planning. For many of these there are specialised packages, but if your needs are simple you may find it easier to use one general-purpose package for many tasks rather than learn your way round several separate programs.

Spreadsheet programs vary in the amount of data they can hold, in the facilities they provide, in performance, in ease of use, and also of course in cost. However, all but the most trivial can handle spreadsheets up to at least 256 columns and 8192 rows. This should be plenty for almost any application a one-person business is likely to have, even allowing for the fact that the spreadsheet must hold not only data but everything associated with it including headings, macros, and the definitions of graphs. All these you simply place in a 'spare' part of the spreadsheet, outside the area in which you will manipulate data. Be cautious about putting them too far from the data, however, as most programs will then store all the blank space included in the ranges of rows and columns that are in use. The whole spreadsheet is held in the PC's memory while it is in use, so very large spreadsheets may call for a computer with more than the usual amount of memory.

A major part of the facilities that are provided is the set of formulas and commands. These always cover a range of mathematical and financial calculations, including such things as discount and compound interest rate. Usually there are also logical functions (such as IF) and often trigonometrical and statistical formulas, as well as those for handling dates – for example, calculating the number of working days between two dates. Some programs have more specialised formulas for use in particular applications such as project management. There is also variation in the range of commands and graph types provided.

Performance is not likely to be a problem while your spreadsheets are small, but your machine may seem slow if you work with very large tables or a lot of complex calculations. The spreadsheets used in weather forecasting are so large that they need some of the world's most powerful computers to run them, but a simple PC will do nearly anything a one-person business is likely to want. One of the biggest tasks for the PC is repeating all the calculations ('recalculating the spreadsheet') whenever you change a figure. You can prevent recalculation being started until you have changed all the figures you want to change, so that it is done only once instead of many times.

The other important factor (besides price) in choosing a spreadsheet is ease of use. The basic functions are much the same for all programs – entering data, headings and formulas, and saving or printing information. However, the method of giving commands varies a lot, as does the control of graphs and of printouts. In some cases there are useful default settings for options and parameters, in others you will have to make a decision on each one. Spreadsheets designed to run under Windows will of course have a lot in common with other Windows applications, but at present they tend to be expensive. If possible, try to get your hands on those programs which meet your needs and see if you feel comfortable using them.

When you come to read the section on 'Database Managers' you will realise that the conventional database is similar in principle to a spreadsheet, in that it holds data in tabular form. The difference lies in the functions provided to manipulate the data, and the means by which this is done. Most spreadsheet programs have commands to do some of the simpler operations associated with databases, such as selecting and sorting data. Similarly, as we shall see later, many databases have some of the functions of spreadsheets, such as the use of formulas to allow the contents of a cell (or 'field' in database parlance) to be calculated from others. In fact some programs have the facilities of both, and of other applications as well, in a simple form. We shall discuss these under 'Integrated packages' in Chapter 5.

Database Managers

Along with word processors and spreadsheets, database managers make up the 'big three' of personal computer applications. All are adaptable to a host of uses, and all have been available since the earliest days of PCs. With a package of each type you will be ready to tackle most of the computing tasks that come the way of a one-person business.

A **database** is a collection of data, and in the present context it is a collection in such a form that it can be managed by a computer program. This implies that there must be at least a certain degree of structure to it. A **database manager** is an application program which manages a database. In fact the program itself is often referred to as a 'database', but this is unlikely to cause confusion although it may upset the purists.

As with a spreadsheet, data in a database is organised in the form of a table. In this case we call the rows 'records' and the columns 'fields'. Usually each record will describe a number of properties of a specific object, with each field relating to one of these properties. Every field, or column, has a name. However, unlike the spreadsheet the field names are not stored as part of the table itself, but in a separate 'header' file. The rows do not have separate headers, so the contents of the fields themselves identify the record. Usually, though not necessarily, the contents of one of the fields will be unique to this record so that all records can be distinguished by this field alone.

Unlike the spreadsheet, the screen does not always display the data as a table. Indeed, one of the main features of a database manager is the range of 'views', or ways in which you can display the data. One of the most useful views is that in which a single record appears on the screen. It can be laid out in whatever way you find convenient, and fixed text can be added to explain the significance of each field. The fixed text is stored only once, as part of the header file, rather than in every record. This is the most convenient view for entering whole new records. If you want to enter or amend data in only one or a few fields of existing records, you can set up a view which shows only those fields which identify the record (say a person's full name) and those fields which you want to change. If you want to read or print the information in certain fields only, you can set up a table of (say) names and salaries, leaving out all the other fields.

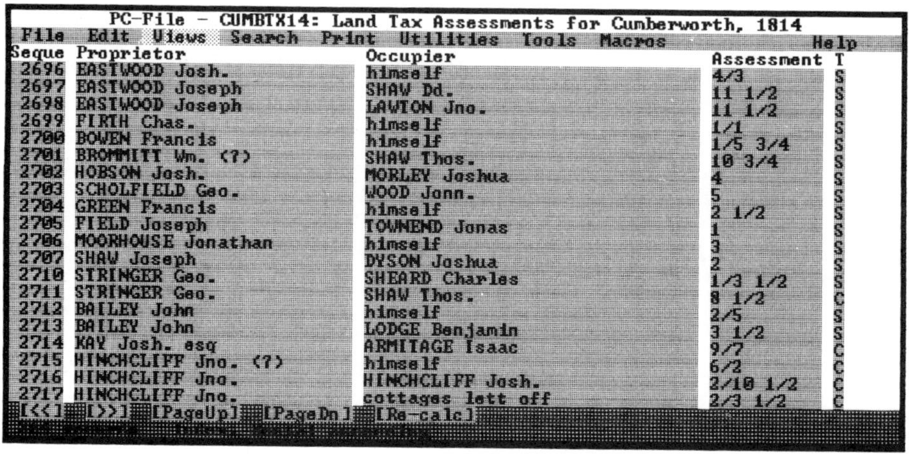

Figure 4.5 A database displayed in 'Table' view ('PC-File')

You may meet the term **report** in descriptions of databases. A report is simply a screen display, or a printout, showing the particular selection and arrangement of data that you need. You can arrange it in whatever format suits you best, and add headings and other explanatory text. However the term is usually applied to a standard output format which you want to use repeatedly, with various selections of data, which is therefore set up as a **template** so that you can call it at any time without further effort.

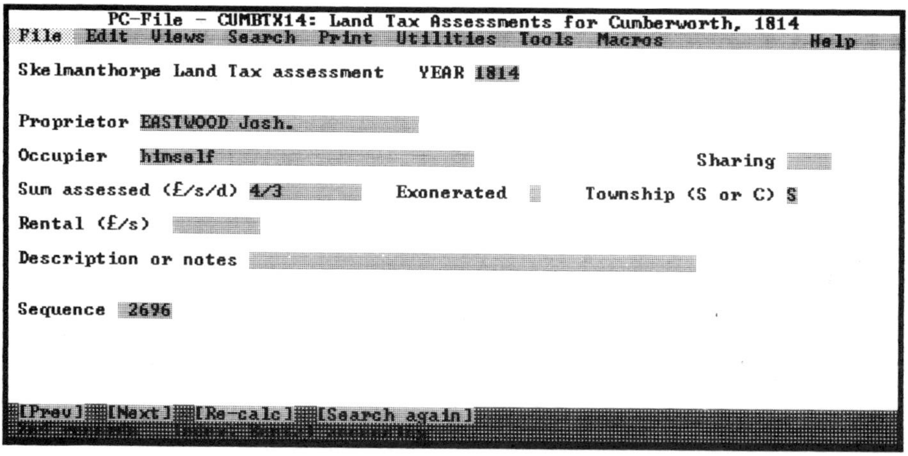

Figure 4.6 A database displayed in 'Record' view ('PC-File').

A major feature of a database manager is its ability to sort records, and to select records which meet specified criteria. As we saw in the last section, we can do this with a spreadsheet. However a database manager can use more powerful criteria for selection and sort order, and will usually do the job faster. It may also be easier to specify the criteria. Simple criteria are easy to set up on most databases, often using menus. Complex criteria can be difficult, and sometimes have to be written out in something akin to a programming language (described in Chapter 5). In an extreme case you may need an expert to do the job for you, though this is unlikely for the sort of problems a one-person business will want to solve.

Databases, like spreadsheets, make extensive use of macros. Here again the most complicated cases call for expert help, but you should be able to deal yourself with all or most of your own needs.

There is usually no limit to the amount of data you can hold in a database, other than the capacity of your disk. However there may be a limit to the size and number of fields in a record. Normally you need to decide the size of each field when you set up the database. This much space will then be allocated to the field in every record you create, whether you use it or not. The tendency then is to make fields as short as possible, and this accounts for the abbreviations and curtailed names and addresses that you often see in mail shots and the like. This is becoming less of a problem as disk capacity becomes progressively cheaper, as we shall see in Chapter 6. However, it is possible to design a database in such a way that only as much storage space is assigned to each field of a record as is needed to store the data. A database which works in this way is called a **variable record length database**. It has the obvious advantage of saving storage space. But you rarely get something for nothing, and what you lose in this case is performance. There are two reasons for this. The first is that if you want to read or update a field in a record, or a series of records, the computer can no longer go directly to that field because it does not know how far along the record it is. It must instead go to the beginning of the record and read through it all, counting the fields until it reaches the one it wants. A more serious problem is that whenever information is added to a field in any record, all the data from that point on must be shifted along to make room for it – which in practice means that the whole file must be rewritten.

There are a few variable record length databases on the market, but they are not very popular. Your choice will depend on how sparse the data is in your database – in other words just how much disk space this kind of database would save you – and on your view of the balance between disk space and performance. You may well want to have several separate databases. Unless you buy two database managers (which of course will take up more disk space – probably more than any data file) you will have to make the choice with all these databases in mind.

Some database managers offer a compromise. While the records in the main data file have fixed length fields, one of these fields contains a pointer to an entry in a separate data file which has variable length records. This is useful in the case where you occasionally want to add variable length information – such as notes or comments – to records which are otherwise suitable for a normal tabular database.

These linked variable-length fields are called **memo fields**. Their presence does not affect performance except when they are actually written or displayed. However, some of the functions that can be used with ordinary fields may not be available with memo fields. For example, they cannot usually be used for sorting data and sometimes not for selecting it.

A special case of the use of memo fields is the **free-text database**. This is of particular use for storing text which is inherently variable in length, such as abstracts from scientific journals, procedures, legal documents, recipes and the like. In this case the free-text data file holds the main database. Sometimes each record will have extra fields which are used to identify the data, such as a short title or reference number, and these can be used to find records rapidly. They may be organised as a conventional database, which in this case serves only as an index. However, a free-text database manager can also search for particular words or phrases within the free-text fields. This, in principle, lets you select all the records in which a particular subject is mentioned. Of course, you will need to watch out for synonyms and paraphrases, and for variations in phrasing. The selection criteria may need to be quite complex. For example, any of several words or phrases may indicate that the item might be of interest, but the presence of other words may then rule it out. Because selection is uncertain, this sort of database is usually used interactively. For example, you might start by asking for all items containing both 'drama' and '16th century'. On the one hand this may find so many records that you need to be more selective, perhaps choosing only those which also contain 'Shakespeare' or 'Marlowe'. On the other hand it may not find the item you want at all, so you need to allow also the (approximate) synonyms 'Sixteenth century' and 'Elizabethan'.

Word processors have similar facilities for searching text, so a free-text database manager may be closely linked to a word processor or even integrated into it. One or two free-text database managers avoid the term 'database' altogether and call themselves **information managers**.

In simple programs, called **flat file databases**, any formulas used to put information automatically into a field can refer only to data in the same database. However, you may have several databases controlled by the same database manager, and you may want one database to be able to refer to data in another. For example, I am interested in the history of my family and I have a database listing each member with dates and places of birth and death. I also have a database in which I list old family photographs. I want to print out lists and labels for these photographs which include the details of each person shown. In the 'photograph' database I only need list a reference number for each person, not all the details about them. However, I include a formula in the definition of this database which tells the program to look in the other database, using the reference number of each person, for the full information, and to include it in the lists and labels. A database manager which can fetch information in this way from a related database is called a **relational database manager**. There are many uses in business for this feature, and all the most powerful database managers are relational to some extent. However, there is no agreed definition of the meaning of 'relational' and some programs are more restricted than others. In particular the number of files that can be open at one time, in other words the number of other databases from which data can be extracted by the one you are using, varies very much from one program to another. Similar to the relational database manager is the **transactional database manager**. This is not fully relational but does have some ability to fetch data from other databases. It is sufficient for many business applications. As terminology is so imprecise, it is important that you decide just what you want your database manager to do and compare this with the abilities of those programs that you are offered.

The database manager is probably the most complex and flexible application program you will use, and it would take far more space than I can spare to describe all the features which you will find in a modern program. Your database may be critical to the success of your business, and in that case you need to be sure that the program you use is dependable and adequate for your needs. If those needs are simple you should be able to find a suitable program for yourself. If they are complex or if the database is vital to your business you would be wise to seek advice from someone with experience of the sort of business you are running, rather than just experience of selling computers.

If you install Windows you will find that a simple database manager, 'Cardfile', comes with it. This will be good enough for some straightforward tasks, although it is not a relational database. You may need something more powerful in the end, but it would be wise to try out your 'free' program first. Apart from anything else, you can note what you don't like about it, so that you can avoid those features next time you go shopping. It is usually possible to transfer data from one database to another without too much effort, though check this before buying a new program if you have entered much data into the old one.

You should be aware that if you store information on individuals in a computer database (or on a computer in any other way, for that matter) you may need to be registered under the Data Protection Act, and to observe the rules laid down by that Act. You can get all the information you need about this from the Data Protection Registrar, Springfield House, Water Lane, Wilmslow, Cheshire SK9 5AX. This applies to computers in the UK only, but there are similar provisions in most other countries.

That's enough for one chapter. In the next chapter we shall look at some of the more specialised types of application packages.

5

Application Software 2: specialised applications

In the last chapter we looked at Word Processors, Spreadsheets and Database Managers, the three general purpose application programs that meet most business needs. Now, we go on to look more briefly at some types of application program which are a little more specialised. These will not be needed by all businesses, but they are widely used. At the end of the chapter we shall look at packages which are more specialised, and at those which are unique to your own system.

Graphics packages

This is a general term for any application package which deals with pictures rather than, or as well as, information in character form. It excludes those packages, such as graphics-based word processors, which use the screen or printer in graphics mode to display only text. Desktop publishers are a borderline case, but these I shall deal with separately.

There are basically two ways of handling graphics with a computer. We distinguish them as **bit-mapped** and **vector** graphics. The difference lies in the way in which images are described and stored. A bit-mapped image is described by listing the state of each individual **pixel** or picture element that makes up the picture. For the moment think of pixels as being the dots on the screen, or in a half-tone photograph, though we shall see shortly that things are not quite that simple. A vector image is described, instead, as a set of mathematical formulas. Each of these describes one of the objects on the screen; for example a circle would be described in terms of its location, diameter, and line width, and the colours used.

A vector graphic image is thus made up of lines (not necessarily straight) and combinations of them, such as rectangles and circles, and so is sometimes called 'line-art'. You will find that you have a choice of line thicknesses, and of 'tints' or repeating patterns which you can use to fill closed shapes such as circles. Each line is described by a set of co-ordinates. These are used to define the image as it is displayed on the screen or printed out. You can change the size and proportions of the picture: the program has only to do some simple arithmetic on each co-ordinate and then redefine the image.

In contrast, a bit-map image is described by a table. This contains an entry for each point in a matrix which represents the image, in the same way as a screen image is defined (in graphics mode) by defining each dot on the screen separately. But the point spacing in the image, as it is held by the program, is not normally the same as that of either the screen or the printer – it may be much finer. So when the image is displayed or printed the program has to work out how best to represent it. The program does this by taking an average of the states of all that group of the points in the image which will be represented by an individual screen pixel or printer dot. This becomes difficult when the point spacing of the bit-mapped image is not an exact multiple of that of the screen or printer, as more image points will be combined into some screen or printer dots than others. For this reason, although you can vary the scale of the image, the results of doing this are not always satisfactory. For example, a line or grid pattern may appear to be superimposed on the image, sometimes giving a 'tartan' effect. You can avoid this by choosing only scales in which the ratio between image points and screen pixels in each direction is an integer. However, since the screen and printer dot spacings may not themselves be related by integers, the printer may not reproduce exactly what is seen on the screen.

Figure 5.1 A 'Paint' program ('Windows Paintbrush').

The two types of graphics are handled by two different types of program. A **Paint** package handles bit-mapped images. You can draw pictures on the screen with a pointer, using the keyboard or, more conveniently, a mouse. Line widths and colours can be selected, and there are also various standard shapes you can make use of – circles, ellipses, rectangles and so forth – as well as drawing freehand. You can fill in any closed shape with a choice of patterns. You can also import drawings from other programs, and many sets of useful drawings and symbols (described as **clip art**) can be bought as files on floppy disks. Besides this, if you add a scanner to your computer you can scan in drawings and photographs from 'hard copy' (which usually means paper) to produce a file holding a bit-mapped image. I shall say more about scanners in Chapter 6, though I should say here that it is not always easy to get good results. Manual cut-and-paste methods may suit your business better.

Vector graphics call for a **Draw** or **CAD** (Computer Aided Design) package. This also will let you draw images by moving a pointer, but shapes and lines can also be drawn by entering co-ordinates and dimensions. This makes drawing more precise. The emphasis is on lines which can be defined mathematically. These include the usual ellipses, rectangles and polygons as well as straight lines, but freehand lines are treated as a series of short straight lines. Again you can fill closed shapes, but the range of patterns is more limited. In a vector image, unlike a bit-mapped image, each object (circle, rectangle, line, or whatever) can be modified separately – moved, enlarged or reduced, or deleted. You can import images only if they are in vector form, which rules out scanned images. 'CAD' packages usually have more facilities than 'draw' packages, often including the ability to create three-dimensional images which can be viewed from any angle.

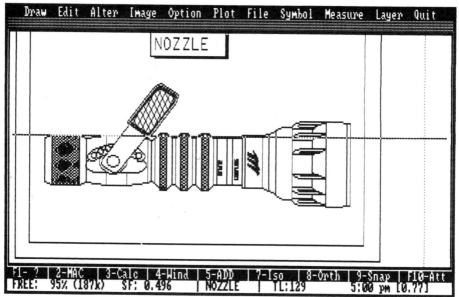

Figure 5.2 *A simple CAD or 'Draw' program ('Draft Choice').*

There is an overlap between the uses of the two types of package, but in general 'paint' packages are useful for freehand sketches and simple diagrams, as well as scanned images, while a 'draw' package is more suitable for complex diagrams and scale drawings. A true CAD package is a draughtsman's tool and is expensive. It needs a powerful computer, and a precision output device rather than an ordinary printer. However, there are scaled-down CAD packages which can be run on a PC and are satisfactory within their limitations.

Unfortunately there are no universal standards for the structure of graphics files. This can make it difficult to transfer files from one program to another, although there are utilities which will help. There should in principle be no problem if both programs are Windows-based.

If you have Windows you will find that a simple 'paint' package is included with it. This will probably serve for all except specialised needs in this direction. If you need a 'draw' or 'CAD' package you will have to buy your own.

Desktop Publishers (DTP)

Just as word processing can replace typewriting, so desktop publishing can replace typesetting – the first stage in conventional printing. The purpose of DTP is to enhance text by presenting it in a range of type styles, sizes and layouts in the same way as a professional printer would do. Most desktop publishing packages will also let you integrate illustrations with the text.

You should think about buying a DTP package if you will need newsletters, leaflets, menu cards, program cards, camera-ready advertising copy or the like with a more sophisticated appearance than word processing will provide. Bear in mind, though, that the size will be restricted by your printer. Most printers can handle only A4 or (in some cases) A3 paper. You will normally be able to work in only black and white, although you can of course produce two or more complementary images and superimpose them in different colours. Some top-of-the-range DTP packages will let you design in several colours on the screen and make colour separation prints directly.

Desktop publishing and word processing complement each other. Text is most conveniently entered with a word processor, and enhanced with a desktop publisher. However, there is a good deal of overlap between the two. Desktop publishers always include simple word processing facilities, so that you can edit text and enter small amounts of new text. For example, if you are designing a simple poster, it is easier to type the text straight into the desktop publisher than to type it first into a word processor and then transfer it to the other package. On the other hand, the more powerful word processing packages include some of the features of desktop publishing, such as a choice of fonts and sizes.

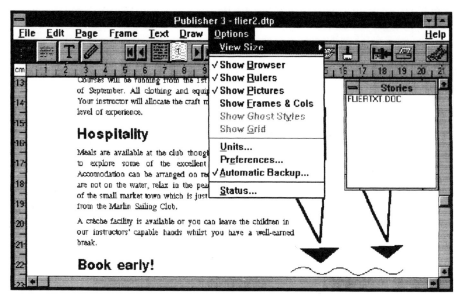

Figure 5.3 A desktop publisher ('Timeworks 3').

There is a major technical difference between DTP and word processing, although it is becoming blurred as top-end word processor packages provide more and more of the facilities of desktop publishers. Word processors normally use the screen and the printer in character mode; desktop publishers invariably use both in graphics mode. This gives DTP great flexibility in the choice of typestyle and layout. However, there are penalties to be paid in speed and in hardware cost. Few DTP packages will run well with less than 640 kilobytes of memory, and many demand more. A hard disk is essential, and even simple work may take up a few megabytes of disk space. A more powerful package or work on long documents or detailed illustrations will call for tens of megabytes. Some DTP packages will run on the simplest of PCs (such as the XT type, discussed in the next chapter) but you will spend a good deal of time waiting for results, so for serious work you will want a faster machine. As to image quality, you can work with a low-resolution (CGA) screen, but you will find it much easier with a higher resolution. The final appearance of your work will depend on your printer. You can get reasonable results with a 24-pin matrix printer, but for anything near to professional print quality you will need a laser or ink-jet printer. A laser printer will limit you to A4 size paper: some matrix and ink-jet printers will handle A3 or larger.

In other words, for serious desktop publishing you should be prepared to buy powerful hardware. You may need to spend two or three times as much as you would pay for a system that handles only straightforward work, such as word processing and simple databases and spreadsheets. So you should think carefully before you go into desktop publishing. If you need to produce a lot of work of near-print quality – say if you publish a regular newsletter, or use menu cards which change daily – it may well be worth doing your own DTP. If your needs are more modest, you will be better off using the services of a DTP bureau or of a conventional print shop.

This is perhaps the place to mention that desktop publishing is a particular strength of the Macintosh computer, and many users whose main business is DTP use this machine in preference to an IBM-compatible PC. If this is your situation, find out more about the Mac before you make your choice – for example from the book listed in Appendix 2. If you do prefer to stick with the PC, you will find that DTP and graphics in general can benefit more than most applications from the use of Windows. You will any case need a powerful PC and plenty of memory to handle DTP, so the extra burden imposed by Windows is less noticeable.

Simple desktop publishing is not difficult to learn, although there is a good deal more to it than to word processing. The more powerful packages have many extra features. These take more learning, but of course you need learn only those that you want to use. Indeed, one of the dangers of DTP is that you may be tempted to use features just because they are there. Some early users of DTP produced unattractive work – particularly advertisements and posters – because they couldn't resist trying out the whole range of typefaces, borders, background 'tints' and other tricks which they had available. In fact simplicity is the key to good results with DTP, just as with any form of printing.

This leads to the point that **graphic design** – the choice of layout, typeface, spacing and so forth – is by no means a simple matter. If you happen to have 'an eye for design' you may be able to produce fair results after a few trials. But even so it will take much practice before your skill approaches that of a trained graphic designer (and the staff of a good DTP bureau or print shop will have had this training). It is remarkable how much difference a subtle change in typeface or line spacing can make to the look of a printed page. For many users, adopting DTP caused a drastic decline in the quality of their printed work. So if you do decide to use DTP, you would be wise to seek some training in graphic design as applied to DTP. Failing this, read some of the books on the subject. It helps, too, to get into the habit of analysing other people's work, whether DTP or printed, of the kind that you intend to do. Look at it critically, and decide just why it does or does not catch the eye in the way you would wish.

An important feature of DTP is its ability to integrate images and text. The images can be in either of the forms that we discussed earlier in this chapter, 'vector graphics' and 'bit-mapped images', although you may find the manual uses different names. Most DTP packages let you draw simple line-art from within the package. With some you can also produce simple bit-mapped images. However you can also import images of either type which have been created or captured outside the DTP package. As we have seen, the two types of images have different sources. Line-art images come from 'draw' or 'CAD' programs. Bit-mapped images are generated either by 'Paint' programs or else by scanning an existing image, such as a drawing or photograph.

The problem of lack of file standards applies to the import of images into a DTP program just as to transfers between different graphics programs. The way in which the image is defined depends on the program which generates or captures it. In fact there are not as many different methods as there are programs. This is because some programs deliberately copy the method used by another program, though even then there may be minor inconsistencies. So if you want to import images, you should take care to choose DTP and graphics programs which are compatible with each other. Most DTP programs claim to handle a range of image formats, and some graphics programs can export images in a choice of formats. In principle, therefore, it should not be too difficult to find a match. However, difficulties do often arise. For example, when you import a line-art image the lines themselves should be correct; but other details, such as the thickness of lines or the pattern used to fill closed shapes, may be lost or distorted. Packages from the same software publisher, or which use the same graphic user interface, are less likely to suffer in this way. Even so, nothing should be taken for granted. A quick demonstration, or a 'demonstration disk', may not be enough to reveal any problems. You should try to see a full demonstration of the packages that interest you doing the type of work that you want to do. Failing this, make sure that the supplier will take the package back if it does not do what you want.

There are fewer problems in importing text from a word processor into a DTP package. There is one format which is standard, called 'ASCII'. Every DTP package can import text in this format, and nearly every word processor can produce text in it, usually as an alternative to its usual format. The catch is that the ASCII format ignores many of the enhancements which word processors can add to text, such as a variety of fonts and styles. It also omits some of the information that controls the layout of text on the page. This may not matter. It is often best to use a word processor to produce text in its simplest form, and then use the DTP package to deal with layout and with text style. However, if you want to do more of the work within the word processor, you must choose a word processor and a DTP package which understand each other. The better DTP packages will import text in the formats used by several of the most popular word processors. As an alternative, some will accept certain codes which can be included in an ASCII file; for example, words enclosed in angle brackets, such as <italic>. You can add these to your text in any word processor. However, there may be limits to what you can do in either of these ways. So if you want to import anything more than bare text into your DTP package, see it working with text imported from your own word processor before you buy. Or, of course, get a money-back guarantee from the retailer.

There are far fewer DTP packages on the market than word processors; perhaps twenty. Of these, a few are powerful, expensive packages designed for the corporate market. They cost several hundred pounds and need a lot of disk and memory space.

At the other end of the market are packages below the hundred pound mark. These have the same basic functions but lack some of the advanced functions of the bigger packages, particularly in respect of image handling. Some of them will run satisfactorily, if slowly, on a simple machine. Others need more memory or a more powerful processor. There are a few packages in between these two areas.

Many desktop publishing programs can only be used with a 'graphic user interface'. Nowadays this is likely to be Windows, but some older DTP packages use GEM. In this case GEM is usually supplied with the DTP program, and included in the price; but check this. If you already use a different version of the same GUI, it is important to check with the supplier that this will not lead to problems.

One of the strengths of DTP is that it lets you select from a wide range of different fonts (or typefaces). In most cases these fonts are controlled by the GUI which supports the DTP package, as described in Chapter 3. Where the desktop publisher does not depend on a GUI it will have its own independent set of fonts. In this case these will be the only fonts you can use, even if you run the package from a GUI which has its own fonts.

You should be aware that font files, especially in large sizes, can take up a up a lot of disk space, so be restrained in your choice. In fact good graphic designers rarely use more than one or two fonts, in perhaps two or three sizes, on any page.

There are two slightly different approaches to desktop publishing; 'page-based' and 'frame-based'. Without going into technical details, the former is said to be more convenient for single-page documents such as handbills and advertisements, and the latter for multi-page documents in which you want the style to be common to all pages. However, each type of package will do either type of work; the difference is just a matter of ease of use.

A brief mention should be made here of 'T_EX'. This is a combined word processing and DTP package designed for the preparation of scientific papers. It is complex and not easy to use, and it takes up a good deal of disk space. On the other hand it is able to handle all kinds of mathematical and scientific formulae. It is in the Public Domain, which makes it relatively cheap (Public Domain software is discussed later in this book). It comes without an instruction manual, but as it is widely used in the academic world there are several books which fill the gap. If you have to prepare scientific papers you should discuss T_EX with others who have used it, or with the editor of the journal concerned.

Outliners

A close relation to the word processor is the **outliner**. This is a program which works with text, like a word processor, but structures the text in a number of 'levels'. For example, if you were writing a book like this one the top level might be the book title, and the second level would be the chapter titles. The third level would be the subheadings, and there might be further levels for sub-sub-headings and so on. Finally the lowest level would be the 'body' text such as you are reading now.

The most important feature of the outliner is that you can choose to 'hide' everything below a given level. For example, if I hide everything below level 2 I see only the book title and chapter titles – in effect a contents list. If I hide only the lowest level I see every type of heading. This is a synopsis, which gives a fair idea of the contents of the book. In fact, like most writers of technical books, I work the other way round. First I decide on the chapter headings, then the main subheadings, and so on, adding more detail until I have a full synopsis. This is not only my guide in writing the text, but also the 'trailer' I use to interest a publisher before I start writing. Here a second feature of the outliner is useful. The text at each 'level' is indented further than that of the next higher level, so the synopsis shows clearly the structure of the book.

The program also lets me 'promote' or 'demote' each item to a higher or lower level, in which case all the entries associated with it (say all the sub-sub-headings following a subheading) are promoted or demoted to match. It is also easy to move an item to another position in the outline, and again all the associated entries go too. And if I choose, I can have items numbered in the conventional decimal system, or lettered and numbered in a choice of other systems. The program takes care of this numbering automatically.

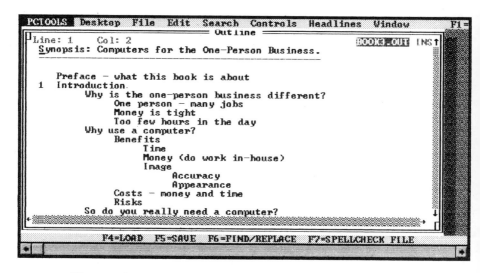

Figure 5.4 An Outliner (part of the 'PC Tools' utility package).

Altogether the outliner is a very valuable tool for an author, at least of a book or report which needs to be well structured – it might not be much help to a novelist.

However, this is by no means its only application. It can be used for organising ideas in any context, for action lists, for company structures, and many other purposes.

Some word processors incorporate an outliner. In this case the outline can be directly expanded into the book, or whatever it may be. More often the outliner is a free-standing program, or one of a set of utilities. In principle outliners could be used as word processors to write the whole book, but in practice they are not convenient to use in this way. There may also be restrictions on the size of the data file they produce.

Accounting programs

These are basically databases in which each record represents a financial transaction. You can define reports to produce summaries, analyses and final accounts. You could perfectly well use a standard database manager to deal with your accounts, and indeed I did this for several years. However, an accounting package will save you the trouble of setting up a database manager to do the job, and is likely to be faster and easier to use. In particular, it will have been based on the experience of people very familiar with standard accounting methods. This will make it easier for your accountant to understand, and for you too if you are already familiar with these methods.

There are two main types of accounting package, based on two accepted methods of accounting. The simpler is based on **cash-book accounting**. This will be adequate for those with few transactions – perhaps up to ten a week – and no complicated requirements. These packages – for example, 'Money Manager' – are easy to use and quite inexpensive. They assume that you want to associate each transaction with a particular 'account' – I use three: cash, bank and credit card. They also let you analyse your spending and income into classes and subclasses. For example one class could be 'office supplies' and subclasses could be 'paper', 'disks', 'stamps' and so forth. When you enter a transaction you include codes representing whichever account and subclass are applicable, as well as the description, date and amount. This is the data entry part of the operation. For reports you can select (usually from a menu) a full transaction list for a specified period, or a selected list showing (say) only your purchases of stamps, or any of a range of summaries or analyses. Most of these packages will deal with value-added tax, and prepare your quarterly or monthly VAT account, and some will also prepare full year-end accounts. A few can display information as a graph.

The more complex type of package is based on **ledger accounting** or double-entry bookkeeping, where there are separate lists or 'ledgers' for each account. Each transaction is regarded as a transfer between two accounts, and so will be entered in two of the ledgers. Needless to say, in the computer version you need only enter the transaction once and it will automatically be 'posted' to the two relevant ledgers. In general this type of program follows traditional accounting procedure closely. All such packages implement the basic 'Purchase' and 'Sales' ledgers. Many of them include further facilities, such as 'Nominal' ledgers and the automatic production of invoices and statements. In other cases the programs to deal with these extensions can be bought separately as and when they are needed. In either case the functions will be (or at least should be) fully integrated so that you need never enter a transaction twice. These packages have a full set of reports and should be able to produce all the summaries, analyses and year-end accounts that you need.

There are many accounting packages on the market. Some are general-purpose. Others are aimed at a specific type of business; for instance one aimed at the retail trade may be automatically linked to the cash register, or even allow you to use the PC as a cash register. Some have links to other administrative databases, such as stock records, payroll systems, and price lists.

Your choice of an accounting package, if you need one at all, must be very much influenced by the nature of the accounting methods that suit your business. This is something you would be unwise to decide upon without the guidance of your accountant. Nowadays most accountants dealing with small businesses are well aware of the potential of PCs, and yours can probably recommend a suitable program. If not, get him or her to lay down your accounting methods first, and then look for a program to match. Your local business computing centre may be able to give you useful advice, but remember that if they sell products their advice may not be impartial. Otherwise try to find a dealer who specialises in accounting programs, or at least one who carries a range of such programs and is familiar with all of them. Remember that in this area more than most, you will want support quickly if you have problems, so a local dealer – if competent – will be an advantage.

It is not usually possible to transfer data from one accounting package to another, so you would have difficulty making a change in mid-year. If you don't make the right choice first time, plan to make the changeover at your financial year-end.

If you are registered for VAT, the Customs and Excise will want to know about any computer program you use in calculating your VAT liability. They are unlikely to object to any established program, but might do if you concoct your own. This could have been a problem when I kept my accounts with a standard database manager, but in fact I only used this to record and summarise transactions and I worked out VAT by hand. If in doubt, consult your accountant.

Organisers and other aids to Management

Personal Organisers – the 'Filofax' and its rivals – have become the hallmark of the modern businessman or woman. Naturally, computerised versions have appeared. There are also many other programs, more specialised than the three standards that I described in the last chapter, which are designed to help managers. These range from elaborate project management aids to simple utilities such as calendars and calculators. I cannot describe them all, but shall look at some of those which are widely used.

Much the most popular is the **Personal Organiser**, or **Personal Information Manager** (PIM). The PC version partly replaces, partly complements the conventional organiser. Usually such packages contain a diary, a 'to-do' list of tasks which need doing but may not be scheduled, an address and telephone number list, and a 'notebook' for miscellaneous information. There are often other functions as well, which vary from one package to another. The telephone number list is linked to a modem, if you have one (I shall discuss modems in the next chapter), so that you have only to select an entry and the program will dial the number automatically. The appointments list is linked to an 'alarm clock' so that it will give a warning on the screen, and audibly as well, a few minutes before an appointment is due. The program is usually memory resident (explained in Chapter 3 under 'Utilities') so that it can be brought into play instantly, without disturbing the application that you are using at the time.

If you happen to have a portable computer this may be all you need, but even then it is often more convenient to refer to a printed copy than to the PC. So all these organisers can print out your information. Most of them will print on paper which will fit into an ordinary personal organiser binder. Although this is obviously a good idea, the need to change the paper in your printer from the usual stock may make it less convenient than it sounds.

If you have to do much travelling you may find a **Route Planner** useful. This finds the best route, by road, from one place to another, and estimates the journey time. The better programs will find a route which calls at several points, either in the most economical order or in an order that you choose. They will also take into account your preference for motorways or quieter routes, and of any temporary delays such as road works that you choose to enter. These programs are based on road maps. The output is available either as a map or as a schedule of instructions for the driver to follow. Packages for the UK and several other countries are available.

Finally there is a wide range of calendars, calculators, reference tables and other minor aids to management. Some of these are sold separately, but more often they are included in suites of utilities. Windows includes a small selection.

Communications packages

Communications, in the context of this book, means passing data electronically between your PC and another computer. There are two main ways to do this. One is the **Local Area Network**, or **LAN**, which links a number of computers which are close together and normally under the same management. The main aim is to let a number of workers share the same data. They can also share resources. For example, some of the PCs may not have printers: the LAN gives them access to printers attached to the other machines. LANs are becoming important in larger companies, but they are unlikely to be of interest to you unless you collaborate with other computer users in the same building. If you do need a LAN you will need appropriate software and also some simple additional hardware. You will also need special versions of many of your application programs. There are several reasons for this, but the most important is to ensure that one user cannot change data while another is using it.

A few highly-simplified LANs exist which connect together a very small number of PCs by way of their serial ports. Though slower and more restricted than a 'proper' LAN, they do permit the sharing of both hard disks and printers.

LANs are a complex subject, and if you do feel the need of one I advise you to get in touch with a competent dealer or consultant. It would be a good idea to read one of the many books on the subject first, so that you know what the possibilities and pitfalls may be.

The other form of communication between computers is a looser link between machines which may be any distance apart, and probably under separate management so that co-operation is less close. It is often referred to just as **data communication**, or sometimes (if several machines are linked within a defined network) as a **wide area network** or WAN. The link is usually a telephone line or radio link provided by one of the utility companies. This link may be 'leased' in which case the connection is always there, whether in use or not, or 'dial-up' in which case it is made when needed and broken when finished with, just like a telephone call. To use the link each computer must be fitted with a **modem**, a piece of hardware we shall discuss in the next chapter. Each PC must also have the appropriate software, a **Communications Package**. This is a complex subject. However, there are some good books available, and after reading one of these you should be able to set up your own modem and communications software. Most dealers are competent to advise you.

There are several ways in which the one-person business can use communications. We can divide them into those where you make arrangements privately with another user, and those where you use a service which is public in the sense that it is available to anyone who chooses to pay for it. In the first case you have only to make sure that the two systems are compatible, and agree what files will be transmitted and how each is to be identified and interpreted. Typical uses for such a system are sending invoices or other accounting data, and exchanging technical information.

In the second case the question of agreement does not arise in the same way, since the service already exists and you have to accept whatever protocols and methods it uses. There are two main uses for such a service. You may want to get information from an **online information system**, which is in effect a database of information of more or less general use. It may, for example, hold commercial or scientific or bibliographic data. Many of these databases are vast, and you will only be looking for a few items each time you get access to one of them. So some sort of **query method** will be made available to you. In some cases you can select items from a catalogue, which may be included in the database or may have been sent to you beforehand. In other cases you can tell the remote computer to search for words or phrases, just as in the 'free-text' databases we described in the last chapter. In others again you may work through a series of menus to reach the item you want. At least part of the charge for using such a database will be proportional to the **online** time, the time for which you are connected to the remote computer. The same usually applies to the cost of the telephone connection. Since many of these services are based abroad this can be significant. So the art of getting value from such a database is to keep the online time as short as possible, and the access method should be designed to help you do this.

As an alternative to getting pre-existing information from a database, you may wish to exchange messages of any type with another user of the remote system. This has come to be called **Electronic Mail**, or **E-Mail**. You can exchange messages just as if you were in direct communication with an associate, except that here you need not make a prior agreement with each individual. You can send a message to anyone who is a subscriber to the E-Mail system, just as you can talk to anyone who subscribes to the telephone system. In fact there are several different E-Mail systems, but the ones with most subscribers are naturally becoming dominant. However, there are links between most of the systems so that you can send a message to a subscriber on a different system.

E-Mail does have a couple of advantages over a direct link. One is that the remote user need not be ready to receive the message when you send it. If he or she is not, the E-Mail system will store the message until the addressee is ready for it. The second advantage is that you can put as many addresses as you like on a message and it will be sent to them all. You do not need to repeat the message for each one. E-Mail is used quite widely within and between big companies, though it has not taken off as fast as the organisers had expected. It is also popular with technical journalists. Whether it would help you depends on whether any of your business contacts are subscribers, and how urgently they need the information. Sending a disk by 'snail mail' (as E-Mail enthusiasts call the postal system) may be fast enough, and will be cheaper.

Another type of communications system which can be used by all, or all who care to pay for it, is the **bulletin board**. This is the equivalent of a notice board on which anyone can post a message for all to read. It is typically used to state a problem, or an opinion, to which other users may want to respond. There may or may not be some particular subject in which the board specialises. Most bulletin boards are aimed at the computer enthusiast rather than the business user, but a few may be more useful. For example, some designers of software will provide support to their users by way of their own bulletin board as an alternative to mail or telephone. This gives other users the opportunity to learn about these problems, and to contribute if they have found solutions of their own.

There is one more aspect of communications to be discussed here, and this is the use of your computer to give you access to the public fax network without having to use a fax machine. If you already have a modem, all you need is appropriate software. Otherwise you will also need a 'fax card' which fits inside your PC. You can think of this as a simplified modem, which can be used only for this purpose. Now you can send documents, prepared for example with a word processor, directly to any fax machine in the world by way of the public telephone network. You do not need to print them on paper first. Similarly you can receive a message from any fax machine and display it on your screen, or put it on paper with your printer. You can receive any sort of fax message, text or picture, but some fax cards will let you transmit only text.

A fax card is much cheaper than a fax machine, but you will need to leave your PC switched on all night if you want to receive fax at any time. If you do have a modem and subscribe to an E-Mail service, you can usually send fax messages through it (though this may be more expensive). You may not be able to receive them in this way.

Similar to the fax card is the **telex card**, which lets you use your PC as a telex machine. In this case you would have to arrange with the telephone company to have a link to a telex exchange, possibly via your own telephone line. If you subscribe to an E-Mail system you can send and receive telex messages this way and you do not need the telex card. However telex is rapidly being superseded by fax, and telex cards seem to have become scarce.

Integrated software

Most PC users are interested in all three of the 'classic' applications – word processors, spreadsheets and database managers. Software publishers soon saw the advantages of offering **integrated packages** which include all of these. Often they include other functions as well, such as communications. Integrated packages vary in the degree of integration. In a few cases there is little in common between the applications but the publisher's name. More often the user interface is common to all of them. For example, the same keystrokes that would save a word processor file to disk will save a spreadsheet, and so on. In the better integrated packages the transfer of data between packages is made very easy. It may even be dynamic in the way I have already described in writing about Windows; changing data in one application of the set may automatically cause another of the applications to alter related data. Of course, if you have Windows you may be able to do this even if the applications are in separate packages.

Besides these advantages, an integrated package is usually cheaper than buying all the basic three packages separately. Indeed, it is often thrown in free when you buy a PC or an operating system. This is almost the case with Windows; it includes two of the three basic applications as well as communications, and Windows itself provides the integration, but at present there is no spreadsheet.

There are two disadvantages to integrated packages. The first is that they take away your choice. You may favour word processor 'A', spreadsheet 'B' and database manager 'C'. If they come from the same supplier you may or may not find them in an integrated version. If not, you will not.

The second disadvantage is that the individual applications built into the integrated packages are rarely as powerful or as flexible as the best of those sold separately. They are usually good enough for occasional use, but if you use one application a lot you may want something which is more powerful, or which fits your own way of working better. As a writer I use a word processor far more than any other package, so it is worth my while to choose one which suits me really well even if it costs more and is not integrated with my other software.

Integrated packages, even expensive ones from the 'big name' companies, vary very much in quality. The result has been to give a bad name to the class as a whole. This is a pity, because a good integrated package will meet the needs of many small business users. It is also the best starting point for a beginner who does not have strong views about what he or she needs. If an integrated package comes with your computer I would certainly suggest that you use it. If in time you find it is not good enough for some of your tasks, that will be soon enough to start looking for an alternative. The same applies if you have Windows. Its built-in word processor will serve for most purposes and it also has a simple database, though not a spreadsheet. If your machine does not come with an integrated package, however, I should not suggest that you rush to buy an expensive one. Get some experience with low-cost versions of whichever application packages you need, or with a simple integrated package. When you find out why you don't like them you will know what to look for next; either a better integrated package, or a separate package for your most important application.

Programming languages

Programming languages are in a different category from most application software. They do not in themselves carry out any of the tasks of your business – unless you are a professional programmer, of course, in which case you don't need me to tell you about them. Instead, they are the tools with which you can write your own software. Whether or not that is a good thing we shall discuss later in this chapter. In the meantime, bear in mind that programming can take up a great deal of time. On the other hand, a home-made program may be the only way of carrying out some simple but essential task.

A programming language is simply a language which the computer can understand, and so – with practice – can you. It is needed because computers do not understand plain English. In principle they could be made to do so. There are already database managers which let you ask questions, and specify reports, in plain English. Their understanding of grammar is fairly good, and their vocabulary is adequate for that particular purpose. They work interactively, so if they do not understand a request they can ask you questions until they are sure what you mean. But although this approach is useful, it does show up two weaknesses of the use of plain English. The first is that it is expensive in resources. English is a very rich and flexible language. It has many ways of saying the same thing, and the computer must understand them all. This means that the computer will be either slower or more expensive than one based on a more formal set of commands. Secondly, plain English is imprecise. You have only to look at a legal document to see how much verbiage is needed to make sure that a meaning is unambiguous. We need a more precise language if our commands are to be concise. A plain English database may be practicable now; a plain English computer system is some way off.

Equally, you as a user would find it very hard to understand computer language, as we saw when we considered system software. The instructions that the operating system sends to the hardware are simply strings of binary digits. An expert can, slowly, interpret a few of them with the aid of tables. None would choose to write any sort of program in this way. We saw that the application programs speak a slightly simpler language to the operating system. Professional programmers make some use of this for critical parts of their programs, but for the most part they use a higher-level language of the type we are discussing here.

From this you can see that a programming language is always a compromise. On the one hand it should be easy to use. On the other it should be precise and concise. Needless to say there have been many attempts to square this circle, and there are hundreds of programming languages about. Of these maybe twenty are in common use. Only a few of them are likely to interest the non-professional programmer.

The most important of these is a language called **BASIC**. Although the name hints at the aim of its designers, it is in fact an acronym for "beginners' all-purpose symbolic instruction code" which makes that aim more clear. It is a language which is designed to be general purpose and easy to learn. Conciseness and power are subsidiary to this. This makes it a very suitable language for the amateur programmer. In fact the BASIC language comes free with most PCs, and so is obviously the one to cut your teeth on.

There is however one more weakness of BASIC besides those mentioned. This is lack of standardisation. BASIC may be supplied with most PCs, but there are many different 'flavours' of BASIC. If you write a BASIC program it will work on your own machine (with luck!), but it may not work on another. So BASIC is suitable for the sort of simple program you may write to get you out of a hole, but not for programs which you want to publish to the world.

At this point I had better explain what I mean by saying that this language is supplied with a PC. Of course a computer language is not something you can buy, any more than you are buying the English language when you buy a dictionary. What you get is in fact a piece of software which will take a program you have written in the BASIC language and turn it into a program in the language which the computer (or more precisely the operating system) can understand. There are two ways of doing this. A **compiler** takes your program and turns it into a program file, which looks exactly like the program files of bought software and is used in the same way. An **interpreter** also starts with your BASIC program, and works out what commands in machine language will give the result you want. But instead of adding each command to a program file, it sends it immediately to the operating system. Thus the program is run at the time that the interpreter reads your BASIC file. If you want to run the program again, the interpreter must read your BASIC file again because the interpreted program is not stored anywhere.

Each approach has its advantages and disadvantages. I shall not go into them here. Both interpreters and compilers are available for BASIC, although not necessarily for every flavour of BASIC. In the past, interpreters have been more widely used, but compilers are coming into favour. For most other programming languages, compilers are preferred to interpreters.

There are many other programming languages, amongst which 'Pascal' and 'C' are the most likely to interest the PC owner as there are low-cost compilers available for both. However, programming is a specialised subject so I refer you first to the columns of the PC magazines, and then to the many books on the subject.

Later in this chapter I discuss whether do-it-yourself programming is really a good idea for the one-person business. In the meantime, if there is a BASIC compiler or interpreter with your machine, I suggest that you find a little time to play with it. Whether or not you want to use it in anger, it will give you a little more insight into what goes on under the bonnet.

You do not need any special software to write **batch programs**, since the language they use is based on the commands and parameters that you can give to your operating system. The operating system includes some extra commands which are only of use in batch files and would not be entered at the command line. Batch programs, or **batch files**, can only operate on complete data files, and cannot manipulate the data within a file. Even so they can be very useful in the management of your system, and particularly in automating activities such as backing up data and selecting actions from a menu. It is well worth while learning how to write them. I shall have more to say about this in Chapter 8.

Task-specific software

In Chapter 4 we looked at general-purpose software that is useful to almost every business, large or small. In this chapter we have looked at packages that are more specialised, but still useful for many types of business. Now we come to software aimed at a single type of business. This is **task-specific** software. Some such packages are promoted as **vertical software**. By this the suppliers imply that the package meets all the computing needs of the business in question.

This sort of software does not differ in principle from that meant for more general use. However it is designed to be easy to use, and among other things this implies that any data transfer between one part of the application and another is automatic. For example, a system designed for a filling station will take information on the amount of fuel supplied from a petrol pump; prepare a credit card voucher and check the validity of the card; keep a total of the sums received in cash and as credit transactions; keep a total of the quantity of fuel sold from each pump; and allow for these to be reconciled with the amount of cash in the till, and the amount of fuel remaining in each tank, daily or at the end of each shift. The system may do other tasks, such as preparing statements for the credit card companies, orders for the fuel supplier, and monthly and yearly accounts, and also predicting cash flow and profitability. If you were to do all these tasks with general-purpose packages you would first have to put a good deal of effort into customising them to your own requirement. You would also have to spend some time moving data from one package to another. This should not involve actually re-keying figures, but you would need to learn the procedure for doing it.

This example demonstrates that the virtue of task-specific software is that it makes your task as simple as possible, by drawing on someone else's planning and experience instead of your own. On the other hand, such software tends to be expensive. It may also be inflexible, so that you have to suit your method of working to the software. This need not be so, but the choice of packages for any particular business is likely to be small.

You will not find specialised packages for every type of business. On the one hand, the business may be so specialised that a developer could not sell enough copies of his package to make ends meet. On the other hand, one of the package types I have discussed in this chapter and the last one may be so near to the needs of your business that there is no point in designing a special package. Or it may be that software developers have just not noticed that your type of business exists.

However, there are packages designed for a wide range of businesses. I cannot try to list them all, but here are some examples. Retail businesses of many types; guest houses; consultants and specialists of various kinds; builders, plumbers, and other tradesmen; haulage contractors; vehicle and other repairers; farmers; estate agents and surveyors; financial advisers, agents and accountants; insurance agents and loss adjusters. A particular area where a lot of 'vertical' software is available (though not cheap) is the medical profession.

A major problem with this kind of package is finding what is on the market, and sorting the good products from those which are not so good. Most computer dealers will not know or stock such specialised software. Computer magazines do not cover it in their editorial matter, though occasionally they carry advertisements. The producers of this software may have stands at some of the larger computer trade shows, but often they are too small to afford this. Your best prospect is trade shows, and the trade press, related to your particular type of business. If there is a trade association it can probably help. In particular it may put you in touch with other users. If all else fails, look in the advertisements and catalogues of the firms supplying 'shareware' – indeed, this is worth doing even if you know of other suppliers. I shall say more about shareware in Chapter 7; briefly, it is a method of selling software which lets you try it out at very low cost before you buy. You then buy directly from the supplier. Because this cuts out so much of the cost of selling, it lets the designer make a profit on quite small sales. If a businessman or woman writes software for the use of his or her own business, it is often put on the shareware market so that others can use it too.

If you don't find what you want, and you cannot do the job with any of the standard packages, you may think about software written especially for your own business. You may write it yourself, or pay someone else to do it. We shall look more closely into this towards the end of this chapter.

Big name or low cost?

Software packages of any one type may cover a wide price range, often as much as ten to one. The most expensive packages usually come from the best-known companies. Naturally these packages tend to have a rich range of facilities while the cheapest packages are simpler, but this does not account for all the difference. A lot depends on the market that the source company wants to be in: the 'corporate', or medium to large company, market, or else the small business and home market. The corporate user is likely to have many copies of the package. There may be varying patterns of use within a large company, but it is convenient to standardise on a single package which must therefore be one with a wide range of features. Cost is unlikely to be important to such a company, and in any case it has the buying power to obtain large discounts. However, the buyer will be aware of the 'safety factor' – to borrow a phrase from the computer hardware field, 'nobody ever got sacked for buying Wordxxxxx'. In the small business and home user market, cost usually is important. You have to consider not only the cost of the program itself, but also that of the more expensive hardware that you may need to run some of the top-of-the-range packages. If you are not going to spend much of your time with any one package, you need something simple and easy to learn. And a limited range of features is acceptable, so long as the particular ones you want are there.

It is interesting that one spreadsheet manufacturer, who used to sell at a 'corporate market' price, recently cut that price by three-quarters to move into a different market sector. Also, several up-market suppliers now sell low cost versions of their products. Some of these are just outdated versions of the primary product. Others are up-to-date but have some of the little-used features removed. This has the side-effect of making the program easier to use, and often of reducing the disk and memory space needed. The difference in price bears little relation to the reduction in features, it is mainly a matter of market position.

So there are three areas to choose from: big-name, high-priced packages; cheaper packages from the same big names; and low to medium priced packages from less well-known companies. For the one-person business the first of these will probably not be the best choice, though if the application is very important to you it will be worth spending as much as necessary to make sure that it really does what you want. But when it comes to choosing between the others, what's in a name? There is no easy answer. A big-name package is likely to have been more thoroughly tested. The suppliers may be able to give more effective help. Even so, such packages may still fall short of perfection in both respects. Cheap packages, unless they are old or cut-down versions of higher-priced programs, may be less well tested and there may be less support available.

Dealers and consultants, or at least those of them whose income depends on the price of the products you buy, will naturally encourage you to buy the higher-priced products. This is reasonable, since you will doubtless expect them to provide you with support. A cheap product will give them less profit and yet, possibly, more trouble. They also prefer to sell packages that they already know well, because these are easier for them to support. If you make the choice yourself you must bear this matter of support in mind. However you can look to alternative sources for help; the software publisher or a user group, for instance. We shall discuss this more fully in a later chapter.

My own inclination (and of course writers are always short of money) would be to look first at the low to middle part of the price range, but treat very cheap packages with caution. I should then base my choice mainly on how well the package met my own particular needs. I should give no weight, or even a negative weight, to features I did not expect to use. If a 'big name' could supply what I wanted I should choose it in preference to an unknown at a similar price. Otherwise, unless I knew more about the companies concerned, I should assume that I could get acceptable support from any company or, failing that, from elsewhere.

It may be that you suspect the publisher is about to go out of business, or to discontinue the product. In that case you might find that you could get no support from the publisher. On the other hand, such software is often drastically reduced in price, which can make it a good bargain if cost is important to you. The brand-new product from a small company should be treated with caution. It may well be inadequately tested and you could find yourself playing guinea-pig. If the product fails in the market the company may disappear, and with it your chance of support.

Bespoke software

As we said earlier in this chapter, it may happen that none of the standard packages will solve your problems. The alternatives are then to write your own software (discussed in the next section) or to have it written for you. Software written for a specific user is often described as 'Bespoke software'. It may be written from scratch, or a standard package which is somewhere near to your needs may be partly rewritten. There are many software houses and freelances who can do this for you. If you want an existing program modified, your choice may be limited to the original publisher, for copyright reasons. However, some publishers will license other companies to do this work. Whichever way the job is done, it is likely to be expensive, and few one-person businesses can afford bespoke software. It becomes more affordable if you can get together with others who have the same problem, and share the cost between you.

Apart from cost, the main point to watch with bespoke software is reliability. The publisher of a standard package can afford to do extensive testing before releasing it for sale, because he can spread the cost of these tests over many sales. Often he releases the package first to a few specially chosen customers who are willing to act as guinea-pigs – this is sometimes called 'beta testing'. With bespoke software this cannot happen, of course. Here you have no choice but to be the guinea-pig yourself, so you must be prepared for some errors and failures in the early days of use. You must also realise that it is hard to predict how long it will take to develop a piece of software. There have been some horror stories in the press about companies which have been destroyed by late or faulty software. Fortunately these are the exception rather than the rule – otherwise they would not be news.

If this gives you the impression that I am wary of bespoke software, you are right. Big companies can afford to employ top-class programmers and to have fall-back arrangements in case bespoke software is late or defective. This is unlikely to be true for a one-person company, and bespoke software will be suitable only in special cases.

Do-it-yourself programs

Much of what we have said about bespoke software applies here too. However, in this case you are your own program developer. This means that cost is less of a problem. It consists of your own time, if you choose to account for it, plus the cost of a compiler (discussed earlier in this chapter) and whatever training and instructional books you feel you need. The compiler will only cost as much as employing a programmer for a day or two. Training varies in cost, but you could buy a fair amount of it for the cost of a week's hire of a good programmer. On the other hand, what it will take is time – lots of time, since you will have to learn programming before you start to do any useful work.

Many sole businessmen and women have written programs for themselves, often because they like a challenge rather than because they can justify the time involved. If you have an interest in programming (and it can be fascinating), and you have time to spare, and the program you plan is an enhancement to your computer system rather than an essential, then by all means have a go. Bear in mind what I said under 'Bespoke programming' about reliability, and remember that thorough testing of a program takes longer than writing it. And start with something simple first. A set of small separate programs may be a safer approach than one big one, even if it will be more tedious to use. You may like to start your programming as I did, by writing something that will help with one of your hobbies rather than with your business. That way you will get experience, both in programming and in estimating the time and effort you need, at less risk. Anyway, if you do decide to try, good luck. If not, I commend your caution!

Hardware

Choose your hardware to suit your software

Choose your hardware to suit your software – the phrase has been so overworked that it has become a platitude, but it is still true. In principle any IBM-compatible PC can run any program written for any such PC. Up to a few years ago this was almost true in practice. Nearly all PCs had at least 512 kbytes of memory, and nearly every program would run on a PC with this memory. But as programs became more powerful, this memory size limit became harder and harder to meet. Eventually some program designers came out with versions which needed more memory. Others followed suit, and now many of the up-market programs need at least twice this amount of memory, and some need more. In particular, Windows and applications based on Windows need a PC with a lot of memory. There are still plenty of programs that will run within the 512 kbyte limit, although some of these will run faster if there is more memory available.

Processor power (or speed) is also an issue. A fast machine is never essential: any program will run on the slowest of PCs. However, for some tasks such as graphics and large spreadsheets the process can become agonisingly slow. In this case a faster processor is well worth the extra cost. As we shall see, the oldest types of processor cannot run some Windows-based programs, regardless of the processor speed.

The third factor that affects compatibility between machine and application is disk capacity and performance. Early machines had only floppy disk drives, but it was soon realised that a hard disk made the machine both faster and easier to use. For some years the software designers kept their programs within reach of the dwindling number who had no hard disk on their machines, but now this limit has gone too. Most major programs will not run without a hard disk, and this certainly applies to Windows and almost anything else that works in graphics mode. Indeed, a machine based on Windows needs a large hard disk to work efficiently, and 80 or 100 megabyte disks are now becoming the norm. Disk performance is also important. In some applications it is more important than processor performance. This applies, for example, in many database applications.

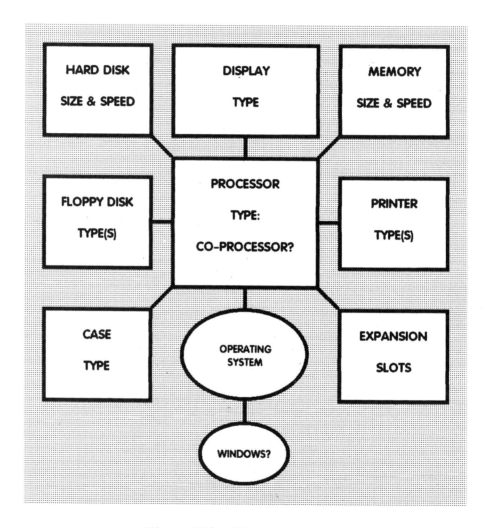

Figure 6.1 Specifying your computer.

If money is not a problem, you can simply buy one of the most expensive types of PC on the market, and feel confident that it will do anything you want to do now and for a few years into the future. Most of us cannot afford to take that approach. So we must buy a machine that will do just what we need, with a bit in hand but not too much. For this reason you should decide first what software you need, and then consider what sort of a machine you must have to run it. If this machine turns out to be beyond your means, you may have to scale down your software ambitions. But if you choose your hardware first – presumably to suit your purse – you may find that you are unable to do some of the jobs you planned to do with the PC. Or even if you can do them, you may find that they run so slowly that they try your patience.

Desktop or portable?

The first hardware decision you must take is whether to buy a **desktop** machine or a **portable** (or 'laptop', or whatever description is fashionable this year). The desktop machine is not designed to be moved frequently. It will take up a space perhaps 15 inches square on your desk, and the display will use a cathode-ray tube (CRT) similar to the type used for television. These tubes are heavy, partly because of the very thick glass used to prevent the escape of radiation. They are thus not suitable for a portable machine. Usually, though not always, the display sits on top of the main box of the computer – the 'system unit' in computer jargon. The keyboard is always a separate item, which you can place where you find it most comfortable. Indeed, recent Health and Safety regulations require that the keyboard must be movable in this way and also that the display must tilt and swivel. (They do not apply to portables unless these are in continuous use). For many programs, particularly graphics programs and those based on Windows, you will want to use a mouse. For this you will need to keep an area of your desktop free, say 9 inches wide and 6 inches deep. It is up to you whether this is on your right or your left. Personally I find it convenient to use the mouse with my left hand, leaving my right free for the keyboard. Some mice are not symmetrical, but may come in right-handed and left-handed versions.

The portable is a very different machine from the desktop, and incidentally a much more expensive one. The biggest difference is that the display is in the form of a thin flat screen instead of a bulky CRT. This display is incorporated in a hinged lid which can be folded forward to close the machine, like a briefcase, or backwards to whatever angle you find most convenient for viewing. A great deal of effort has been put into developing flat screens, but unfortunately they are still far less satisfactory than the CRT. In particular, colour flat screens are expensive and therefore not widely used. Even the monochrome display has less contrast than a CRT, although modern LCD displays are much better than those of a few years back. However, those who choose to work with portable PCs find these screens acceptable.

The keyboard of a portable PC is invariably built into the machine and cannot be separated from it. The larger portable PCs have a keyboard which is similar to that of a desktop PC, and this prevents the size of the machine being reduced very far. Usually it is about the size of a briefcase. Smaller machines (often called 'laptops') are about the length and width of a sheet of A4 paper – just over 8 inches by 11 inches. To fit the keyboard into this space, some keys have to be left out. These may include the numeric keypad, the arrow keys used to move the cursor, and possibly the function keys (we shall discuss all of these later). The remaining keys can be made to take over the functions of those that are missing, but this is obviously less convenient than using a full keyboard. In some cases the keys are made smaller and closer. If you only use this machine, and you have normal size fingers, this may be acceptable. If you use another machine besides this one, different key spacing may cause you problems.

Early portable computers did not always have disk drives, but now a 3.5 inch floppy disk drive has become the rule and there is often a hard disk as well. This may be limited in capacity, although disk drives get more compact every year. A mouse may be provided but if travelling you may not be able to use it. The alternative is a tracker ball, which serves the same purpose, and may be built into the keyboard.

Portable computers run off batteries, usually the rechargeable type, and many can also be run off the mains. Battery life is still a problem. It can vary from two or three hours to ten or more, depending on the particular machine. If you intend to use a portable PC away from the mains supply, choose one with adequate battery life.

The conclusion is that in many ways, the portable computer is not as satisfactory as the desktop machine. However, for some people its obvious advantage – portability – makes it worth having. Only you can decide if this applies to you.

Processor type

The other fundamental choice you must make is that of processor type. The processor is the heart of the PC, and is one of the factors that decide how fast your programs will run; or even, in some cases, whether they will run at all. Processor design has improved steadily, and several generations have been used in IBM-compatible PCs. The terminology can be confusing, and is not always consistent. However, the most usual way in which the different processor types are identified is by the numbers 8086, 286, 386, 486 and 586. There are others, but they are not widely used. The sequence may go further by the time you read this book, as a new type appears every couple of years. Needless to say the new introductions are always more powerful, and more expensive, than their predecessors. The numbers (apart from 586) are a shortened version of the part numbers which one manufacturer, Intel, gives to its processors. So strictly speaking they apply only to the processor itself, but they are now generally used to describe the PC as a whole. This applies even if the processor is made by a different company. Intel refers to its '586'processor family as 'P5', but '586' is likely to remain the generic term.

Just to confuse matters, machines using the 8086 type of processor are often called 'XT' machines, since IBM first introduced the 8086 in its 'XT' version of the PC. The IBM machine using the 286 processor was called the 'AT' and you may still meet this term, though as 386 and 486 machines are also 'AT's the term has become confusing and is not now widely used.

8086 machines are the oldest, cheapest and least powerful type still on sale. They were the first type to cater for the mass market, as Amstrad introduced an 8086 machine (the PC1512) in 1986 at about half the prevailing price for a typical PC, and this caused a general fall in prices. By modern standards they are slow, and they are not really suitable for running graphics programs. Indeed, the latest version of Windows will not run on an 8086 machine. If your needs are simple – say word processing and small spreadsheets and databases – an 8086 machine may suffice. However, these machines are rapidly disappearing from the market, and future versions of your applications may not run well on them.

The 286 is faster than the 8086, and more expensive. Most software will run satisfactorily on it; but although Windows will run on this machine, some of its facilities are not available. For a while the 286 has been regarded as the 'entry-level' machine, but for technical reasons it is little cheaper than a 386. For this reason, and because Windows is becoming so popular, many manufacturers have withdrawn their 286 machines from the market.

This brings us to the 386, which is now regarded as the entry-level machine. This machine will run Windows with all its facilities, and has ample speed for most purposes including graphics. The 486 and 586 are more powerful still. However, the extra power is aimed mainly at companies who have several machines linked together in a network. As a sole user you are unlikely to need this extra power unless you are doing complex tasks such as CAD (Computer Aided Design) or using very large databases or spreadsheets.

The 386 is available in various versions. The two that will concern you are the 386SX and 386DX – there are variants of these to suit portable PCs. So far as you are concerned, the main difference is that the DX is faster. Just to confuse things, sometimes the term '386' is used to cover all versions of the 386 chip and perhaps newer chips as well, and at other times it refers only to the faster versions of the 386 in contrast to the 386SX. All versions of the 386 processor are available with a choice of 'clock speeds'. For example, if you ask for a 386SX machine you may have the choice of 16, 25, 33 or 40 Mhz processors. The difference in speed between the SX and DX is less easily defined, but in any case processor speeds alone do not directly correspond to the performance of the PC as a whole. Your best guides are the reviews published in PC magazines. These usually include 'benchmark' tests, which are tests typical of the work done by users.

There are even more versions of the 486, and I shall not try to list them here. They range from those which are slower and not much more expensive than the fastest 386s up to much more powerful and expensive machines. The 586 is not yet on the market as I write, but will presumably be still faster and more expensive.

As we saw earlier, there are some applications where the effective speed of the program depends very much on the processor speed, and others where it has little effect. The 386SX is the most popular processor at the moment. It should be more than adequate for the needs of most one-person businesses. For Windows you will need a 25 Mhz or faster machine, otherwise a slower version will do. If you expect to use complicated graphics or large spreadsheets, it is worth paying for a faster version.

As this book goes to press 486 prices are falling rapidly, so by the time you read it you may find a 486 machine costs little more than a 386. In that case, obviously, the extra power of the newer machine will be worth having.

Co-processors

Another way to improve processor speed is to add a 'co-processor'. This is a second processor which takes over some of the arithmetic operations from the main processor, and does them faster. Most 286 and 386 machines have a socket for a co-processor which you can add to your machine at any time. However, not all the programs which are sensitive to processor speed can actually use a co-processor. If you expect speed to be a problem you would be wise to start off with a fast machine. If you only hit this problem later, and then only if you are performing mainly numerical tasks (e.g. with very large spreadsheets), the co-processor may be the best way out.

Memory

For many applications, the size and speed of the PC's memory affects performance more than the choice of processor type does. This applies particularly to recent programs or recent upgrades of older programs. The earliest popular PCs, including the Amstrad PC1512, had 512 kbytes of memory (meaning 512 kilobytes, which in computer circles means 512 x 1024 rather than the usual 512 x 1000). This was regarded as generous at the time. However, as we saw in an earlier chapter, as programs have grown more powerful they have grown larger, and the 512 kbyte limit has become irksome. Some program designers have abandoned this limit, so their applications can no longer be run on the simplest machines. Others have kept within it only by using technical tricks. These usually allow the program to run with 512 kbytes but only slowly, with a larger memory needed to get full performance. For a while that larger memory was 640 kbytes, but for many programs it is now 1 Mbyte (1 megabyte, i.e. 1 x 1024 x 1024 bytes) or more.

This leads to some problems with 8086 and 286 machines (though strictly speaking the problem is in the operating system as much as the hardware). These machines cannot have more than 640 kbytes of ordinary memory. In the case of the 8086 it is possible to increase the memory by plugging a 'memory expansion' card into one of the expansion bus slots, although this is not always desirable because you may need these slots for other purposes. In any case, it is useful only where the application program is written to take advantage of this **expanded memory**, and many applications are not. The expanded memory can be used only for storing data, not software.

Expanded memory can be used on a 286 too, but this machine can also use **extended memory**. This is more flexible, since it can be used either as expanded memory or in other ways, but it still takes up an expansion bus slot.

With the 386 and later machines (and the operating systems supplied with them) this limitation has been eased. Most such machines will take at least 8 Mbytes of memory, and some will take more. However, few users really need this much. Usually the machines are supplied with only a few of the memory slots filled. You can add more at any time, relatively cheaply, and it does not use up expansion bus slots. Most 386 machines are supplied with 1 or 2 Mbytes of memory. 1 Mbyte is enough for simple applications but 2 is recommended for most purposes, and is the least with which Windows will run satisfactorily. If you want to run Windows application programs, you will find 4 megabytes of memory almost essential. Even on a 386, memory beyond the first 640 kilobytes is technically extended memory and is treated separately by the operating system, but there are ways of making it useful to most application programs. The manual will explain what you need to do; if you find it hard to follow, I can recommend the book listed in Appendix 2.

The other feature of memory is its speed. The memory units for 386 and faster machines are available in various speed ratings. However, unless you have some particular reason for making the change you should stay with the memory speed that the manufacturer installed in your machine. Faster memory will not automatically improve performance, there may be other limiting factors.

Disks

The memory in a PC is made up of electronic circuits (or 'chips') which are made in much the same way as the processor. This memory is essential, but it does have two disadvantages. Firstly, the information held in it is lost when you switch the computer off. Secondly it is expensive in relation to the amount of data it will hold. So every PC also has disk storage (or, in computer jargon, 'Direct-access storage'). Information is stored on disk as a magnetic pattern, much as music is stored on a cassette tape. Once stored, this information does not need power to retain it; it will stay on the disk until you deliberately remove it. So software and data are normally held on disk. But disk storage is much slower than memory, so a program must be copied into the PC's memory to be executed. Data may also be copied into memory, in which case it must be copied back to the disk after use if it has been altered. Programs need not be copied back because they are not changed when they are used. Some programs, such as spreadsheets, hold all the data they are using in memory. Others, such as databases, usually read only one record at a time from disk and write it back as soon as they have finished with it.

There are two sorts of magnetic disks; **floppy disks** and **hard disks**. The names refer to the materials from which they are made, but this need not concern us. The important thing is that a floppy disk can be removed from the PC, while a hard disk is built in and cannot be removed. (There are exceptions, but they are for specialised purposes and you are unlikely to meet them). Floppy disks come in two sizes, 3.5 inch and 5.25 inch; the former is rapidly becoming the standard.

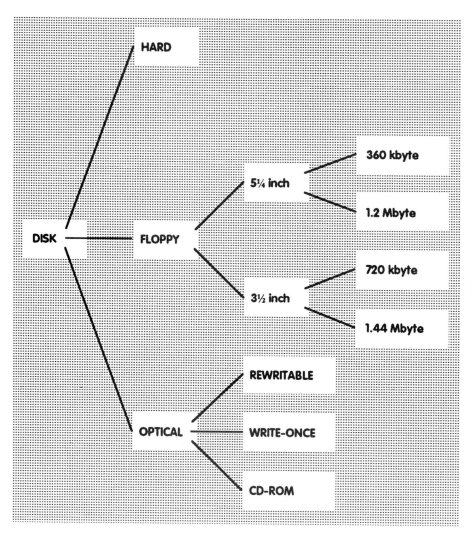

Figure 6.2 Disk drive types

The difference in material and the fact that floppy disks can be removed leads to different characteristics for the two types of disk. Floppy disks are slow, and only store a small amount of data; 360 or 720 kbytes for 8086 machines, and usually 1.2 or 1.44 Mbytes in faster machines although larger capacities are planned. Hard disks are much faster. 8086 and 286 machines usually have hard disks of 10 to 32 Mbytes, but later machines often have disks of 100 Mbytes or more.

Every PC needs at least one floppy disk drive, as software is always supplied on floppy disk and this is the only way to get it into the PC's memory. Early PCs had only floppy disk drives – usually two, so that one could be used to hold programs while the other held data. It was possible to manage with only one drive, but this meant the user had to change disks often. Because the capacity of a floppy disk is small, there is usually only one application program on each disk. As programs grew, they came to take up more than one disk – sometimes dozens. As a result, using a machine which only had floppy disks became complicated and slow. The solution is to fit a hard disk with enough capacity for all the programs and data you need. Programs and data are then copied to the hard disk before use, and kept there. The floppy disk drive is used only to introduce new programs or data to the system, and for backup (which we shall discuss later). It is still possible to buy a PC without a hard disk, but this is only useful for some special applications. For normal use a hard disk is almost essential, and some software (including Windows) cannot be used without a hard disk. The price of hard disks does not increase very rapidly with size, and it is worth getting a bigger one than you may at first think you need: certainly at least 32 Mbytes. If you intend to use Windows it would be wise to have a hard disk of at least 80 Mbytes.

Hard disks also vary in speed, in two ways. Firstly there is **access time**, the time it takes to find a particular piece of data or software on the disk. Secondly there is **data rate**, the rate at which data or software can be copied from the disk to memory once it has been found. The first is particularly important in applications which access the disk often, such as databases. The second mainly affects the time taken to change from one application to another, although it may also be significant within the application – especially if you do not have as much memory as the software would like to use. Access time is usually quoted in advertisements and specifications. In principle the shorter the better, but it would be uneconomical to put a very fast disk on a slow PC. The PC manufacturer will fit or recommend a disk of suitable access time. Data rate is rarely quoted in specifications, partly because it depends on the PC itself as well as the disk drive (as we shall see when we discuss 'interleave' in a later chapter). Again the PC manufacturer will choose a suitable disk drive.

There is one more type of disk which you may meet, and this is the **optical disk**. Technically this is very different from the magnetic disk, because the information is written and read by a laser beam. What this means to us is that the capacity can be much more than that of a hard magnetic disk, and that all optical disks are removable like a floppy disk. There are three types of optical disk. The first is the **rewritable** type. Data can be written on this, and replaced by other data, just as on a magnetic disk. The second is **write-once**, or 'WORM'; you can write data on to this, but once written it is permanent and you cannot replace it with new data. Finally the **read-only** disk has data placed on it at the time of manufacture; you can read it but not write to it.

Optical disk drives come in various types and sizes. You are likely to meet only two types at present. The first type is designed for rewritable disks, and will often handle write-once disks as well. The two common sizes are 5.25 inch, which will hold about 300 megabytes, and 3.5 inch which holds about half this. New versions are appearing all the time, and these capacities will increase. You might use this type of drive instead of a hard disk, with the advantage that you can remove the disk from the machine if you choose. However it is at present both slower and more expensive than a hard disk of similar capacity. Most one-person businesses will not need this type of disk drive.

The optical disk you are most likely to meet is the **CD-ROM**. This is a read-only disk and is very similar to a compact audio disk. In fact you can tell the difference only by reading the label. It is just under 5 inches in diameter and holds about 600 megabytes. The drive is the same size as a 5.25 inch floppy disk drive and will fit within most PCs, or can be a separate unit. A few of the drives designed for this disk can also handle a rewritable disk of the same size. The CD-ROM is becoming quite widely used for distributing bulk data, including graphics, and occasionally also for software. While most one-person businesses will not need this sort of disk drive, yours may have a need for data which is best bought in the form of CD-ROM rather than on paper. The advantage is that you can use the PC to find the particular item of data you want – and 600 megabytes is a lot of data to search through; this book takes up about half a megabyte. However, data on CD-ROM can be expensive. Find out if you can afford it before you buy the drive!

Screens

If you buy a portable PC you will have to accept the screen that comes with it, and that may well affect your choice of PC. Otherwise you may or may not have a choice of display. The reason is that the 'video' circuits within the PC must match the type of display, and some PCs have these circuits built in so that they cannot be changed. However most desktop PCs have the circuits on a removable 'video card' and you can then fit the card that matches your choice of display.

You will nearly always have a choice of colour or mono display with a desktop PC. Colour is unlikely to be essential, since most printers work only in one colour (usually black, of course, but you can get ribbons of other colours). Colour printers are available, but satisfactory ones are expensive. But even if you do not plan to print in colour, a colour display can make many programs easier to use. Most programs are written with colour displays in mind, and use colour to distinguish different kinds of information on the screen. For example, a warning message may be displayed in bright red. In spite of this, nearly every program can be used with a monochrome display if necessary. So colour is certainly useful if you can afford the extra £100 or so, but if cash is short you can live without it. Portable computers rarely have colour displays because they are expensive to make as flat screens.

The other feature to consider is definition (or resolution), which in effect means the size and pitch of the dots which make up the image on the screen. Here there are four standard types of display to consider, with the cryptic names CGA, EGA, VGA and Super VGA (or SVGA). These vary in the definition of the display, and also in the number of colours available.

The oldest and cheapest standard is **CGA**. There are probably over a million of these screens in use, so evidently many people find them acceptable. However, the dot pitch is coarse and the characters can clearly be seen to consist of a matrix of dots. Graphic images also appear 'grainy'. There are six colours available, besides black and white, and in some circumstances each of these can be used at either 'full' and 'half' brightness. Not all programs can support all these colours. A few early ones can support only three.

Whether this standard is acceptable is a matter of personal choice. I have used a CGA screen for six years and find it good enough for word processing, though a higher definition would be easier on the eye. For graphics work it is a definite handicap. It is worth noting that the mono version of this standard gives, at least subjectively, a sharper image so may be preferable where colour is not important.

The next standard is **EGA**. This has a closer dot spacing than CGA and so is more comfortable to work with. However, it has never been very popular and many programs do not support it. You would therefore be wise to avoid it.

The standard which is now most widely accepted is **VGA**. VGA displays are more expensive than CGA but the dot pitch is much closer and the range of colours (for programs which fully support it) is much wider. This standard is excellent for most of the purposes for which you are likely to use a PC. Only if you are working on elaborate graphics, or need to have one colour shade imperceptibly into another, are you likely to want anything better.

Super VGA gives higher definition still, and an almost infinite range of colours although you will normally have to select a more restricted 'palette' from amongst them. The snag, at the time of writing, is that SVGA is not actually a standard. Different manufacturers have different ways of implementing it, and these are not compatible. So you can only use SVGA if your application software supports the particular implementation that your display happens to use. This could well be a problem for you. If you use Windows-based programs the problem is less; Windows rather than the application program controls the screen, and most displays are supplied with software (a 'screen driver') which makes Windows compatible with their version of SVGA. The problem may in any case be resolved in a year or two.

IBM has introduced further standards, but they have not yet been widely taken up because VGA is good enough for most purposes.

Nearly all displays, except on portables, are in '14 inch' size. This means that the CRT screen is 14 inches measured across the diagonal, which gives a working area of about 9 inches by 7 inches. Some compact desktop PCs are supplied with a 12 inch screen, and portable PCs also have smaller screens. Larger screens are available, especially 17 inch, but they are expensive. It is now possible to buy a 'flat-screen' display to use, instead of a CRT, with a desktop computer. However these displays are also expensive and so unlikely to be used unless desk space is very short, or the user is particularly worried about radiation (which is discussed in chapter 8).

Quality of most displays (covering things like flicker and reflection) is adequate, though there is some variation between makes especially in SVGA displays. One point to watch is the screen surface. Some screens are plain glass; others have the surface etched to reduce reflections. Try to see the screen of your choice before you buy. Failing that, you will find that the reviews in PC magazines usually comment on screen quality.

The circuits that drive the display may be an integral part of the PC or may be on a 'video card' plugged into one of the expansion slots. In the latter case the card will often be supplied with the display. If it is not, get the display supplier's advice on a suitable card. Video cards for VGA and Super VGA displays may offer a choice of video memory capacity, usually between 256 kbytes and 1 Mbyte. If you can, get 1 Mbyte. Less than this may make colour screens appear sluggish, or limit the range of colours you can use.

Keyboards

There are two standards for desktop PC keyboards, the 'standard' and the 'extended' types. The first usually has about 83 keys, the second about 102 keys, although there are slight variations between manufacturers. These keyboards were first introduced with the IBM 'XT' and 'AT' machines, but have been imitated with minor variations by all other manufacturers. The extended type is the one you are most likely to meet.

The 'feel' of the keyboard, and details such as the rake of the keys and whether they have flat or hollowed tops, vary from one manufacturer to another. All this is very much a matter of personal preference. Keyboards are usually discussed in reviews, but because choice is so personal you should try to get as much experience as you can on a keyboard before you buy. It may affect your choice of the whole PC since a manufacturer will rarely offer a choice of keyboard. However, most (though not all) keyboards are connected in a standard way, so you may be able to buy a more satisfactory replacement elsewhere.

Portable PCs are a different matter. The keyboard is an integral part of the machine so you will not be able to replace it. Also, space considerations mean that some of the standard keys will be omitted, or the key spacing reduced. This is definitely a case of try before you buy.

Mice and tracker balls

The mouse has become very popular and nearly every PC now has one. For Windows and other programs with graphic interfaces, the mouse is almost essential. For programs where you need to use the keyboard anyway, using a mouse as well may be an inconvenience. In most cases you have the choice of using the mouse or the keyboard, in any combination that suits you.

There are times when a mouse cannot be used. For example, if you are using a portable computer when travelling there may be no flat surface to hand. An alternative to the mouse is the **tracker ball**. This consists of a ball in a small housing which either stands on your desk or is fixed to the side of your keyboard. By placing your hand over the ball you can move it in any direction, and this controls the screen pointer just as a mouse does. A few portables have a tracker ball built in.

The choice between a mouse or a tracker ball is one of personal preference. Most people seem to prefer the mouse, but the tracker ball is better for portable computers and cluttered desks. There are other devices for moving the screen pointer, such as light pens and touch screens, but the mouse and tracker ball meet most needs.

Expansion slots

A feature of the basic design of the PC is that it has **expansion slots**, or sockets, within the system unit. These allow extra circuit boards to be plugged in so that you can expand the capability of your PC by adding extra devices, such as a scanner or a modem. Often some of these slots are taken up by devices we have mentioned already, such as the video card which controls the display, or a controller for the disk drive. This varies from one model of PC to another. Sometimes these items are included in the 'motherboard' (the main part of the PC which carries the processor and memory), but this means you are unable to change them for other types if you wish. In any case there will be some slots left free for you to add devices of your own choice. The number varies from one machine to another, and must be a factor in your choice of machine. It is complicated by the fact that some of the slots may be only 'half length'. Some of the devices you may wish to add will fit in half-length slots but most will need the full length. Beware of slots which are obstructed by other parts of the machine. Note also that some devices you may wish to add are wider than the spacing between slots and so effectively take up two slots. 'Hard cards' (discussed below) and modems are the most likely problem here. I would suggest that you choose a machine with at least three free full-length expansion slots, preferably more, unless you are sure that you will not want to add anything to your machine. Bear in mind that if you have an 8086 or 286 machine, extra memory will take up expansion slots.

Disk bays

Another feature of the PC design is that there are slots, or bays, for disk drives in the front panel of the machine. These nowadays come in two sizes, '5.25 inch' and '3.5 inch'. If you measure one of them you will find that this is not actually the size of the slot. A '5.25 inch' bay is designed to hold a drive for 5.25 inch floppy disks and a '3.5 inch' bay takes drives for 3.5 inch floppy disks. These bays may be used also for hard disks, although sometimes these are mounted out of sight within the system unit. Hard disks may fit either size bay, but nowadays the smaller size is more usual. The number of bays provided varies from one machine to another, and many have bays of both sizes. 8086 machines usually have only 5.25 inch bays, and recent machines may have only 3.5 inch bays. It is wise to choose a machine with one or two spare bays in case you want to add another floppy or hard disk drive, or a CD-ROM drive. For CD-ROM you will need a 5.25 inch bay. If you don't have a spare bay you can buy 'external' drives which stand on the desk instead of using a drive bay; they cost more than 'internal' drives.

Upgrade capability

All the hardware we have discussed so far is closely associated with the PC and will probably be bought as a single package, although if you prefer to pick and choose the separate parts you can usually do so. Buying a complete package avoids any problems of compatibility. Before we go on to look at hardware which is less closely tied to the PC we should give a little thought to the future.

You will obviously choose a PC which will do all the tasks you have in mind at the time. If you can afford it you will buy a machine which is a bit more powerful than you need, to leave room for development in the future. But you cannot be sure how your own needs will change. Nor can you tell what new software will appear on the market. So you may find, in a year or two, that you wish you had a machine which was more powerful in at least one of the respects that we have looked at – processor power, memory size, or disk size and speed. What can you do, when choosing your computer, to keep your options open for the future?

The most common situation is to find that you have not enough room on your hard disk. You can get round this for a while, by weeding out programs and data that you don't use any more, or perhaps by buying one of the programs which 'compress' your data so that you can fit more of it on to the disk; these can be surprisingly effective, giving up to 100% more data storage with only a slight loss in performance. But sooner or later this will become impracticable, and you will need a bigger disk.

Fortunately this is a simple matter. In nearly every case you (or your dealer) can simply remove the disk – after you have preserved its contents on floppy disks – and replace it with a new one with a higher capacity. Disk drive designers get more and more capacity into the same space as time goes on, so you are fairly sure of finding that the drive you want will fit into the existing space. While you are about it, you may choose a drive that is faster than the old one. Again, newer drives usually have better performance than the old ones.

As an alternative to replacing the disk drive, you may be able to add the new drive alongside the old one. This has the advantage that you can retain the information on the old drive without copying it, besides giving you more capacity. Not all PCs have room to add a second drive in this way; it would be wise to choose one that does. You may have to add a new disk controller, which will take up one of the expansion slots, although if the new disk is of the same type as the old one it may be able to share the same controller. You, or your dealer, will have to do a little extra work in arranging the software to suit a two-disk machine. You don't need to stop at two hard disks, but is unusual to use more.

Another way to add a second disk is to fit a **hard card**. This is a disk drive which is fitted on to the same expansion card as its controller, rather than into one of the drive bays. It is thus easy to install, and can be used even if there is no room for a conventional drive. However it cannot share the existing controller and so will definitely take up an expansion slot, and in some case two because of its width.

We saw earlier that some programs run slowly (or not at all) if the PC has too little memory. If you have a 386 or later machine, it is easy to add extra memory, up to a limit set by the design of the particular machine. Most will accept 8 megabytes, some more – but check this before you buy the machine. Adding memory involves opening the case of the machine and plugging the new units in. Sometimes you can keep the existing memory units, sometimes they have to be discarded. This is a job you can usually do yourself, although in some machines there are other parts in the way which you have to move first. Otherwise your dealer will be glad to do it for you.

Think twice before you replace your memory units with faster ones. Although this is feasible, it may not give the improvement you expect. In some cases it can cause unexpected problems. You should definitely ask your dealer, or some other expert, first.

Replacing the processor by a faster one is not so easy. A few PCs are sold as 'upgradable' meaning that the processor can be unplugged and a faster one put in its place. This is easy to do, but may be expensive. In many other machines it is possible to replace the whole 'mother board' of the machine by one with a faster processor. This is definitely a job for a dealer, and you may have to hunt for one who is interested. Another possibility, as we saw earlier, is to fit a 'co-processor'. Most PCs allow for this and it is easily done, but not all processor-limited software can take advantage of a co-processor. On some 486 machines a 'clock doubler' chip can be added to improve performance.

Whichever way you increase the processor power it is likely to be expensive. It is worth considering whether it would not be more economical, in the long run, to replace the system unit of the PC as a whole with a faster one. You should be able to keep the display unit, mouse, and hard disk, and probably the keyboard and floppy disk, so the cost of replacing the system unit may be little more than that of upgrading it.

Printers

Practically every PC user will need at least one printer, but unlike the items we have already discussed a printer is rarely included as part of a package deal. This is largely because the choice of printer types is wide, and is not related to the type of PC – you can use any printer with any PC. Over the lifetime of the computer there have been many different types of printer, starting with adapted typewriters, but the only types likely to interest the one-person business are matrix, ink-jet, laser and possibly daisywheel printers.

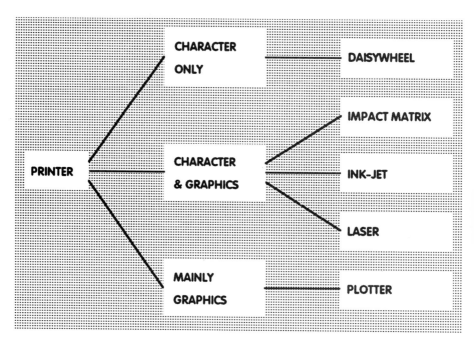

Figure 6.3 Printer types.

Daisywheel printers

This is the oldest type we shall discuss. It works on the same principle as a typewriter, in that a type slug carrying the required character in relief is pressed against the paper, with an inked ribbon in between. The type slugs are carried on a rimless wheel, each on a separate radial spoke giving the appearance of a many-petalled flower, hence the name. The wheel is moved to the position where a character is to be printed and spun to bring the right spoke to the top, and this is then struck by a hammer.

The design of the characters (i.e. the font) is obviously built into the daisywheel. If a different font is wanted the wheel can easily be replaced by another, but it is not really practicable to make changes within a document.

These printers use a ribbon similar to a typewriter. It can be the conventional ink-impregnated fabric ribbon, which is reversed when the end is reached and re-used until the print becomes unacceptably faint. Or it can be a 'one-time' ribbon, which has a carbon film on a plastic base. Some printers can use both. Text typed with a one-time ribbon looks much better than the other, but the ribbons are more expensive to use because each lasts for only a single pass. However, daisywheel printers are so slow that ribbon cost is unlikely to be important. Normally the ribbon is black, though you can use a different colour if you want.

The daisywheel printer can print only those characters which are on its wheel. It cannot print any other characters or symbols, nor can it print graphic images. On the other hand it produces better print quality than any other type of printer, although ink-jets and lasers are not far behind. It has the advantage over these types that it can print multiple copies, using carbon paper or self-copying forms.

Daisywheel printers are going out of fashion because of their slowness and inflexibility, though there are still a few on the market. If you need to produce multiple copies with good print quality, you should consider a daisywheel printer. Otherwise one of the newer types will suit you better. You may, like me, find it convenient to have both.

Matrix printers

These should strictly be called 'impact matrix printers' since other types also use the matrix principle, but 'impact' is nearly always omitted. Like the daisywheel, these printers work by pressing a ribbon against the paper to print each character in turn. However, instead of having a set of preformed character slugs they have a vertical row of small pins. These are struck in any combination, as the 'print head' moves across the paper, to form the required character shape. Since there are no fixed character shapes, any character or symbol can be produced by striking the right combination of pins. The printer can also be used to print images.

These printers can work in two modes, 'character' and 'graphics' modes. In character mode the character shapes are determined by software which is built into the printer and cannot be changed. Thus in this mode the printer has a fixed set of characters in a particular font. In fact modern matrix printers often have several such fonts, which can be selected by the application software (such as a word processor) which is controlling the printer. Fonts can thus be mixed within a document, and even within a line of print. Sometimes there is provision for additional fonts or character sets to be added, either by plugging a 'font cartridge' into the printer or by 'downloading' the font information from the PC into a small memory within the printer.

In graphics mode, the printer itself has no control over what is printed. It receives the image to be printed as a 'bit-map' which determines which individual pins are to be struck as the print head moves across the paper. Thus it can print any image, which may or may not include characters. This is the method used by programs which work in graphics mode, including those based on Windows. It allows an unlimited choice of character shape and size, but its disadvantage is that printing is much slower than in character mode.

Two factors determine print quality in character mode. Firstly the number of pins in the print head. This is usually either 9 or 24, though other numbers are sometimes used. 9 pins are the minimum needed to print reasonable characters. Where there are 24 pins they are placed much closer together (in fact in two staggered rows) and so the character shape is better defined. Secondly, nearly all printers give the choice of 'draft' or 'NLQ' (Near Letter Quality) mode. In the second of these, the print head may move across each line of print twice, with the paper moved a small distance vertically in between. This gives the effect of a printer with twice as many pins, and so improves the character shape, but makes printing slower.

In graphics mode the number of pins has less effect on print quality, since the head can make as many passes as necessary to give the required definition. The number of pins does affect printing speed, and the 9-pin image will be slightly coarser because the pins are larger.

All the matrix printers I have met use fabric ribbons, with special ink which serves also to lubricate the pins. All these printers can use single-colour ribbons, but some can also use multi-colour ribbons. This allows printing to be in colour. The print head passes over each line three or four times, using a different coloured section of the ribbon each time; the sections are in the three primary colours, and sometimes also black. This means that printing takes at least three times as long, and ribbon costs are at least three times as high. The quality of colour printing produced by a matrix printer is not high, but is good enough for some types of work.

Matrix printers are popular because they are cheap to buy and run, and the colour versions cost little more than black-and-white. They are also much more versatile than the daisywheel. Because they are impact printers they can print multiple copies, like the daisywheel. They are moderately noisy; less so than the daisywheel, producing a buzz rather than a clatter. However the print quality is poorer than that of the other types. 9-pin draft mode is not always easy to read. 9-pin NLQ mode or 24-pin draft mode is good enough for drafts and internal documents. Many people will consider 24-pin NLQ mode good enough for correspondence, although still well below the standards of the other types of printer. A 24-pin printer is usually faster than a 9-pin printer in the same mode.

The 9-pin matrix printer is about the cheapest that you can buy, and a few come under the £100 mark. Unless cash is very short it is not really suitable as your only printer, although if you have another printer for 'best' the matrix will produce drafts at low cost. The 24-pin matrix printer costs more than the 9-pin but is faster and produces much better print quality. It is probably the best general-purpose machine. If you need better quality or less noise, consider either an ink-jet or a laser printer. These (especially the laser) cost more, and are expensive to run, but they give good print quality and are almost silent.

Ink-jet printers

This is a more recent type. It is again a matrix printer, but there is no impact and no ribbon. In place of the pins of the matrix printer is a set of tiny nozzles. As the print head moves across the paper, ink is squirted from each nozzle as required to print the character or image. Performance and definition are much as for the impact matrix printer, and again there is usually a choice of 'draft' and 'NLQ' modes. The printer is almost silent, and print quality in NLQ mode is good. How good depends on the number of nozzles, which also affects the price.

Some ink-jets can print in colour, although these tend to be a good deal more expensive than the black-and-white versions. The colour quality can be very good. Unlike the impact matrix printer, all the colours are printed in a single pass over the paper by dividing up the nozzles between three ink colours. This does reduce the definition, of course, so a printer with many nozzles (and so a high price) is needed for the best results in colour.

Ink-jet printers are relatively expensive to run because the ink cartridges are costly and last for a limited number of pages. In the past there has been trouble with the nozzles clogging, but this has been largely overcome. In many cases the nozzles form part of the ink cartridge, which ensures that they are replaced often. Ink-jet printers are also more fussy than others about the type of paper. Some need special paper, which can be expensive; others will run with any reasonably smooth paper, such as copier paper. Find this out before you buy. If you use a 'prestige' paper, such as laid or wove, for your correspondence you may have trouble. Again, try before you buy.

Some ink-jet printers are very compact, and so this is the best type if you want to carry it about with your portable computer.

Laser printers

Laser printers differ from all the others in being 'page' rather than 'line' printers. Instead of having a moving head which covers the paper line by line, the printer collects all the information for a whole page, and when this is complete it prints the whole page in one action. This has the advantage that there is no problem of registration in graphics mode, and so no risk of the striped effect which is often seen with matrix printers and occasionally with ink-jets. It is also faster than other types of PC printers, and is silent. On the other hand it is more expensive to buy and run than the other types and tends to be bulky. Most laser printers print in black (or some other single colour) only; colour versions have just started to appear, but they cost several thousand pounds. The process is similar to that used in a photocopier, and laser printers use the same sort of paper as photocopiers. In fact most paper is suitable, although a reasonably smooth surface gives the best results. The toner powder needs replenishing, and the drum replacing, at intervals. Both are expensive, so the laser printer is one of the most expensive types to run as well as to buy. However, print quality is good, and this is the fastest printer likely to be used with a PC.

The laser printer needs a large memory since it has to hold the information for a whole page of print. In character mode this is a moderate amount, but in graphics mode it can be over a megabyte. Laser printers are often supplied with only enough memory to work in character mode, but extra memory can easily be added (at a price) to make the printer suitable for graphics mode. The printer works more slowly in graphics mode, in that there is a longer interval between pages. This is mainly because the interface between the PC and the printer can pass information only at a restricted rate.

Some laser printers will also work in 'Postscript' mode. This is in effect an extension of character mode to cover a much wider range of character shapes and sizes, as well as vector graphics. Its advantage is that it allows most of the flexibility of graphics mode together with the performance of character mode. Postscript printers are more expensive than standard models, because they incorporate a powerful processor as well as memory. 'Postscript' mode is useful only with software that is designed to support it. Windows provides this support for all Windows-based applications.

Plotters

Like printers, these produce an image on paper. The difference is that the plotter draws an image by moving a pen over the paper in any direction, rather than scanning the paper systematically as all types of printer do. It is thus ideal for line drawings, avoiding the stepped effect that is visible when diagonal lines are printed. Characters have to be drawn, so only simple typefaces are possible. Plotting tends to be slow, particularly if large solid areas have to be filled in. The line width is determined by the width of the pen. Most plotters can handle several pens, and so can work with several colours and line widths. The right pen is picked up automatically at each change of colour or width. The plotter can only be used with suitable software, but 'Draw' and 'CAD' programs usually provide support for a plotter. Most plotters are limited to A4 or A3 paper, and such a plotter will be priced in the same range as a laser printer. There are plotters which will handle much larger sheets, but they are very expensive.

The plotter is thus a specialised device. If you are much concerned with line art or CAD, or with plotting graphs and charts, you may find it worth having a plotter as well as a printer. Otherwise a printer in graphics mode will usually give adequate results.

Paper handling

The methods of handling paper are much the same for daisywheel, matrix and ink-jet printers, so are dealt with together here. Paper can be handled either in single sheets ('cut sheet') or as a continuous strip. All these printers will allow single sheets to be fed by hand, since this is essential for letterheads and forms. Usually there is a guide to ensure that the paper is in the right position, and the paper is gripped by rollers as in a typewriter. In some cases loading is semi-automatic; once inserted, the paper is fed automatically till the top of the page is in the right place to start printing.

A development of this is automatic sheet feed. Many sheets of paper (usually up to 50 or 100) are placed in a hopper, and a new sheet is fed automatically when the previous page has been printed. The application program can signal the printer to say when a new sheet is to be fed. If it does not, one will be fed automatically when the print reaches a set distance from the bottom of the previous page. All laser printers, and a few others, have automatic sheet feeders built in. In many other cases a sheet feeder can be added as an option.

Nearly every printer, other than lasers, can also use continuous paper. Continuous paper can be fed from a roll, as with a fax machine, but this is not usually satisfactory for a printer. The problem is that the position of the paper cannot be controlled well enough, and it is difficult to separate it into pages. Continuous paper is therefore used in **fanfold** form. This means that the individual sheets are divided by perforations, which makes them easy to separate after printing, and the paper is folded in alternate directions at each line of perforations to form a neat stack. If you are lucky it will also drop into a neat stack after printing, but this takes a little arrangement. Fanfold paper also has a row of large holes down each side, at half-inch spacing, which engage with sprockets on the printer platen roller. This makes sure that the position of the paper is accurately controlled. Often the side strip of the paper which carries these sprocket holes is separated from the body of the sheet by vertical perforations, so that it can be torn off to leave a standard size sheet. Modern fanfold paper has very fine perforations ('microperforation') and can hardly be distinguished by eye from cut sheet once the pages are separated.

If you use fanfold paper, you must leave enough room behind your printer for the paper stack and also provide a tray to catch and re-fold the printed sheets. Printer stands can be bought which take care of this. It is difficult to load fanfold paper into some printers. Try for yourself when you are choosing a printer.

The most widely used size of cut sheet in Europe is the international A4 size (210 x 297 millimetres). In the USA and Japan $8^1/_2$ x 11 inches or $8^1/_2$ by 12 inches is common. Most printers can handle all these sizes, and usually also the obsolescent 'foolscap' size which is 8 x 13 inches. These printers are usually described as having an 80-character carriage. This means that they can handle paper which is wide enough to take 80 characters, at 10 characters per inch – in other words an 8 inch print line – with reasonable margins. Most printers are also available, at a higher cost, with a 132-character carriage. This will handle A3 paper (297 x 420 millimetres), or A4 or similar paper placed horizontally.

Fanfold paper is available in these and other sizes. The dimensions are always quoted after the perforated side strip, if any, has been removed. However the height of the page must always be closely related to the sprocket spacing, and in practice this means it must be defined in inch rather than metric units. Fanfold A4 paper is therefore $11^2/_3$ inches deep. This is a fraction of a millimetre different from true A4 but the difference is not perceptible in practice.

Most printers, and most software, are of American or Japanese origin and so are designed for 11 inch or 12 inch paper. Usually it is possible to set either the printer or (more often) the software to use A4 fanfold, but in a few cases this is difficult so you may need to keep some 11 inch paper in stock. The problem does not arise with cut sheet. Some software makes specific provision for the use of an automatic sheet feeder, but some does not. In this case you may have to experiment to find how many lines you should tell the software to put on a page.

It is worth noting that fanfold paper costs nearly twice as much as cut sheet. An automatic sheet feeder may well be a good investment even if it is not a standard feature of your printer. It also makes it easy to turn used paper over and print on the back for draft work, which is a further economy, and it saves you the trouble of tearing along the perforations. In addition you need not leave room for a paper stack behind the printer. Against this, sheet feeders do occasionally misfeed, although on modern devices this is infrequent. I suffer a misfeed perhaps once a week, and it is easily corrected, but I have met sheet feeders of other makes which gave more trouble.

Connecting printers and plotters to your PC

Every PC has a parallel port which is normally used only for a printer. This is the most convenient way to connect a printer because it is absolutely standard and needs no setting up. The parallel port is an oblong 25-pin socket on the back of the PC system unit. It may be mounted on a card plugged into one of the expansion slots. Sometimes there are two such ports. Your printer should come with a cable, one end of which plugs into this socket. That's all there is to it as far as the hardware is concerned, except that you may have to move a switch inside the printer to select the UK character set (or whichever set you want to use). You will need to tell your software what make and type of printer you are using. If you don't have a cable, or need a longer one, any dealer should be able to supply it. Be careful to get one that suits your printer, because the plug on that end may vary.

It is also possible to connect a printer to the serial port of your PC. This is another socket on the back of the system unit. It may be similar to the parallel port, or it may be smaller with fewer pins, since only four or five are actually used. There are often two such ports. Some printers have both serial and parallel interfaces; others have to be ordered in the appropriate version. There are two disadvantages to connecting a printer this way. The first is that you may want to use the serial port for something else, such as a modem or a mouse. In this case you may have to add another port, in the same way as you would add a parallel port, or use a switch. The other snag is that you will need to set both the printer (which will have some tiny switches hidden within it) and the software to suit this port, and this can involve quite a lot of trial and error. However, once it is done the printer should work as well as on a parallel port. The serial connection is not as fast as the parallel one; for most printers this will not matter, but it may slow down a laser printer. In general you should prefer the parallel port, but if like me you have two printers and only one port of each type, it is convenient to use one of each. Put the slower printer on the serial port if you can.

Other peripherals

There are other peripherals which you may want to add to your PC, but these are more specialised and only a few users will need them. These peripherals are not themselves mounted inside the PC, but each is connected to it by a controller card which takes up one of the expansion slots within the system unit. This is why I suggested choosing a machine with plenty of free slots.

The two types of peripheral you are most likely to meet are scanners and magnetic tape drives, and we shall now look at these. You may also wish to connect either a CD-ROM drive or an extra floppy disk drive in this way if there is not room for them inside the system unit. Also you may need to use expansion slots for extra parallel or serial ports, or (on an 8086 or 286 machine) for expanded or extended memory cards.

Scanners

We saw in connection with graphics software that a scanner can be used to convert an image on paper into a data file which the computer can use. There are two types of scanner that you are likely to meet. The first is the hand-held scanner. This is a T-shaped device, about 15 centimetres long and wide, with a window and rollers in the bottom face of the cross-stroke. You place it on the document you want to scan and draw it slowly downwards over the page. The software associated with the scanner may be sold to you with the device, but some 'paint' packages also support the more popular makes of scanner. This software will create an image file, which you can view on the screen or manipulate with the paint package just like any image file.

The scanner head is only about half the width of 'A4' paper so you will often have to scan an image as two separate files. The software will allow you to link them up again to re-create the whole image, although this is not always easy. You can buy this type of scanner for well under £200, though one which will record an image in colour will be a good deal dearer.

The other type of scanner is large enough to deal with a whole 'A4' page at once. You may put the document face down on a glass plate, or you may feed it through a slot. These scanners are considerably more expensive, but more convenient to use.

Most scanners can be used with any PC, though there can be difficulties with 8086 machines; check with the supplier. You may find that the size of image you can scan is limited by the amount of memory in your PC.

Scanners have obvious uses, but it is not always easy to get good results. This applies particularly to the character recognition software which is available with some scanners. You should see a detailed demonstration, preferably on your own PC and on documents of varying quality, before you buy anything.

Magnetic tape

Magnetic tape was used on early PCs as the main storage for programs and data, but was soon superseded by disks. However, there is one function for which you may find magnetic tape useful, and that is backup. I explain elsewhere why it is important to backup the data on your hard disk regularly, by copying it to another medium. Usually the data on the disk is backed up piecemeal, and the software is not backed up because you can reload it from the original floppy disks at any time. In this case floppy disks serve well for backup. However, another strategy is to backup everything on the disk. This makes it easy to recover if you do have trouble with your hard disk. But now that hard disks of 100 megabytes or more are common, this full backup takes a long time. It also takes a lot of floppy disks, and these have to be changed by hand so you cannot go away and leave the PC to do the job overnight.

One solution is to backup to a rewritable optical disk drive, since one optical disk will hold all the contents of your hard disk, but this is expensive. A cheaper solution is to use a tape drive. There are several types, but all of them have the tape in a cartridge, not unlike a music cassette. These come in various capacities, and obviously you choose one with a higher capacity than your hard disk. Transfer to tape is quite slow, but this is not important as you can start the process just before you leave your office for the night. Tape cartridges have a limited life, so it is important to check that the contents of the disk have in fact been recorded and can be recovered. A good tape system will do this for you. Expect to pay a few hundred pounds for a tape system to be used in this way.

Communications

In chapter 5 we saw what software you need to communicate with another computer. Here we shall look briefly at the hardware that goes with it. However, communications is a complex subject and if you really intend to go into it you should consult a dealer, preferably after reading one of the many books on the subject.

Modems

The essential piece of hardware for communicating with a remote computer is a **modem**. This may be a separate box standing on your desktop, connected to the serial port on the back of your computer. Alternatively it may be a card which fits into one of the expansion slots of your computer. The modem must also be connected to the telephone line, of course, and so it is essential (in the UK) that you buy one with the green 'BEAB approved' label. Strangely, it is legal to sell a modem without this approval although it is not legal to use it. There are similar rules in most other countries. Setting up a modem can be quite complex, and is beyond the scope of this book. If the modem and software (which also must be compatible with each other) do not have adequate instructions, buy a good book on the subject.

Local area networks

This method of linking PCs which are a short distance apart also needs the appropriate card which you must plug into one of the expansion slots. In this case you will not connect it to the telephone line but to cabling which should be supplied with the card – the details vary from one system to another. However, the software implications of a LAN are considerable, and you may need special versions of your application software. The one-person business is unlikely to need a LAN, but if you do you should seek expert advice.

Linking a portable to a mainframe

This is a much more likely situation. You may have a desktop computer in your office and a portable which you use elsewhere, and want to transfer data from one to the other.

The simplest and safest way to do this is to write the data on to a floppy disk with one machine, and read it with the other. You should make sure that each computer can read disks written by the other. This does not necessarily mean that both drives should be designed for the same density (though obviously they must both be the same size). It is possible to exchange data between a 720 kbyte and a 1.44 megabyte drive. However, in this case you should be careful that any disk is always written to by only one of the drives, and is of the type designed for that drive. If you try to write on a disk of the wrong type you may have problems. If possible, avoid this situation by choosing machines with matching disk drives.

If you want to transfer data electronically, you could install a local area network, but this would be using a sledgehammer to crack a nut. A much simpler way is to connect the serial ports of the two computers together (you do not need modems). Most communications software will then let you send data from one computer to the other, but it is simpler to use a program such as 'Laplink' which is specifically designed for this purpose. This will usually come with the special cable needed to connect the two serial ports. If not you can get one from your dealer.

Cables and mains leads

The cables that connect your display unit, keyboard and mouse to the system unit should be supplied with each item – if not, complain to the supplier because the connectors are not always standard and you may have difficulty getting them elsewhere. The printer should also be provided with a cable, and so should any other peripherals. So you should not need to buy any cables separately. If you do, for any reason, take careful note of the connectors needed on them, or if possible take the units you want to connect along to your dealer.

You will need several mains sockets. There will be one mains lead for the system unit and possibly also one for the display unit, although in some cases one of these connects into the other so that they need only one socket. The printer will have its own mains lead. Some other peripherals will also have mains leads, although others will take their power from the system unit. The power consumption of PCs is low, so a 3 amp or 5 amp fuse will suit each unit. For convenience and reliability it would be wise to have an electrician install as many power sockets as you need, but if you have only one it is safe to connect all the units to it through a suitable adapter. The type which plugs in with a short cable is more reliable than one which has plug and sockets in a single block.

In some cases you may find that interference from the mains can cause occasional problems, usually erratic behaviour when some other electrical equipment is switched on or off. This is most likely if there is heavy electrical machinery nearby, or if your premises are supplied by overhead cables. If you suspect this, or just want to guard against the possibility, you can fit a device between the mains and the computer which will improve matters. The simplest and cheapest is simply a special plug, incorporating a 'surge protector', which replaces the normal mains plug. Alternatively you can buy this as an adaptor which fits between the existing mains plug and its socket, or as a multi-way socket on the end of a short lead. Except in the last case you would be wise to use a separate device on your printer mains lead, to avoid the possibility of the printer interfering with the PC by this route. If you still have problems there are more elaborate mains screening devices, but you should consult an expert about these.

Choosing your hardware

We began this chapter with the first rule – choose your hardware to suit your software. You should now know enough about hardware to see that this means choosing a suitable processor, the right amount of memory, a hard disk of the right capacity and speed, and an appropriate display unit. You will also need a printer that meets your business requirements, and possibly other peripherals.

This still leaves you with a wide choice, as there are over a hundred PC suppliers in the market and nearly all of them will be able to offer a machine that matches your specification. In the next chapter I shall discuss where you can get information on what is available, and how good it is, and how to decide where to buy.

7

Buying your system

What should you buy?

Your first step, as we have seen, is to decide what sort of software will benefit your business. Chapters 3, 4 and 5 will have shown you what is available, and you may be able to get more specific advice from business associations, enterprise centres and other advisers. Next, for each type, you must decide which of the many packages on the market will suit you best. Later in this chapter we shall see where you can get information to help you make that choice. We shall also see where you can buy what you need. You may decide that one package suits you much better than all the others, but in general you will probably find several that will do. Keep your options open for the moment. What you want to know now is what sort of hardware you need, so that the software of your choice will run satisfactorily.

First you need to decide whether you will use Windows. If so, you should be looking for a 386 machine with at least 2 Mbytes of memory, preferably 4 Mbytes. You should also have a hard disk of at least 80 Mbytes which is reasonably fast; say under 20 milliseconds access time. If you intend to run applications concurrently – and one of the reasons for using Windows is to allow this – you will need at least 4 Mbytes of memory. The slowest version of the 386 (such as a 16 Mhz 386SX) will do for most tasks, but a faster one will be better for complex graphics applications and for very large spreadsheets. If in doubt, buy a fast one if you can; the price difference is fairly small. You are not likely to need a more powerful machine than a 386 for the sort of tasks that a one-person business has to do, and at the moment the 486 machines are quite a bit more expensive although prices are falling fast. You should choose a VGA display if you can afford it, or possibly SVGA if you will be doing much graphics work. If you need to save money, buy a mono display in preference to one with lower definition.

If you do not use Windows you can manage with less memory, 1 or 2 Mbytes. For most applications you can also use a smaller, slower, hard disk. However, for complex graphics and large databases a fast disk is worth having. In principle you do not need a 386 machine, but these are now almost as cheap as 286 machines and have several advantages, so it is worth paying the little extra. Don't buy an 8086 machine unless you are really short of cash; these machines are obsolescent and an increasing number of applications will not run on them. Again, choose a VGA display if you can afford it; but you can manage with CGA if graphics applications are not important to you.

The next question is whether to buy a machine from one of the up-market suppliers, or a cheaper clone. There can be a substantial price difference. If you buy a machine with a famous name (and there are several of these besides IBM), are you really getting good value? Or are you just paying a lot for the name label? There isn't an easy answer to this. The up-market manufacturers are very conscious of their image, and so they will put a great deal of effort into quality control, servicing, and customer satisfaction in general. You are unlikely to have problems; if you do, you can expect a rapid response. However, the lesser manufacturers have improved in this respect, and many of them now have excellent reputations. It is now normal for them to offer a satisfactory maintenance service, usually through a third party. Only you can decide how much it is worth paying for the extra peace of mind. If money is not a problem, by all means go for a big name. If not, you will find plenty of manufacturers to meet your needs at a lower price. Be cautious about very small or very new companies; they may not last long enough to solve any problems that crop up. A few of them may skimp on quality, although that is unusual nowadays. And notice what deal each offers on maintenance. My own inclination would be to avoid very cheap offers, unless there is a respectable reason for them. The most likely reason is obsolescence, and buying an obsolescent machine will limit your options in the future.

Much the same applies to software, as we saw in an earlier chapter. But here pricing is more artificial; we saw how the price of one spreadsheet was cut by three quarters to bring it into a different market sector. You are unlikely to need the most expensive package of its type, but you may be disappointed if you buy the cheapest. There is plenty of choice in between.

Now you should have a good idea of what you want, and you can work out what it will cost you. Any good PC magazine will have many pages of advertisements from which you can find the current prices. Can you afford it? If not you will have to go through the process again, starting with less ambitious aims. If and when you have defined a system within your price range that will do what you want (though preferably with your options reasonably open) you are ready to decide where to buy it. This we shall discuss later in this chapter.

You may still be unsure whether you need a computer, or what you would use it for. In this case, perhaps you should ignore all the advice I have given above. Buy a really cheap computer – perhaps second-hand – and cheap software (such as 'shareware', described later). You can play about with this, and get some idea of what computing could do for you. You will also learn what features of the hardware and software are important to you and which are not. Then, if you do decide to take computing seriously, your experience will help you decide what sort of hardware and software you really need. The old machine didn't cost you much – ditch it, or give it to your children to play games on.

What is on the market?

I suggested above that once you've decided what sort of software you need, you should find out just what there is on the market that will meet your needs. How do you do this, when there are hundreds of software and hardware companies and thousands of products? There are many sources of information; we shall look at each of them in turn.

Advertisements and data sheets

The most abundant source of information, and the easiest to get hold of, is advertising in the press. There are dozens of magazines dealing specifically with the PC, and every newsagent offers a choice. These magazines depend for on their income mainly on advertisers rather than buyers. Indeed, some are given away free, although these will not be on the newsagents' shelves. So you can get a lot of advertisements for very little money. There's no point in buying every magazine you see – at least, not just for this purpose – as the advertisements are much the same in all of them. Just buy one of the fattest.

Some magazine advertisements are very useful, giving a full specification of each product. Others give briefer information, and some are no more than 'brand advertising' – trying to persuade you that theirs is the only company to deal with, but telling you little about their products. However, in nearly every case you have only to write or telephone and the company will be only too glad to send you detailed data sheets on its products.

Exhibitions

There are several major exhibitions each year which deal with computers in general or PCs in particular. These vary from time to time, but at present the biggest are the 'Which Computer' show at the National Exhibition Centre near Birmingham in the spring, and the 'Business Computing' and 'Computer Shopper' shows in London in the autumn. There are other London shows, and also smaller shows in provincial cities. Here you can see products working, and talk to salesmen about them. Sometimes data sheets are laid out on the stand for the taking. In other cases you will have to ask a salesman, and the data may then be posted to you. Most of the stands are run by manufacturers rather than dealers. You may or may not be able to place orders on the spot. I advise you not to do so – take the information home and think about it in a calmer atmosphere.

There is usually an admission charge to these shows, but anyone in the trade is bombarded with free tickets so see if any of your friends has one to spare. Exhibitions like this give an excellent chance to see the actual product, and often to see it demonstrated or even to get your own hands on the keyboard for a few minutes. Some stands, especially those selling up-market software, have rows of seats and run demonstrations at frequent intervals. These are often worth watching, even if only to give your feet a rest. Usually you will be invited to leave your name and address or a business card. Often a card is drawn out of the hat after the demonstration and you may win anything from a cheap pen to a computer. You may even be entered in a draw for a sports car. You may not be impressed by this approach to advertising, but why refuse anything that's free? Apart from this you are unlikely to get free samples of anything significant, unless you can persuade the salesman that you are in the market for several hundred of whatever it is. What you will be offered free is sample issues of various journals and newsletters. If you can carry the weight, take them.

The disadvantage of a show of this kind, apart from the time and energy that it takes up, is that only a selection of suppliers and manufacturers take part. This applies particularly to the provincial shows, which are often staffed by local dealers rather than manufacturers. If your interest is in seeing a particular piece of hardware or software you may well be disappointed. Indeed, on some stands you will see only the products that are new this year. But if you do have the time to visit one of these shows it will give you a chance to see demonstrations, and to ask questions, about a wide range of products.

Reviews

Advertisements, exhibition stands and data sheets will tell you what is on the market, but of course you cannot expect advertisers to point out the weaknesses of their products. So what you need next is an independent source of advice. Here again, the press is a good starting point. Most of the PC magazines give a good deal of space to reviews of hardware and software. Sometimes these are reviews of a product in isolation. At other times there may be a group review of several closely competitive products. For example, the cover of a magazine on my desk this month proclaims '12 £1000 business machines reviewed – need you pay more?' In most cases the reviews include some scientific testing as well as just opinion. Of course time is money to a reviewer, so he or she will not have spent long enough with a product to find out everything about it. Nevertheless these people have the experience to know what weaknesses to look out for, and in general their opinions are useful. If possible, compare the views of several reviewers on the products that interest you.

Of course, if you just go out and buy one or two magazines you won't find reviews of every product that interests you. Apart from group tests, a product is usually reviewed when it is new or has had a major upgrade. Even group reviews often cover a small, and perhaps arbitrary, selection of what is on the market – although one magazine did recently review a group of 100 PCs of the 386 type. You may be able to find back numbers in a library, or with a friend. Otherwise choose one or two magazines which you think have the best reviewers, and write to their circulation departments to ask for a contents list of recent back numbers. Things change so rapidly in this industry that a review more than a year old will not be much use to you.

Another source of independent information is the surveys that come out from time to time which list the products of many manufacturers. Some are in book form. They usually have titles which describe their purpose, such as 'The guide to good Software'. They may simply list products, with a more or less brief description, or they may include a critical review. Most of these books deal with software though there are one or two for hardware. They can be useful if they give a comprehensive survey, not least because they give the suppliers' names and addresses so that you can write for further information. The difficulty is that the process of book publishing means that each of these works is several months out of date by the time it is published. It may be a good deal older than that by the time you read it. PC hardware and software can change a lot in this time. So just use the book as a pointer, and get more up-to-date information about anything of interest that you find in it.

Some magazines issue supplements, one or more times a year, which serve the same purpose. They will be more up to date, although not as up to date as the magazine itself. But they are often very selective and do not cover anything like the full range of suppliers. Some PC magazines include a comprehensive list of products every month. This gives only very brief information, but you can write to the suppliers of anything that looks interesting.

Demonstration disks and shareware

Some software suppliers offer demonstration disks, either free or for a small charge. They may be given away free at an exhibition, or attached to the cover of a magazine, or you may be invited to write to the suppliers for them. The idea is that you can learn about the program in your own time and on your own machine – or a friend's, if you've not bought one yet.

There are two kinds of demonstration disk. One of them is really just a slide show. Once you have started the demo it tells you what the program does, and shows you what its screen displays look like. You have no interaction with it, except perhaps to press a key to move on to the next screen. The other sort of demonstration disk includes a simplified version of the program itself. This lets you get the feel of it in use. You can also try out some of the tasks you would want to do in your own business. The demonstration is usually limited in some way to make sure that you do not use it instead of buying the full program. For example, it may not let you print out results, or it may only handle a small amount of data. Or it may die on you after a few hours of use. Even so, this sort of demonstration can be very useful in helping you to assess a program.

The problem with many demonstration disks is that they are not prepared with enough care. I have had several such disks which simply did not work, or which upset the computer in some way – for example by altering the screen colours, and not resetting them after the demo. Needless to say, these did not tempt me to buy the software although it may in fact have been good.

You could think of **shareware** as the ultimate in demonstration disks. A shareware disk carries a complete and fully working version of a program, though it may not be the latest version. There is usually an instruction manual (sometimes a shortened version) as a text file on the disk. The idea is that you can play with the program as much as you like, to decide whether it does what you want. If and when you decide to make serious use of it, then you are morally obliged to pay a registration fee. You may in fact be legally obliged to pay, but this is academic as it would be almost impossible to enforce. However, shareware authors depend on registration fees to stay in business, so it would be mean to cheat them. Often there is an added incentive to register, such as the latest version of the program and a properly printed and bound manual. Of course you can only expect support from the author if you register.

When you buy a shareware disk, therefore, you are only buying the disk itself and the opportunity to try the program; you are not buying the right to make full use of the program. So shareware disks are very cheap. There are quite a few dealers specialising in shareware, and they sell disks for a few pounds each. Many user groups sell disks a little cheaper than this, and they will sell to non-members although they may charge them a pound or so extra. The price you pay for a shareware disk should cover only the cost of the disk and of copying the program to it, plus reasonable overheads such as advertising. Some shareware appears on the 'free' disks given away with PC magazines, or sometimes with hardware. You can also get disks from your friends, since copying is allowed – indeed, even encouraged – although of course there is still the obligation to register if you continue to use the program. If you have a modem and communications software, you will find many bulletin boards have a stock of shareware which you can download. Watch the cost of this, particularly the telephone charges; it is economical for small programs, but for bigger ones it may be cheaper to buy a disk.

In contrast to shareware, **public domain** (or PD) software really is free. The author has declared it available to all, and you can use and copy it without charge. Most PD software falls into one of two groups. Firstly, simple utilities and games, which often form part of the collections on magazine cover disks (the magazines make a small payment to the authors). Secondly, specialised software written by US government agencies. For a time, US law required that such software be placed in the public domain. Such programs are distributed in the same way as shareware.

Shareware and PD programs vary very much in quality, although the better dealers will list only those programs that they consider to be good. A few are up to the standard of the best commercial programs. For example one database manager, which happens to be the one I use, is used in larger numbers than any of its commercial rivals. Many of the programs are simpler than their commercial equivalents. They do the basic tasks just as well but lack some of the 'bells and whistles'. This is not always a bad thing. Others are specialised programs which would not sell well enough commercially to be viable. A few shareware programs are the work of substantial companies, which could sell their programs commercially but prefer the shareware method. Sometimes they use both methods for different products, or even for different versions of the same product. Most shareware authors, however, work on their own, often in their spare time. The attraction of shareware to them is that they do not need a marketing organisation.

The true cost of shareware is the registration fee rather than the cost of the disk. It varies with the type of program, of course. Shareware usually costs much less than an equivalent commercial program, as nothing has been spent on advertising and little on marketing. The better shareware dealers, and some user groups, will handle registration for you, though sometimes for only some of the software on their list. You send them the registration fee in UK currency (assuming a UK dealer) and they either send you a registered copy themselves, or arrange for the author to do so. Otherwise you have to send the registration fee direct to the author. This is simple if the author is in the UK, but more of them are in the USA and a few in other countries. These nearly always want payment in their own currency. You can get any bank to do this for you, but it can be expensive. Many authors are prepared to charge to the major credit cards, and this is often the simplest method.

Support varies between authors, although obviously you have no right to support unless you have registered. A few just don't reply to letters, or have moved house. Some of the largest firms only support the latest version, and may make a charge for support. In most cases reasonable support is provided free of charge. One US author regularly sends me, free, disks upgrading an inexpensive program I registered some years ago. You cannot expect any support for public domain software.

You may have heard rumours that viruses are carried by shareware. In fact you are most unlikely to find a virus in a registered copy of a program, or in a shareware or PD disk supplied by a reputable vendor or a user group. These go to great lengths to stay free of viruses – their reputation depends on it. One or two magazines have looked into the question and found that the risk is indeed less than with commercial programs. On the other hand, there is always a risk in taking copies from friends or acquaintances. They are not likely to pass on a virus deliberately. But somewhere down the line, someone may have unknowingly had a virus in his or her machine, and passed it on in the disk copy. It is only a small risk; you must decide yourself whether to take it. If in doubt, invest in an anti-virus package; these are discussed later.

It can be difficult to find what is available in shareware and PD software, since many suppliers show very little detail in their lists and advertisements. One or two of them produce good catalogues. These are expensive to produce, so either you have to pay a pound or two for them or that supplier charges more for shareware disks.

There are really two reasons why you may be interested in shareware. Firstly you may believe that a shareware program will do the job you want done, and that its registration fee is good value. Secondly, you may find it difficult to decide just what features you want in an application program – a spreadsheet, say. In that case it would be premature to spend a lot of money on a commercial program. Instead you buy one, or several, shareware versions and play with them until you have enough experience to know just what you need. Then you can buy a commercial program, or register shareware, with less risk of wasting your money.

Where to buy

There are many ways in which you can buy your hardware and software. They range from a quick telephone call to a personal visit to Hong Kong. We shall look at the more practicable of them.

Dealers

This is the safest way to buy, though not the cheapest. There are PC dealers in every sizeable town, and they will be listed in the 'Yellow Pages' and may advertise in your local paper. Some of them are excellent; most of them will do a competent job; a few are rogues, or just incompetent. Neither the Yellow Pages nor their advertisements will tell you which. You can get some idea from their manner and the state of their premises, but the only reliable basis for choosing is personal recommendation. Ideally you want to ask people who are in your own line of business, or at least use the same sort of computer and software as you have in mind. You may be able to get advice from your trade association or from an enterprise centre. Microsystems centres and similar groups can advise, but many of these either sell equipment themselves or are linked to particular dealers or suppliers, so they may not be impartial.

A good dealer will not only help you choose your hardware and software, and supply it, but will install it and may give you a certain amount of training in its use. He or she will also be willing to come back and help you out whenever you have problems. Thus buying from a dealer makes things as easy for you as they can be. But of course this has to be paid for. The dealer may charge for training and for after-sales service, but most of his overheads will be absorbed in the price of what he sells you. So you will naturally pay more than if you bought the equipment without any of this support.

The other problem with dealers is that most of them carry only one make of hardware, or a very limited range, and likewise with software. These will not be among the cheaper makes, since those bring less profit to the dealer. That makes it harder for him to give you the support you expect. Besides, the more expensive brands are (or should be) more reliable and so cost him less to support. So a dealer may, with the best of intentions, talk you into buying what he happens to stock rather than what you think you want. Keep in mind that you know far more about your business than the dealer does, and go home and think about it rather than accepting his suggestions on the spot. Of course, your trade association may recommend a dealer who specialises in your kind of business. You are then more likely to get the best system for the job, but it still will not be cheap.

Consultants

A consultant, like a dealer, should take most of the work of choosing and buying a system off your hands. The dividing line between consultants and dealers can be a bit hazy because some consultants sell equipment. But, at least in theory, the difference is that the consultant puts your interests first, and should be able to recommend whatever software and hardware suits you best without any vested interest. This, of course, should mean that he makes no profit or commission on the goods, so you will have to pay him directly. His fee may be quite high. Make sure that you are aware of it beforehand.

The advantage of a consultant, if you choose the right one, is that he or she understands business as well as computers. Obviously you want one who understands your own business, or at least businesses of a similar type. It may be difficult to find a consultant who fills the bill. Your trade association, or the local enterprise centre, may be able to suggest one.

Your consultant may simply advise what you should buy, or he may obtain it and install it for you. Naturally the more the consultant does, the higher the fee. He should pass on to you any discount or commission he is offered, to ensure his independence. Find out what happens if you have problems later; the initial fee may cover this, or there may be a further charge.

High street stores and computer supermarkets

Quite a few high street stores now sell PCs and software, alongside hi-fi or books or whatever. They carry a limited range. In a few cases they choose to call their computer departments 'business centres' and in this case the staff should know something about computers. They are in effect PC dealers. However, they are again unlikely to know much about your own type of business. Find out what after-sales support is offered. It may not include setting up the system, and they may only be prepared to sort out problems if you can convince them that their kit is at fault. However, the high street store will be much cheaper than a PC dealer. So it is a reasonable option if you know enough about computers to look after yourself, or have some other source of help.

Much the same applies to computer supermarkets, except that here the range of products on sale is wider. There is usually limited technical help available, but this is unlikely to extend to setting-up or to dealing with problems unless these can be shown to be faults in what you have bought. Against this, they offer very keen prices. These supermarkets are new at the time of writing; it remains to be seen how they develop.

Mail order dealers

If you know exactly what you want, you can buy it by mail order. The name is slightly misleading, as you can equally well order by telephone and charge the goods to your credit card. There are many mail order dealers, and you will find them advertising in all the PC magazines. You can judge the prosperity of the firm from its advertisement, to some extent, but a personal recommendation is more useful if you can get one. These firms are strictly 'box shifters' with no formal after-sales service, though if you ring up with a problem you can sometimes find someone to advise.

Most of these firms carry a wide product range, though some specialise in a particular field such as printers. Their prices are keen, and you can compare them from their advertisements. Sometimes these say 'ring for prices'; in that case you can reasonably expect to pay no more than the lowest price advertised elsewhere. Find what that is before you ring.

Watch out for the hidden charges. The advertised prices normally exclude VAT and delivery, although this may only appear in very small print. If the items are in stock, delivery should be fast (sometimes faster if you pay more) but otherwise it may be slow. If time is important you may be wise to arrange that the order is cancelled if it cannot be met within, say, a week.

Sometimes you will see advertised a 'special offer for a limited period'. By all means consider this, but don't let it rush you into a decision. Computer hardware is one of the few markets in which the trend of prices is downwards, and this month's 'special offer' may be the prevailing price next month. If you decide you are interested but have missed the deadline, it is worth haggling with the salesman. If he could afford to sell it at that price last month, he can afford it this month. Software specials tend to be different. They may be end-of-line sales because a new version is due, in which case they are good value unless you really need the new features. If the price is very low, it may be cheaper to buy the old version and upgrade later than to wait for the new version and buy that. On the other hand, a brand new product may be offered cheaply to get the market moving, and then revert to a normal price. This can be good value too. New products are more likely to have bugs than established ones, but in this case the suppliers will probably let you upgrade to a bug-free version for nothing or a nominal fee. They ought to, after all – you are doing some of their testing for them!

A rather special case of mail order is the few firms which specialise in getting software direct from the USA. This is rather a controversial subject. If you buy US-sourced application software in the UK it is often priced much higher than it would be in the USA. In some case the dollar sign is simply replaced by the pound sign, which means the price is nearly doubled. For this you should get an anglicised version of the program, though beware of one or two firms that don't do this. You should also get support from an agent in the UK. The rights and wrongs of this pricing practice are not my concern, but one or two firms have taken the opportunity to buy software in the US and sell it to UK customers at much keener prices. If you take advantage of this, you will usually get the 'US' rather than the 'UK' version of the software. This may or may not matter to you. It may show in little things like the '£' sign and the date format, and the absence of support for the A4 paper size. More seriously, in the case of a word processor the spell checker may expect American spelling. You are unlikely to be able to get support in the UK, though you could telephone to the USA for help.

Buying Direct

This is not quite the same as 'mail order'. It is the term used for buying equipment direct from the manufacturer or importer. A number of hardware and software manufacturers supply only in this way, and not through dealers or mail order suppliers. This does away with the middleman, and so lets them offer keener prices. They find their customers mainly by advertising in PC magazines, and sometimes through their stands at exhibitions. Their products are likely to be reviewed in the magazines at least as often as those sold in the conventional way.

Software companies often sell both direct and through dealers and mail order suppliers. In this case you may find that buying direct from the software company is actually the most expensive option.

If you deal directly with a manufacturer or importer, either by mail or by telephone, you should be able to get detailed information about the product and possibly some about its suitability for your business. PCs will usually be supplied with the operating system installed and ready to use, and also Windows if you order it. On the other hand you will not expect any on-site service, except that maintenance will usually be available. Sometimes this is included in the price, at least for the first year or two; in others you pay separately for a maintenance contract. The companies doing business in this way vary in competence, like any others. Your best guide is the reviews in PC magazines. If several machines from the same supplier score well, that should be a good firm to deal with.

A word of warning: several suppliers of hardware have gone out of business while holding customers' money. Since you have to pay in advance, it is wise to use a credit card, as this will offer some protection in most cases – check your credit card company's terms of business.

Buying abroad

If you travel abroad, particularly to the Far East, you may find that hardware and, especially, software is very cheap there. Buy only if you know exactly what you are doing, as you will have no come-back at all if the product proves unsatisfactory. You will be liable to duty when you import the goods, which may still leave them looking cheap. However, there is a good chance that the software is an illegal copy. If so, not only will you get no support, you may be liable to legal action. Be particularly suspicious if there is no manual, or the manual looks to be a photocopy or a locally printed copy rather than the original.

Buying US software in the States is a much safer proposition, and can be quite a money saver although again you will have to allow for duty. You may or may not be able to get support in the UK depending on the policy of the supplier. You can always telephone the USA for help, of course. See above under 'mail order' for possible problems arising from using software that is not anglicised.

Buying second-hand

You may get a good bargain by buying second-hand, but you should bear in mind that computer design develops rapidly and so a machine more than two or three years old is near obsolescence. In particular, if you buy an 8086 or 286 machine you may find that you cannot run some of the software you need. Apart from this, it's largely a matter of knowing exactly what is being offered and what condition it is in. In general there is not much about a PC that wears out; possibly the disk drives and the keyboard, though these are easily replaced (at a price). The CRT may lose some of its brightness after several years use, but this is something that you can see for yourself. Probably the most likely component to wear out is the cooling fan if there is one, and this costs little to replace. On the other hand, printers do wear out and are probably not worth refurbishing.

Some very cheap equipment can be bought at government or bankruptcy sales, especially small ones which do not attract dealers. But you will probably not have a chance to try things out, and they may well be incomplete – in particular the manuals are likely to be missing. So you do need to have a very good idea of what you are buying, and whether it would be worth while if it did turn out to be incomplete. There's an element of adventure here – you might find something very interesting on the hard disk!

Checking your shopping list

If you use a dealer or consultant, it is their job to make sure that everything you need is there and that there are no compatibility problems. Otherwise you must look after this for yourself. Most of this we have covered already, but there are a few things that are worth saying again.

What is included in the basic package

Usually the essential hardware and the system software are sold as a complete package, though you may have some say as to its contents. For example you often have a choice of memory capacity, of disk capacity, and between a mono and a colour screen. If you order parts separately, you would be wise to get them all from the same supplier so that there are no incompatibilities. You need to make sure that you get all the following, and that they are compatible with one another:

❑ System unit

❑ Hard disk drive and controller

❑ Floppy disk drive (one or more) and controller

❑ Keyboard

❑ Mouse (in most cases)

❑ Display unit, with a video card to support it

❑ Interconnecting cables and mains leads

❑ Operating system

❑ All relevant manuals

If you want Windows, try to get this as part of the package as it is likely to be cheaper that way.

You may be able to add some options to this package for less than the cost of buying them separately. For example a different type of case, a co-processor, a tape drive, or some application software (often an integrated package).

It is not usual to include a printer in the package, but you may be offered a choice of printers at a discount price if you buy one at the same time as the PC. Make sure you get a connecting cable and mains lead with the printer. Consider whether the standard cable is long enough – you may need a longer one to suit your office layout.

Hardware compatibility problems

If you buy everything from the same source, and make it clear that you intend to use all the items together, you should not have compatibility problems. If you do, it's up to the supplier to sort them out. Otherwise, when you buy an item you should tell the suppliers what other equipment or software it must work with, and get their assurance that it will be compatible. If they don't know, maybe you should try another supplier, or maybe you can get advice from the original manufacturers. Failing this, arrange that the supplier will take the item back if you have problems.

Since a printer is the item most likely to be bought separately from the PC, this is where most compatibility problems arise. You can be fairly sure that you will have no trouble in printing the alphabet and numbers, but there is more likely to be trouble with symbols. The commonest problem is to do with the '£' sign, since this is represented differently within the PC in UK and American (and Japanese) practice. Nowadays most printers can be set to suit either practice, and so can most PCs and software. But do check before you buy. If you want to use accented letters, and in particular if you want to use a character set other than that of the UK or USA, take particular care to check that this will work.

Software compatibility

Here again, if you buy from a dealer or take advice from a consultant you ought not to have any problems. Otherwise it is up to you to make sure that everything will work happily together. We have covered the need to have a PC with enough processor power and memory, and a suitable disk, to support your choice of software. Beyond this, compatibility problems between hardware and software are rare. The only thing that may cause difficulty is an American program that has not been anglicised. If your PC is set up as a UK system, which it normally will be, you may then have difficulties over displaying and printing the '£' sign and over handling A4 paper. There are utility programs that may help, and user groups are used to advising on problems like these. Otherwise you will have to accept it as one of the penalties of buying software not intended for UK use. Much the same is likely to happen if your PC is set up for some nationality other than USA or UK, though here you may also have problems with accented letters. It is reasonable to expect a program advertised and sold in the UK to be properly anglicised unless you are told otherwise. There are one or two rogue suppliers about. If you are caught this way, complain to the supplier and to the advertising manager of the magazine which carried the advertisement.

Reliability and bugs

Application programs can be extremely complex, and inevitably some errors creep in. Most of them are found in the course of the rigorous testing which reputable companies apply before they start to sell a program. But the occasional 'bug' often remains, usually in some part of the program which is little used. So if the program behaves oddly it is not necessarily your fault. See whether you can reproduce the fault and note down exactly the sequence of events, and then get in touch with the supplier. Often someone else has already reported the fault and they can fix it immediately. If they seem not to be interested, don't use that supplier again. Of course, you should read the manual carefully to make sure that what you are doing is legitimate.

Bugs can become apparent in many ways, but producing a plausible but incorrect answer is one of the least likely. Usually the program will behave oddly in some other way. The most common is refusing to respond to a legitimate keystroke or command. Often it will not respond to any key or command, except (sometimes) the combination which resets the machine. In computer jargon, the machine has 'crashed' and the problem is fairly sure to be in the application program or possibly in the operating system (including Windows if you are using it). Switch off the PC, wait a minute or two until the hard disk has stopped turning, and switch on again. The machine should be back to normal. If you can reproduce the fault by going through the same sequence of events, make a note of the sequence and get in touch with the supplier.

Copying and copy protection

When you receive software on disk, the first thing you should do is to set the 'write protect' slider or tab on each disk. The next is to make a copy of the disk (your Operating System manual will tell you how). Put the original disk in a safe place and use the copy to load the program into your PC. This way you should always have the original to come back to if any accident happens. The licence conditions sent to you with any program normally allow you to do this, but not to make copies for any other purpose. In particular it is both immoral and illegal to give or sell a copy of the program to anyone (except in the case of shareware or PD software), or to use more than one copy at a time yourself.

Occasionally you may come across a program which is **copy protected**, which means that it has been treated in some way so that it cannot be copied. As most users run programs from their hard disks, this kind of software can be run in that way but only if the original program disk remains in the floppy disk drive. This can be a considerable nuisance, and of course you are in trouble if some hardware fault – or just a mistake in operation – corrupts the program disk. Fortunately copy protection is rare these days, except on a few computer games. Personally I would not buy any other copy protected program, and I advise you not to. You may buy a program and find without warning that it is copy protected; this has happened to me. If so, send a strong complaint to the supplier and ask if they will promise to replace the program disk if it is accidentally damaged. If you do not get a satisfactory answer, ask for your money back and avoid that firm in future. One can understand that firms are concerned about illegal copying, but this sort of protection harms the honest users more than the rogues, who have access to ways of defeating copy protection.

Viruses

These are an increasing problem, but one which you can avoid with a little care. Viruses can only be transmitted by software, not by data. Once a PC has been infected by a virus, any program disk which is inserted in it may be contaminated. Any program which is copied on to another disk may also be affected. The effect of viruses varies very much from one to another. They may simply display a message on your screen (one of the best known says 'This computer is stoned') or corrupt the display in some way. The most vicious can destroy all the information on your hard disk. This may not happen as soon as the virus enters the machine. Some viruses wait for a certain date (a recent one chose Michaelangelo's birthday) or until the disk has been accessed a certain number of times.

You can best avoid viruses by buying software only from a reputable dealer, whether commercial or shareware. They check all their disks carefully. In the unlikely event that a disk does carry a virus they will help you sort things out, for the sake of their reputation. Other sources such as bulletin boards, dubious dealers and friends are more risky, although the risk is still small. The greatest risk is in shared computers and in communications networks where you cannot control who has access to your system – as may happen in schools and universities. If your children want to play games on your computer, make very sure that they got their disks from a safe source.

You can buy various kinds of anti-virus software. One kind looks for all known viruses, and is updated from time to time as new viruses are discovered. This can be very effective, but is expensive because of the frequent updating, and you may still be caught by a new virus before the update reaches you. The other kind looks for changes in any program which suggest that a virus may have been added. This does not need updating, but some recent viruses can outwit it. All anti-virus programs are likely to slow the loading of programs from floppy disk somewhat.

It is up to you to decide whether you need an anti-virus program. If you are the only person who uses the PC, you take care where you get your software, and you are not exposed to interference over a communications link, then you are at very little risk. You may still want to get protection for the sake of peace of mind, or to reassure you that odd behaviour of the machine is due to a common-or-garden bug and not a virus.

Supplies

From time to time you will need to buy supplies for your PC; floppy disks, paper, printer ribbons and so forth. You can get these from most of the places where you can buy hardware and software. The most convenient sources are dealers, high street shops, and mail order. Some mail order companies specialise in supplies rather than hardware and software; they advertise in PC magazines. Most companies dealing in office supplies, and some stationers, keep a limited range of computer supplies. Mail order companies – especially the specialists – offer the widest choice and are often cheapest, though watch out for delivery charges. Since computer supplies do not deteriorate in storage, you may as well buy enough at a time to take account of any discount that is on offer.

Floppy disks

You must of course buy the right disks for your disk drive, and the manual for your PC will tell you what these are. There are two sizes, 3.5 inch and 5.25 inch, but each of these is obtainable in two capacities and further varieties are on the way. However, disk suppliers may use other descriptions than the capacity. Thus

3.5 inch 720 kbyte or 5.25 inch 360 kbyte = DS/DD (double sided, double density)

3.5 inch 1.44 Mbyte or 5.25 inch 1.2 Mbyte = DS/HD (double sided, high density).

However there are variants of these terms. In particular the 'DS' is often dropped since single sided 5.25 disks are obsolete, though still sold for some old machines, and there have never been single-sided 3.5 inch disks. 'Single density' disks have long been obsolete. 'Hard sectored' disks are sold for old machines, but will not interest you; your disks will be 'soft sectored', though this is usually taken for granted. You do not need to buy 'preformatted' disks.

Many drives will now handle two densities, such as 720 kbyte and 1.44 Mbyte disks. You should buy disks that correspond with the higher of these densities. The lower density disks will fit in your drive, but some cases have been reported of drives which cannot write on lower density disks without error. Worse, data which appears to be satisfactory now may be found to be unreadable when you try again in the future. The most recent high-density 3.5 inch drives should not suffer from this problem, but 5.25 inch drives are more critical.

Disks come in various qualities. It is unwise to be too thrifty when buying disks. Cheap disks may appear to be satisfactory when you first write on them (if not you should throw them away) but may be found to have errors when read later. They may also not stand up to wear as well as better disks, which makes them unsuitable for backup. In most cases the value to you of the information on a disk will be far higher than the price of the disk. So I advise you to buy branded disks, or unbranded disks from a supplier you can trust, when you want to store data. This includes backup, of course. There's no need to go for the most expensive brand, any reputable brand should be good enough. Of course, if you have data of particular importance, buying a few top quality disks may be worth while for the sake of your peace of mind. Where the information on the disk is easily replaced, such as the working copies of your software, you can economise if you wish. It is almost impossible for any disk to damage the drive, but if you use cheap disks you may need to clean it more often.

You should buy cleaning disks for each size of drive, preferably the 'wet' type. Don't use these too often as they do wear the head slightly. Once every month or two is enough, unless you use very cheap disks. However if you have any trouble reading or writing a disk, always run the cleaning disk before you try again.

Printer ribbons

Daisywheel and impact matrix printers use a ribbon similar to a typewriter ribbon. It is always held in some sort of cartridge, for ease of handling, and there are almost as many types of cartridge as there are makes and models of printer.

There are two types of ribbon; one-time (often called 'multi-strike') and fabric. Most printers can only use one type, though a few can use either. A one-time ribbon has a coating of pigment on a plastic backing, and passes through the machine only once. When the whole ribbon has been wound from one spool to the other, the printer stops and a new ribbon must be fitted. Usually printing can then go on, and there is no sign of the change on the printed page. Throw away the used cartridge. Some firms (which advertise in the PC magazines) will reload your cartridge with a new length of ribbon, but this does not save much of the cost.

Fabric ribbons pass through the printer many times. In some cases the ribbon forms a continuous loop. In others it is wound from one spool to another, and automatically reversed when the end of the spool is reached. The print will gradually get fainter as the ribbon is used, but it is left to you to decide when it needs to be replaced. You can economise by using a new ribbon for good work, and keeping a well-used one for drafts.

There are firms which will re-ink fabric ribbons. You can buy a machine and do it yourself, but this will not be worth while for the one-person business. You can also open some ribbon cartridges and spray the ribbon with new ink. How practicable this is depends on the design of the cartridge; in many cases you will find it hard to open without damage. My experience with this method has not been encouraging. I have found it difficult to get the ink evenly distributed, and some of the cartridges have jammed in spite of care in re-assembly. You may like to experiment to see if you can do better. If so, make sure you buy ink which is designed for the job, even though it is quite expensive. The ink in a matrix printer ribbon contains a trace of lubricant, and this is essential to keep the pins working smoothly. If you use ordinary ink, or worse still spray the ribbon with 'WD40' or some other fluid to redistribute the ink, you risk a seized-up print head. That could be expensive to replace.

In any case, a fabric ribbon will become unevenly stretched in use and this may make it not worth re-inking. Some firms will reload the cartridge with a new ribbon; compare their charge with the price of a new cartridge. A colour ribbon cannot be re-inked, but it may be possible to reload it in this way.

Many suppliers offer the choice of 'original' or 'compatible' ribbons. The 'original' ribbon is that supplied, or at least recommended, by the printer supplier, and should give you no trouble. 'Compatible' ribbons come from some other manufacturer, and vary in price and quality. Cheap ribbons are sometimes shorter, which means they will fade out sooner. They are also more likely to jam in the cartridge, which usually means throwing the cartridge away. I would advise you to avoid the cheapest ribbons, but a good compatible ribbon should serve you as well as an original.

If you have an unusual printer you may find ribbons hard to get. Look in the magazine advertisements, or at an exhibition, for a firm which specialises in printer ribbons.

Ink cartridges

Ink-jets use these in place of ribbons. Again there are almost as many designs as there are printers. They are fairly expensive, especially those which include the nozzles. At present you are only likely to be offered original cartridges; compatibles may appear in the future. In some cases you can buy ink in bottles and refill the cartridges. As long as the ink is of the same quality as the original, this should be satisfactory. However, if the cartridge includes the jets this is done because new jets are needed frequently. You should not refill these cartridges many times.

Laser printer supplies

Laser printers use a powder toner instead of ink. This has to be replenished from time to time. In nearly all cases it is supplied in a cartridge, and you replace this as a whole. The cartridge is complex and expensive, so it is worth considering one of the firms which will refurbish and refill cartridges. Do not try to do it yourself, as there are parts which wear and need to be replaced or at least checked. However, one firm has recently introduced a special design of cartridge which can be refilled. I have not seen this done so do not know how easy it is.

Laser printers also use a photosensitive drum or belt which you must replace occasionally. In some printers you replace it separately from the toner cartridge, and less often. In others the two are combined in a single unit, which you replace as a whole. I have not come across any firm which offers to refurbish drums. Be careful how you dispose of the old drum, as it may have harmful chemicals on it. There should be advice on disposal in the printer manual, or on the box round the new drum. Incidentally, all this applies also to photocopiers.

Paper

We saw in the last chapter that paper comes in two forms – cut sheet and fanfold. Some printers can handle either, others only one. The quality of the paper must suit the printer. Daisywheel and impact printers can print on almost anything, except that if it is too stiff it may not feed satisfactorily; something like 80 gm per square metre is suitable for most purposes. If you use cut sheet, ordinary copier paper will do very well and is cheap. Laser printers will print on any reasonably smooth cut sheet, and again copier paper does very well. Ink-jets are more particular as the absorbency of the paper is important as well as its smoothness. Look in the manual to see what is recommended.

Most types of printer will also handle other materials, of which the two most useful are acetate sheet (for overhead projector transparencies) and self-adhesive labels. There is more than one type of acetate sheet, and you should buy the sort intended for your kind of printer. You may need to use a special type of ink cartridge in an ink-jet printer – see the manual. Acetate is invariably supplied as cut sheet, and usually only in A4 size. Self-adhesive labels are supplied stuck to a backing sheet, of tough glossy paper, which you discard after use. Again there are different varieties to suit the different types of printer. They are usually supplied in fanfold form, except for lasers where they are cut sheet. Labels are available in a wide range of sizes, and often with two or three labels across the width of the backing sheet. Make sure your software can handle these before you buy them.

Labels can be troublesome where the diameter of the printer platen is small; the labels may peel off the backing sheet of their own accord, and jam inside the printer. Be careful how you remove them, as fragments in the wrong place can cause damage. The problem usually arises with cheap labels or with old stock. If it persists, you may have to print on plain paper and then photocopy this onto label stock.

Maintenance

PCs and printers need no regular maintenance, apart from cleaning the disk drives and a little general cleaning now and then. There is little to wear out in a PC (though rather more in a printer) and with luck you may have no trouble for several years. However, if you do have trouble it can be expensive; the most common operation is to replace the hard disk. If the PC is vital to your business, you want it mended as soon as possible and preferably on the spot. So you may think it worth while to take out a maintenance contract. For this you will probably pay £100 to £200 a year, depending on the type of machine and its age. Sometimes the maintenance is done by the manufacturer or importer, but more often it is done by an independent firm which has an arrangement with the supplier. This arrangement is not essential, but it does ensure that the maintenance firm can get parts and information.

Nowadays many PCs are sold with free maintenance included in the price, usually for a year but sometimes for longer. In this case you do not need the maintenance contract until the second year, though you may be invited to subscribe to it when you buy the PC. In other cases maintenance is optional. You will usually be given an application form when you buy the machine. Most maintenance contracts provide maintenance on site. There may be a higher charge if you want to be sure of same-day service. Free maintenance bundled with the PC may only provide for repair if you return the machine to the seller. Find out what the maintenance arrangements are before you buy the PC as they can have a significant effect on the cost.

Training

One more thing you may want to buy is some training in the use of your PC and its software. This is a personal matter. Some people find that they can learn best from a training course. Others manage better with a manual or book, and the program itself to play with. If you do want training, there are plenty of courses around. Your dealer, or the supplier of the hardware or software, may be able to arrange or suggest one. Some are advertised in PC magazines or in the local press. Training can be expensive. If commercial prices put you off, you may find something more economical at a local college or training organisation, or at an enterprise agency.

Starting work

Setting up your system

The main purpose of this book is to help you decide what PC and what software to buy – if you need a computer at all. When your new purchase lands on your desk, it will include a pile of manuals. These will tell you everything you need to know about setting up the system and using it. They will run to several hundred pages, and may not be easy reading. So there are many books by independent authors which aim to lead you gently through the process. One reason why these books are easier than the manuals is that they don't try to explain everything. They tell you about those features which you are likely to use most, and deal with the commonest problems. This makes them good beginner's guides, but sooner or later you will need to refer to a manual. The manuals, between them, should cover everything you could possibly want to know. That is why they are so large, and often difficult to read.

This chapter does not try to replace the manuals or the books that supplement them. It will have done its job by the time you become a proud computer owner. But I do propose to go briefly through the process of setting your computer to work. This will give you some idea of what you may be letting yourself in for, and what help you may need. It may also be useful if you can't find the operating system manual, or can't understand it. A few points, such as the working environment and the use of batch files to help organise your work, are not always covered by the manuals. I shall deal with these in a little more detail.

The working environment

You must arrange the office furniture so that you can use your PC in comfort. The most important aspect of this is your own posture when working. Your chair should encourage you to sit up straight, and provide support for your lower back. The height of chair and desktop should be such that your forearms are more or less level as you work at the keyboard. This implies a desktop which is lower than an ordinary desk, or a higher chair. Ideally the display unit should be low on the desk so that you need not move your head as you raise your eyes from the keys to the screen, but this is less critical.

It is important that you arrange your office so that light reflections from the display screen do not obscure the image. This goes for both daylight and artificial light, of course. Some screens have a smooth surface, and the reflections will be obvious. Others have an etched surface. This breaks up the reflections; they are less noticeable, but they are still there as a sort of fog over the whole screen. You can buy a filter which claims to reduce glare. It may improve matters, if you clean it often, but it is much better to avoid reflections in the first place.

Continuous use of a computer makes your eyes work hard, and if they feel tired after a session with the machine you should have them tested. Eyes become less able to adapt for distance as they get older. You may find, like me, that it helps to have a special pair of spectacles for computer work. Mine are bifocals, with the lower section corresponding to the distance from my eyes to the keyboard, and the other to the distance to the screen.

You may want to put your printer where you can reach it without leaving your chair. This will depend on the way you use it. If you will be loading many single sheets, such as letterheads, it will help. On the other hand, leaving your chair from time to time to attend to the printer will give your muscles a welcome change.

Don't work at the keyboard for too long at a time. This is a strain on your muscles, particularly those of the wrists. In extreme cases it can lead to a condition called 'Repetitive Strain Injury' or 'RSI'. This is very painful and can keep you away from the job for several months. If you start to get pains in the wrist, or a tingling sensation, stop and take a rest. If this happens often, suspect that these may be early symptoms of RSI and get medical advice. Secretaries and copy typists are the usual victims; most of those running a business on their own will have many tasks away from the computer, but some such as authors need to be aware of the risk.

There has been a great deal written about radiation risks. Most authorities now think that the risk is negligible. Radiation is certainly produced within the display if is the CRT type, but a very thick glass faceplate absorbs it. For this reason, screen filters which claim to stop radiation will have little effect. 'Low radiation' monitors are now on sale, mainly to suit those countries whose regulations are tighter than those in the UK and USA. The question of low-frequency magnetic fields (such as from the mains) has also been raised but again there is little evidence that it can do harm. If you are really worried about either of these, a portable computer may suit you better; it is battery powered, and the LCD screen cannot produce radiation. Or you can, at a price, get an LCD screen to use with your desktop PC. But there seems little doubt that the real health risks in using a computer are to do with poor posture, eyestrain, and over-use of the wrist muscles.

Noise should not be a problem with a PC. There will only be a hum from the hard disk and possibly the cooling fan. Impact matrix printers, and particularly daisywheel printers, are quite noisy. You can buy acoustic hoods for them, but these are large and expensive and make it difficult to load and unload paper. Try to hear a typical printer in surroundings like yours, and decide whether you can stand it for the limited time that it is likely to be working. If not, the best solution is a laser or ink-jet printer.

Poor installation of the electrical supply in your office may be both a safety risk and a fire risk. If you have any doubts, call a qualified electrician.

Most of these points, and some others, are covered by regulations produced by the Government in response to a directive from the European Community. At the time of writing they are still in draft form. Ring the local office of the Health and Safety Executive for the latest news about them. Legally they may apply only to employees, but obviously you should take equal care to protect your own health.

Assembling the system

Your first job is to get all the bits of hardware out of their boxes, and check that everything is there. There should be a list in the hardware manual, or loose in one of the boxes. Read the instructions carefully. You may have to remove some packing pieces before you switch on – this is most likely in printers. There will be cables to connect the various parts together, and to the mains. Read the manual to find what goes where. There may be switches hidden inside the printer or on the back of it which you must set to suit the system. If so, the manual will tell you what to do. You may have to install a dry battery in the PC, though no harm will be done if you leave this till later; the machine will just be unable to remember the time and date. Turn the display 'brightness' and 'contrast' controls to maximum for the time being, unless you know that they are adjusted correctly.

When you have double-checked everything, you can switch on the power. The machine will spend a few seconds checking itself. It will display a message at the top of the screen while it does so. If it doesn't, maybe you turned the display controls the wrong way, or the display unit has a separate power switch, or perhaps power is not reaching the mains socket. If this is not the problem, switch off and re-check all the connections. If there is still no response, and the manual has no suggestions, ring your supplier for advice.

What happens when self-checking is complete will depend on whether the supplier has loaded the operating system for you. If not, you will see a message inviting you to put a 'system disk' into drive A. You should then load the operating system on to the hard disk. The manual will tell you how. If the operating system is already loaded you will see a 'prompt', such as 'C:>', at the top of the screen. Or you may see a Windows screen or one of your application programs, if the supplier set up the system that way. When the operating system is loaded, you are ready to work on the software. But first adjust the display brightness and contrast controls to settings which suit you. You need to be able to distinguish colours easily. This adjustment is easier if you have a 'test card' utility. There may be one with the system; if not, you can buy one as shareware. Don't turn the brightness up further than you need, as it has some effect on the life of the CRT.

Configuring the system

Once the operating system is in control, you will want to get on to your application software. You can try some of it now, just to get familiar with the machine. You must see the individual manuals to find how to use each program. Or if you want a quick introduction you could try Phil Croucher's book (see Appendix 2) or something similar. For the moment, run the programs from floppy disk rather than installing them on the hard disk. If you can't do that, read on.

Before you get down to serious work, see what the operating system manual has to say about 'configuring' the system. This means choosing options to make the machine work in the way that suits you best. For example, you may need to tell the system whether you want to work to UK, USA, or some other standards. This will affect things like the date format and the display of the '£' sign. If your choice is not UK or USA it will affect the language of messages from the operating system which appear on the screen. (It will not affect anything an application program puts on the screen). If you have Windows, you can configure this in turn once you have sorted out the operating system. Later on, your application programs will need configuring too.

If you have bought virus protection software, you may need to install this before any of the application software. This is not because the applications are likely to carry a virus, but because some of this software will note certain features of each application as it is loaded. It will then check from time to time to see if there has been any tampering. The manual will tell you what you should do.

The operating system manual will tell you about two special files, called CONFIG.SYS and AUTOEXEC.BAT. The latter is just a batch file; the special thing about it is that it is run automatically when you switch the machine on. These two files are closely associated with the operating system although they are not part of it. In fact you can alter their contents yourself. This will let you arrange some features of the system to suit your own way of working, just as configuring the operating system did. Installing the operating system will probably load simple versions of these files, though it need not do so as the system will run without them. I advise you to 'write protect' these files before you install any other software – the operating system manual will tell you how. The reason is that some application programs may want certain commands put into these two files. Most applications will tell you, when you install them on the hard disk, that they would like to alter the files, and ask your permission to do so. Others will ask you to make the change yourself. But a few programs will try to make the change without asking. This is bad program design, because it can interfere with the working of some other program. If you protect the files, then you will know what is going on, and you can make a copy of them before you let them be altered. Then at least you can get back to where you were.

If you use memory-resident programs or utilities (TSRs) you may want them to be loaded each time the machine is switched on. You can arrange this by just putting the name of the program into the AUTOEXEC.BAT file. See the manuals for details. You can do this with several TSRs, though occasionally you may find that the order in which they are listed is significant. Very occasionally you will find that two TSRs simply cannot be used together. Once a TSR is loaded in memory, it can be difficult to get out again, especially if you have loaded more than one. So if there may be circumstances where you do not want the TSRs loaded, list their names in a separate batch file instead of in AUTOEXEC.BAT. You can then load all of them by typing the name of that file when you see the operating system prompt. It is still difficult to get rid of them; the easiest way is to reset the machine (you need not switch it off), although there are others. If you have a 386 or later machine and MS-DOS version 5 or later, there are ways of loading TSRs which economise on memory. See the manual, or the book by Gookin mentioned in Appendix 2. There is also a set of Public Domain programs called 'Mark' and "Release' that will de-install TSRs prior to running an application.

Now that you have prepared the basic system, you can start installing your application software on the hard disk. You will need to read the manuals to find out how to do this. Often you will be asked which directory, or what path, to install into; or you may simply be told to copy all the files into a directory of your choice. (If there are no installation instructions, this is what you should do). If you are not sure of the implications of using directories, see the next section.

You will find a 'registration card' with most software packages, and probably with hardware as well. Take the trouble to complete and return these cards. You will then be kept aware of upgrades and possibly special offers. Some software houses will only offer support if you have returned the card.

Organising your hard disk

We saw earlier that the most general unit of data is the **file**, which is simply a collection of data grouped for your convenience. Each file is identified by a **file name**, which is given by the user. The file name is limited to eight characters. These can be numbers or letters, or certain punctuation marks (but not spaces or full stops); subject to that you can choose any name whatsoever. In fact you also have the use of three more characters, called the **filename extension**. A full stop separates the filename from the extension, thus: 'FILE.EXT'. Some programs use extensions to distinguish between files of different types, and in this case you cannot choose your own extension. Some extensions are reserved for special purposes. In particular you should never use the extensions BAK, BAS, BAT, CFG, COM, EXE, PRO, SYS or $$$ unless you are quite sure what you are doing – there may be a longer list in your operating system manual. Some applications also assign particular meanings to a few extensions. For example, a database manager may give all its data files the extension DAT. Other extensions have conventional, but not mandatory, uses; for example TXT or DOC may identify the user instructions for a program. With these exceptions you can choose your own extensions, though again it helps to make them meaningful. If there are to be several versions of a document it may be useful to put the version number in the extension.

Programs are stored in files, in the same way as data. In this case the names and extensions are assigned when the program is written, and most of them are of no interest to the user.

If you find a file amongst the application software with a name like 'READ.ME' or 'README.1ST', do read it (with the DOS command TYPE or your word processor). It may contain last-minute amendments to the manual, normally in ASCII text format.

You will probably find before long that you have many files of data, and in addition your software may take up hundreds of files. I see that at present I have over a thousand files on my hard disk. If these were all stored together the result could be chaos. So you can arrange these files, in any way you choose, into groups called **directories** or **folders**; the two are to all intents and purposes the same thing. Each directory has a name, and the rules for directory names are exactly the same as for file names. This includes extensions, though in practice extensions are not often added to directory names. You can have several levels of directories, though it is wise to stop at three or four. Thus any one directory may hold not only separate files but also further directories, which themselves contain files. The directories on the highest level, which you have not put inside other directories, are regarded as all being contained within a single directory which you cannot name. It is called the **root** directory. Your arrangement of files and directories can be shown as an inverted tree, as in Figure 8.1.

You will find it best to put all the program files concerned with a particular task into a single directory bearing the task name, or an abbreviation of it. When you install the program according to the instructions in the manual, this is often done for you. Sometimes the program will treat data files in the same way, but more often it is left to you to decide how to arrange them. It is best to set up a logical grouping, with not too many files in any group. Fifty is too many for convenience, although there is no absolute limit (except in the root directory, which is limited to just over 100 files and directories). It is wise to keep data and program files in separate directories.

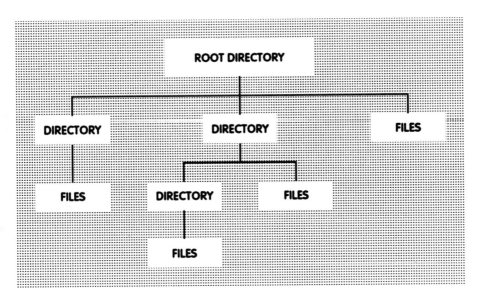

Figure 8.1 A typical directory structure.

Prompts and Menus

If you use Windows and have not configured it to suit yourself, soon after you switch on you will see the Windows desktop displayed on the screen. The same will happen when you finish with any application program. From the desktop you can start a program by pointing to it with the mouse and clicking the left button. If the program icon is not displayed, you may have to make other selections first until the directory (or folder) containing the program is shown on the screen. All this is explained in the Windows manual. When you want to use an operating system command, you can display a menu and select the command from that. There are alternatives to this way of working, for which you must see the Windows manual.

If you do not use Windows, what you see in these circumstances is simply the 'DOS prompt'. You can change the form of this to suit yourself. Until you do this, the prompt will be the name of the current disk followed by a colon and an arrow, thus

```
c:>
```

The prompt is an invitation to you to type in the name of a program, or one of the operating system commands, as we saw in Chapter 3. You need to remember all the commands and programs that you want to use, and also the hierarchy of directories which leads down to each program file. The best way round this is to use a menu system, as we shall see in a moment. However you will still need to use the DOS prompt from time to time, so it is worth altering it to make it more useful. The operating system will tell you how (under 'PROMPT command'). One of the most useful things to do is to add the path (that is, the current directory and any directories above it) to the prompt. Thus the prompt might be

`C:\DIRECT3\DIRECT5>`

if the current directory was DIRECT5 which was itself within directory DIRECT3.

It is also possible, and useful, to display the prompt in a different colour from the commands that you type in yourself.

Most users have a few applications which they use often, and perhaps others which they rarely use. A menu system is the easiest way to select the application programs you use often. It is simply a list of these programs, from which you can pick any one. The menu need not show the actual program names; it can display something more self-explanatory such as 'Word processor', 'Database' and so forth. There are no restrictions on the text. You can set up your menu so that you choose an application by typing its initial letter, or a number representing its position in the list. I find myself that the latter is the fastest way, since it is easier to find a number than a letter at random on the keyboard. Or you can select by moving a pointer or a 'highlight bar' with the mouse or cursor keys.

Ideally a menu should only have a few items on it, maybe eight or ten. If you use more applications than this, one of the choices can be 'Next menu', and selecting this leads you to a further list of choices. Personally I don't go further than this. Programs which I use rarely are left to be called from the DOS prompt; but there is no reason why you should not use menus for everything.

It is perfectly possible to use a menu of this type with Windows, and indeed if there are only a few applications that you use regularly this is easier than working with the Windows desktop. It is also a good approach if you run some programs under Windows and others, for the sake of performance, directly under DOS.

The disadvantage of menus, and the reason why they are not more widely used, is that you have the trouble of setting them up. You also have to alter them when you add or remove applications. This is not difficult, but it does take a little time.

Some operating systems give you the means to set up simple menus, and you can do much the same thing from within Windows though in this case you cannot bypass the Windows desktop. For a more flexible way of making your own menu system you could use one of the **menu generator** programs that are on the market – several of them as shareware. These were discussed in Chapter 3. If you want even more flexibility, you can write batch files which will produce a menu system of your own. This takes more time, but writing batch files will give an insight into elementary programming so you may think it is time well spent.

Batch files and macros

Batch files and macros are very useful tools for making it easier to use your computer system. In principle, both are ways of storing a sequence of keystrokes that you could enter from the keyboard, and feeding them automatically to the operating system. A **batch file** contains a sequence of operating system commands and program names, and the file itself has a name. This name can be anything you choose, but the extension must be BAT. Now if you enter the filename (without the extension) at the keyboard, the PC will carry out each of the commands in turn, just as if you were entering them yourself. Batch files are limited to ASCII characters. You can create them with any word processor that will produce an ASCII file (most of them will). Or you can use a text editor, which is in effect a simple word processor whose native mode is ASCII. AUTOEXEC.BAT is a special case of a batch file. Instead of waiting for you to type its name, it runs whenever the PC is switched on or reset. Apart from this it works in exactly the same way as any other batch file. All PC operating systems can support batch files, but later versions often have a wider range of commands. Some of them are there just for use in batch files.

A **macro** is similar to a batch file, but is not limited to DOS commands and program names. It can include any keystrokes you choose. A macro is called by pressing a preset combination of keys. You can usually create a macro with a word processor or text editor, although some keystrokes may have to be represented by combinations of symbols which you will have to learn, or look up. However macros can also be created in 'Learn' mode. In this case you simply go through the sequence of operations in the normal way, and a macro generator records your keystrokes and creates a macro from them. There is a limit to the number of keystrokes that can be included in a macro, and in general macros are used for simpler tasks than batch files. Some versions of operating systems do not support macros, although most shells (see Chapter 3) do, and there are utilities available to add macros to any operating system.

Although I have described macros in the context of the operating system, many application programs also let you use macros. The rules for making and using these depend on the particular program, so you must read the manual. A few applications offer the equivalent of batch files, sometimes called **exec files.**

A useful feature of batch files is that if you start a program by including its name in a batch file, the rest of the batch file will be executed when the program finishes. This happens because PC programs are written to certain rules. Occasionally you may find programs which ignore the rules and cannot be used in this way. These are mostly games and simple utilities written by amateurs.

There are two ways in which this ability to embed a program within a batch file is useful. Firstly, if you want the batch file to do something and there is no suitable command, you can embed a simple utility program to do the job. This was particularly useful with earlier versions of the operating system which did not let the user key in data while the batch file was running. The trick is to call a utility which detects (say) which number key has been pressed, and stores it in a place where the batch file can find it and act upon it.

The second use of embedded programs is to carry out some operations before and after calling an application program. For example, your batch file can first set a printer to use a particular font, and after the program has finished, it can back up any data files that were changed. Such a batch file can be combined with a menu system to make your PC very user-friendly.

I have not room to show how to write batch files to do all these tasks. You will get a little help from the operating system manual, possibly more if you use a shell that extends the repertoire of batch file commands. Otherwise the subject is often treated in PC magazines, and there are a few books about; one is mentioned in Appendix 2. One important point that is not always made clear is that a menu, or any other message, is best put on the screen by creating it as a separate file (there are utilities to help with this). You then use a 'TYPE' command in the batch file to put the message on the screen.

Using your system

Everything you need to know should be in the manuals, and much of it in books which are meant to be easier reading than manuals. I should not need to repeat any of it here. However there are a few points which are sometimes missed, perhaps because they fall between the operating system and the application program. I shall touch on some of them briefly.

Saving data

Many, though not all, application programs hold a lot of data in memory. This data would be lost when the application program finished if it was not 'saved' by copying it to disk. Modern programs will do that automatically, or at least will remind you before they let you leave the program.

However, there are other ways in which you can lose this stored data. If the power fails, for example, it will be lost. You can inadvertently destroy it all by giving the wrong command, or some fault in the software or hardware can wipe it out. If you have just keyed in a long report or a book chapter, or any other vital information, this can be most depressing. The answer is to get in the habit of saving your data often, say every ten minutes. Some application programs can be set to do this automatically. Others will issue a reminder at set intervals. Failing this, you will have to get in the habit of doing it yourself. A kitchen timer may help to form the habit.

Backing up

Your data should be safe on your hard disk. Unfortunately, it may not be. Hard disks usually run for several years without trouble, but they do fail sometimes. When a hard disk fails, there may be no way of reading the data on it, though there are specialist firms which can sometimes help – at a price. If all the data you use for running your business is on the disk, this can be a catastrophe. Indeed, businesses have been destroyed in this way. A more likely disaster is the loss of a single file because you entered the wrong command by mistake, or less frequently because of a fault in a program.

You should avoid these risks by backing up your data; in other words by copying it to some other medium. Then if the hard disk does fail, you can get another one and copy all the data back on to it, or of course you can copy back individual files if you have just lost a few of them. You can back up all your software as well. This is less important, because you still have all the original program disks which you stored in a safe place, and probably your working copies of these disks too. However it will take some time to re-install all that software. You can cut this down by backing up the software in a way which makes it easy to restore.

Every PC has a floppy disk drive, so the most popular backup medium is the floppy disk. Its disadvantage is that each disk only holds somewhere around a megabyte, depending on the disk type. You may need a lot of floppy disks and a long time to backup a hard disk, although there are utilities which compress files while backing-up, by a factor as high as three. An alternative is the tape drive, which we mentioned in Chapter 6. This is simple to use and can hold the whole of the hard disk contents on one tape cartridge. However it is something extra to buy, and find room for, and tape is not always trouble-free. There are other possibilities, such as optical disks or removable hard disks, but they are expensive at present.

You can choose from several backup strategies. As we saw, backing up everything on the hard disk makes restoration easy. But it takes a lot of time and is not convenient if you want to use floppy disks. So you will probably backup only the data files. A common practice is to do it at the end of work each day. How long it takes depends on the amount of data you have, but it would typically be 5 to 20 minutes. You should have at least two sets of backup disks which you use in rotation. Then if something goes wrong while you are backing-up or restoring data there is always another version, not too old, to fall back on. At least one set should be kept in a safe place away from the computer, in case of fire.

You can cut down on the time taken if you back up only those files which have changed since the last backup. This can be done automatically, since the operating system labels every file with an 'Archive bit'. This is set one way when the file is created or altered, and can be set the other way when you back it up. However, the problem here is that you still need to back up every file from time to time – perhaps each week. You must then keep all the backup disks you make after that till the next total backup, since you will need them all if you are to restore every file.

A variant of this is to copy only those files which have been altered since the copy on the backup disk was made, leaving other files on the backup disk undisturbed. This too can be done automatically. However it means that you cannot clear everything off the backup disk before you copy to it. This may not matter too much, but it means that any files which you no longer need, and clear from your hard disk, will remain on the backup disk. Eventually such files may fill the disk, and you will need to have a clear-out.

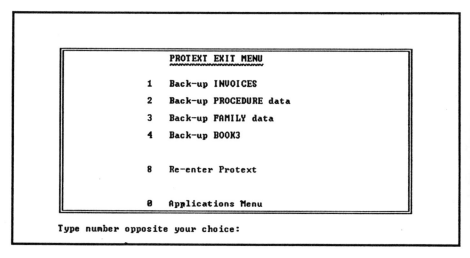

Figure 8.2 A menu displayed by a batch file to simplify backup procedure.

I use a variant of this last method. Instead of backing up daily, I back up all the files that may have been changed by any application at the time when I leave that application. This can be done automatically, by embedding the application program in a batch file. After the program finishes, the batch file displays a screen which asks me whether I want to back up. If I key 'Y' it tells me which disk to insert, checks that it is the right one, does the copying, and tells me to remove the disk. This makes backup so easy that it is never forgotten. An application may be able to work on several different sets of data files. I deal with this in either of two ways. The screen which invites me to backup may ask me which set of files I have used (Figure 8.2). Or I may have specified the file set when I called the program (by attaching a parameter to the program name). The batch file remembers this, and backs up the right file set. This is a good example of how much a simple batch file can contribute to the ease of use of a computer system.

Security

Backup is one aspect of security, but there are others that you should consider. Larger firms are very much concerned with privacy – making sure that their data does not get into the wrong hands. This is far less of a risk if no one but yourself has access to your PC. If you do think it is a problem, you can arrange that the machine will not perform until the user has entered a password. Some operating systems provide for this, as do many shells. However, do not put too much confidence in passwords. They will discourage casual prying, but someone who knows his way about PCs will not be held up for long. If you really need privacy, you had better consult an expert. Don't expect too much. The PC and its operating system were not designed with privacy in mind, and it is not easy to bolt on afterwards.

Other aspects of security are virus protection, which we have dealt with, and protection from hardware failure. We have already seen that you can take out a maintenance contract which will give you a rapid response. This is usually the same day or the next. If the PC is critical to your business, you must be able to move your work to another machine at short notice. You could buy a cheap second machine for this, though if you keep it in the same room it may not help you recover from fire or theft. Or you could make an arrangement with a friend who has a similar machine. Either way, do have a trial run or two to make sure that you really can run your work on the other machine. There are disaster recovery services which specialise in providing time on replacement machines, but these are likely to be too expensive for the one-person business.

You should make sure that your vital data, including backups, is protected from fire or theft. If this should happen to you, your insurance should replace your hardware and software but it cannot replace your data. For two or three hundred pounds you can buy a fire resisting box which claims to protect your floppy disks from any likely fire hazard including collapse of the building. Don't rely on an ordinary fire safe, because paper will stand much higher temperatures than disks. Otherwise, keep a second copy of essential data somewhere off the premises, and remember to keep it up to date. This may not be practicable for your backup disks. I keep mine in a box by the front door, and the theory is that I shall grab them as I flee from the flames. Needless to say, I haven't tested that part of the system.

Here is a reminder of three simple things you should do to protect both data and software from accidental corruption, either by your own mistake or some fault in the hardware or software. Firstly, 'write protect' every floppy disk except when you need to write on it. Secondly, set the 'read-only' attribute on every file on the hard disk that should not be written to. This goes for all program files, unless you are told otherwise. When you copy from one data file to another, it is wise to make the source file read-only. This will protect the file if you make an error in the command and copy in the wrong direction. Thirdly, configure your operating system so that all floppy disk write operations are 'verified'. Then after each file has been written, it will be read by the PC to check that it was written correctly. This does double the time taken to write, but without the precaution you might backup your data for weeks before you realised that a fault was leaving the disks blank. The operating system manual tells you how to do all these things.

Housekeeping

This is the term used for keeping your hard disk tidy. Unless you are more systematic than most of us, you will tend to accumulate files on your hard disk which you no longer need. For example, if you make several drafts of a report, the earlier ones may stay on your disk. Many programs will automatically keep the old version of a file, changing its extension to BAK, when you save a new one. Some programs which use temporary files do not always delete them when they are no longer needed. These usually have names which you can easily recognise, such as DELETE.ME or $$$. When I create files which I don't want to keep, I give them names such as TEMP. Now and again you should have a look at your hard disk and delete any files that are obviously not needed. This will be a lot easier if you have arranged files logically. In particular, if you have kept data and software well apart, you will not risk deleting a file which is part of an application program just because you do not recognise the name.

There are two reasons for regular housekeeping. The obvious one is that, sooner or later, you may run out of disk space. The other is that as the disk gets fuller, many operations get slower. If you leave housekeeping too long, you may find it hard to remember what some files are, even if you gave them meaningful names.

Closely linked to housekeeping is the problem of **fragmentation**. As you use your system, you will add files to the hard disk and you will also delete some. When the operating system has to write a file, it starts in the first vacant space it can find. If this space has been made by deleting a file, it may be shorter than the new file. In this case, when the space is full the system goes on to the next space, linking the sections of the file so that they can all be found when needed. We say that such a file is **fragmented**. But finding linked sections takes time, so as more of the files on your disk become fragmented the machine will become slower. To overcome this, there are programs which will de-fragment your disk. Sometimes they call the process 'compression', but this is misleading because the term is more often used with a different meaning.

A de-fragmentation program will rearrange the files on your disk so that none is fragmented. Some programs can choose an order for the files (based on their extensions) which should reduce the amount of fragmentation in future. In principle no files can be lost during this process. All the same, I would advise you to do a full backup first, just in case. Obviously you should do your normal housekeeping – removing unwanted files – before you start defragmenting. Once you start, the process is likely to take several hours, depending on the disk capacity and how full it is. Some programs let you interrupt the process while you do other work, and resume it later.

De-fragmentation programs are often included in comprehensive sets of utilities. Others are sold separately. It would seem logical to include them in operating systems, but as far as I know this has never been done.

The best de-fragmentation programs will test the disk thoroughly before they start work, so that any faulty part of its surface can be noted and avoided. You can also get separate programs to this. Some of these can also do more technical things to your disk such as 'low-level formatting' and 'interleave checking'. These have been useful in the past, but can cause problems with the more recent types of hard disk. Consult an expert before you use them.

Technical maintenance

You should keep the outside of your PC reasonably clean, and in particular clean the screen from time to time. You can buy special computer cleaning products, but a damp (not wet) cloth is as effective as most of these. Switch off first. You should also clean each floppy disk drive occasionally, using a cleaning disk, as I explained earlier. Now and again, turn the keyboard upside down and blow out the dust. It also helps if you cover the keyboard and printer, and perhaps the screen, after you switch off, to keep the dust out. If you have a daisywheel printer, the typewheel may need occasional cleaning. The materials sold for typewriters are suitable.

Apart from this, your PC needs no regular maintenance. As they say in the trade; 'If it aint broke, don't fix it'.

When something goes wrong

PCs are pretty reliable machines when you consider how complicated they are, but they do go wrong occasionally. When this happens, the first rule is

DON'T PANIC

The reason is that if you start trying everything at random, you may well lose data files which could otherwise be saved. Of course, if there's smoke coming out of the machine, you should switch off and unplug it from the mains. But otherwise, the first move is to sit back and think. Try to remember just what happened, and what you were doing at the time. You may be able to work out, with the help of the manual, what went wrong. Do NOT do anything which would cause a file to be written on to the hard disk, as this could wipe out some of your data. If you can, copy from the hard disk to a floppy disk any data files which may have been changed or created since the last backup. Only then should you start trying to put things right. Use the DOS command CHKDSK, or a more powerful utility, to see if the problem is that a file has been corrupted. If so, try restoring it from your backup disk. But don't copy from it straight on to the hard disk. Copy it first to another floppy disk (using another machine, if that is possible) and use the copy. This reduces the risk that your backup disk might get damaged. If you don't have a backup copy, there is file recovery software that may be able to retrieve some or all of the damaged file. Read the instructions carefully, and keep a cool head while you try it – never be in a hurry. If all this fails, there are firms which specialise in recovering data from corrupted disks. Their services are not cheap, and they may not be able to save all your data. At least some of them work on a 'no cure no fee' basis.

Beyond this, I can give no general advice because problems can vary so widely. This is when you will be glad to know a reliable dealer, or some other source of help. Your maintenance contract, if you have one, will deal with the fault but will not cover retrieval of your data. The service engineer will probably replace the hard disk with another one. After that it's your problem to get the system set up again.

Performance problems

We saw how different types of application program make different demands on the hardware. If you chose your hardware to suit your software, you should find its performance satisfactory. If not, you have either yourself or your dealer to blame. However there are one or two points to be mentioned here.

Firstly, many application programs need a lot of memory. Some will not run on a machine with less than 640 kbytes, and a few need a megabyte or more. There are more programs which, while they do not have an absolute lower limit like this, run much more slowly if they are short of memory. This is because such a program uses 'overlays'. Part of the program will be in memory all the time, but those parts which are less often used are written as separate units called overlays. These are called into memory only when they are needed, and are removed when the space is needed by another overlay. If the process you are carrying out needs more overlays than will fit in the memory at once, the PC frequently has to wait while an overlay is copied from disk. This can have a drastic effect on performance. Suspect this if you can hear or see that the hard disk is working hard while nothing much is happening on the screen.

The obvious answer is to add more memory, if you can. This is easy on 386 and later machines. On 286 and 8086 machines, you can only do it if you have spare expansion slots, and if the application program is designed to work that way. However, you may be able to manage without more memory. The problem may simply be that you have TSRs (memory-resident programs) which hold on to some memory indefinitely, so that the application cannot use it. Try running the application without any TSRs (remove the names of the TSRs from AUTOEXEC.BAT and reset the machine) and see if this improves performance. If you have a 386 or later machine and a recent version of the operating system, there may be further ways to make more memory available. See the operating system manual or Gookin's book.

Secondly, you may be short of processor power. Suspect this if a large spreadsheet takes a long time to recalculate, or a graphics program with complex images seems sluggish, while performance with smaller spreadsheets or simpler images is normal. The answer to this is to fit a co-processor, or change to a faster machine, but neither is cheap. Think, first, whether you could re-organise your work to reduce the load. It may be that a different application program of the same type will run faster on your machine. Often a simple program will run faster than a more complex one of the same type.

Thirdly, your disk may be holding things up. This will be less obvious, but may affect database programs and also slow down the loading of an application program. The problem is most acute if the disk is wrongly **interleaved**. When the PC reads a sequence of records from the hard disk, it must finish handling the first before the next one appears. Some PCs cannot do this if they are asked to read two records which are adjacent on the disk surface. The solution is to 'interleave' the records so that, for example, the record that is to be read next is actually the next but one on the disk surface. This is an interleave factor of two. For a slow PC the ideal factor may be three or more. If the factor is too high, a little time will be wasted while the PC waits for the right record to arrive. But if it is too low, the PC cannot read the record when it appears and so must wait a whole revolution of the disk till it comes round again. This drastically reduces the rate at which data can be read; it can easily take three or four times as long as it should. The PC manufacturer or supplier ought to make sure that the right interleave is chosen, but mistakes have been made – I happened to find myself with one of them. You can buy, or find as shareware, simple utilities which will test whether the interleave is right. If not, you should consult an expert. There are programs which will change the interleave on older types of disk, but these must not be used on the most recent types. In fact you are unlikely to have a problem on 386 or faster machines.

If the interleave factor is correct, there is little you can do to improve the data rate, which is what affects the time to load an application. You can improve the access time, which is more important when small amounts of data are being read from the disk as in a database program. You could do this by fitting a faster disk. But in many cases a cheaper alternative will do at least as much good. This is to use a **disk cache**. The idea is that when you read a record from the disk, there is a good chance that the next record you need will be one that is close to the first. So instead of reading just the record you ask for, the machine reads several more and puts them in to a section of memory which is called the **cache**. Then when another record is needed, the memory is checked to see if it is there already. If so it can be used instantly, without waiting for it to be read from the disk. There is rather more to it than this, but I hope that you have now got the basic idea.

There are two forms of disk cache; software and hardware caches. The former is controlled by a program, and uses part of the main memory (or extended memory, if you have it) as the cache. In most cases it will release that memory if an application program needs it. This sort of cache is cheap, but may have limited effect if memory is short. The alternative is a hardware cache, in which case the cache is a separate memory added for the purpose. This gives the ultimate in speed, but is more expensive.

If you suspect that disk access time is a problem, you could buy a shareware software cache and see how much difference it makes. If it does help you can then register it, or buy a more powerful program or a hardware cache. If you have Windows or a recent version of MS-DOS, you should find a software cache program called 'Smartdrive' on one of the disks. Read the manual to find how to use it. Be aware, however, that it is not easy to predict how a disk cache will affect the performance of any particular program. Get expert advice if you have any doubts.

If you happen to have lots of extended memory, another way to speed up a disk-bound program is to set up a **ramdisk**. This is an area of memory which simulates a disk. It is much faster than disk, but of course its contents are lost when the machine is switched off. Your operating system manual should tell you how to use a ramdisk, or (once again) consult Gookin's book.

A few pitfalls to watch for

This is no more than a check list; most of the matters have been covered already.

First, you can lose data. This is most likely to be the result of an error on your part. In some programs, pressing the wrong key can lose data, though nowadays most programs ask you to confirm that you meant to do it. It is also possible that a hardware or software fault will destroy data. Apart from taking care where you put your fingers, the best precaution is regular backup.

Secondly, you could catch a virus. Many problems are blamed on viruses which are really due to wrong operation or to faults in the PC. If something odd happens, suspect this first. Virus writers are usually proud of the damage they have done, and will put a message on the screen to tell you so. You can protect yourself from most viruses with the software we looked at earlier. If you do get a virus, you should get expert help unless you are quite sure what to do about it.

If you have a modem and communications software, and use it in such a way that others can access your computer, you may have trouble from **hackers**. These are malicious people who call your machine and attempt to destroy or steal your data. If you must use your system like this, read one of the books on PC communications to see how to protect yourself.

Health hazards – mainly due to poor posture or eyestrain – were dealt with earlier in this chapter. So was the need to check that your electrical installation is safe. These are probably the biggest risks involved in computing, so take them seriously.

Finally, one hazard that you may not have expected – computer addiction. This is something that one associates with children playing computer games. But there is no doubt that it is easy to become fascinated with the PC. You may find yourself spending hours working out how to solve a problem with the computer, when you know very well that you could have done it in ten minutes with pencil and paper. There is only one cure for this: will-power!

Afterwards

At last you are in business with your computer. With the help of this book and a pile of manuals, and perhaps a dealer or a friend, you have installed your hardware and software. And, let us assume, it works! Do you need to know any more about computing?

Well, maybe not. Not until something goes wrong, anyway. But software and hardware are improving all the time. Now that your name is known to the trade, junk mail from suppliers will start to fall on your doormat. Some of it will be tempting, especially offers to upgrade your software to the latest version. And you may wonder what you are missing; might other suppliers have something even better to offer?

So in this last chapter we shall see how you can keep in touch with developments in the PC world; where you can get help and advice when you need them; and whether and how you should upgrade your system. And finally, in case what you have read so far seems too abstract, we shall look at a real one-man business to see what all this means in practice. It will be the business I know best – my own.

Keeping in touch

Magazines

The best way to keep up to date is to read the PC magazines. There are many of these. Typically they have a news section, reviews of new or updated products, group reviews of particular product classes, instructional articles, and comment. Perhaps more important to you, they are packed with advertisements. These do not vary much from one journal to another. Some of the magazines come with a 'free' disk (in other words one which is included in the price). These vary from moderately interesting to almost useless. The disks all carry, from time to time, demonstration versions of commercial programs – sometimes of an old version, to encourage you to buy the latest. Some carry complete shareware programs. The rest of the contents will be simple utility programs and games. These will usually be either shareware or 'public domain' – meaning that you can use them as much as you like without payment. Sometimes there is material which is closely related to the magazine itself, such as illustrations to a tutorial article.

There are dozens of magazines on the market which are aimed at the PC user, besides others which treat computing more generally. Some have a particular bias; for example towards games, or 'Windows', or shareware. Others cover the whole spectrum. My favourite among these is 'PC-Plus', but try them for yourself. You can get some idea of their popularity from the amount of advertising they carry, since advertisers go for the widest circulation. By and large the best magazines soon become the most popular. However, none is expensive. Try a few and see which you like. See what you think of the disks too, if they have them. My opinion is that few cover disks would persuade me to buy the magazine. However, I do occasionally find utilities on them which are useful – perhaps an average of one every three or four months. And of course you can always erase the disk and use it for your own purposes (it will be 'double density' rather than 'high density). If possible, choose 3.5 inch cover disks. They are more robust, and so less likely to be damaged on the way. Cover disks are unlikely to carry a virus when they leave the publishers, though there have been one or two cases. But if the disk looks as if it might have been tampered with while on the newsagent's shelves, beware.

Once you've decided which magazine you prefer, you may want to take out a postal subscription to it. This makes sure you get it regularly, and there is less risk that the disk has been tampered with.

Books

Books take much longer to reach the market than magazines, so do not carry topical news or reviews of the latest products. Nor, with the odd exception, do they carry advertising. Some are aimed at beginners, telling them how to set up their systems and get to work. Many are concerned with particular items of software, or less often hardware. Others cover some aspect of computing more generally. An obvious example is communications, another is CD-ROM.

So you are not likely to buy a book to get news of the latest developments. On the other hand, if your interest in some aspect of computing has been aroused by a magazine article, a book will give you a more comprehensive view. Also if you are wondering what a particular piece of software would do for you, a book about it will tell you more than an advertisement or data sheet. See if your local library can help. Computer books can be quite expensive – those published in the USA are often much thicker, and much more expensive, than those published in the UK. Sometimes this means that they are more comprehensive, which may or may not be what you want.

Sometimes they are simply more verbose, which makes them harder to read as well as more costly. Have a good browse before you buy.

Some general bookshops have a shelf of computer books, although I suspect their choice depends more on the energy of the publisher's representative than on quality. Other books you will have to order specially. There are a few firms which specialise in computer books. They issue comprehensive catalogues, though these may show no more than the title. Individual publishers issue more detailed brochures. Some of the specialised booksellers have small advertisements in the press. Most of them have stands at exhibitions, where you can buy books on the spot. These stands can be very crowded, so try to get there early. Appendix 1 includes a couple of names and addresses.

User groups

You may find it useful to join a user group. Some of these deal with PCs in general. They are always represented at the major exhibitions, and sometimes advertise in PC magazines. You will find the addresses of two in Appendix 1. Others are concerned with specific products, usually application programs. These are run by the suppliers of the products, or at least with their approval, and the suppliers will put you in touch.

Each of the general groups issues a journal, often monthly or quarterly, and these include a lot of correspondence from members about problems or ideas. There is usually a section in which experts offer advice on members' problems. Sometimes there are special offers on a few items of software or hardware, or on training courses. There will also be small advertisements from members. There may be reviews of products, which usually reflect much longer contact than reviews in commercial magazines. They may also take a different viewpoint, though they are not necessarily less biased.

These groups also hold meetings of members in London and elsewhere. Some of these are informal, giving members a chance to get together and swap ideas and problems. Others include a talk or a demonstration on some aspect of PC computing. Only a small proportion of members go to meetings. Whether you could go depends on where the nearest meetings are held, so find this out before joining if meetings are important to you.

Most of these groups offer an advice service or 'Helpline'. This will operate by telephone or mail, often both. Some also have a 'bulletin board' where members with modems can state problems, and both the group's staff and other members can suggest answers. The groups may also put you in touch with other members in your district, who can help you with particular problems or give general guidance to beginners. The advice service is probably the most useful feature of these groups.

Finally, most of these groups also sell shareware disks. Their prices tend to be a bit lower than those of the best commercial dealers. Some will also sell to non-members, at an extra charge. The amount of information in their shareware lists varies from one group to another.

The specialised groups also have their journals, and these will keep you up to date with the development of the product. They may also give you news of plans for the future. They will carry members' letters, and solutions to problems. There will also be more general articles on how to make the best of the product. Sometimes the magazines are run by the staff of the product supplier, and you cannot expect a critical view from them. Others are more independent, and are prepared to discuss weaknesses in the product and perhaps to press for improvements.

Naturally these groups do not sell shareware, but a few of them have local groups. I belong to a user group concerned with a good product that happens to have a particularly poor manual, and I have found that meeting other members informally has been a great help.

Watch out for so-called 'user groups' which are actually just commercial businesses, selling shareware or other products, or promoting the interests of a particular supplier. A real user group is controlled by the users, even if it has full-time staff.

Trade associations

If there is an association of people who follow your particular trade, you may find that they can help you with PC problems and advice. In particular, they may have reviewed software which is written to suit that trade. This sort of software is rarely reviewed elsewhere. These associations vary very much, but you can probably expect a newsletter and contact with local members. You may be able to get discounts on hardware or software through them.

Dealers and consultants

If you bought your system through a dealer or employed a consultant, you may hear from them occasionally with suggestions for upgrades, or just a general invitation to ask for advice. They will not usually know more about developments than you read in the press, unless they specialise in a particular trade. However their views may be of interest. Remember to allow for any bias that their own interests may cause.

Friends

Finally, friends and business contacts. Unless they are in the trade, they get their information in the same way as you so will be no more up to date. But they may have been to a trade show, or tried out some new piece of software. They may even let you try it out on their own machines. (They cannot legally give you copies to try on your own machine, except of shareware, so don't embarrass them by asking). Only you can judge how much their opinions are worth; it is always a good idea to get another opinion if you can. And remember a beautiful friendship may end if you recommend something to a friend, and it turns out not to suit them.

Getting help

Sooner or later you will need help. Perhaps something has stopped working as it should. Or perhaps you can't understand the manual, or you want to do something and the manual doesn't tell you if you can. When you need help, you usually need it quickly. Where can you get it?

If you bought your system from a dealer, he or she should be your first port of call. When something has gone wrong, and it's not obviously your fault, the dealer should be willing to put it right without charge. If you can't understand the manual, or you want to know something that it doesn't tell you, you can ask your dealer. If there's a quick answer, you will probably get it free. When there is more work involved, the dealer may have to charge you for it, or perhaps recommend a training course if that seems to be what you need. If you bought the system on the advice of a consultant, you should get similar help there.

However, if you bought the system by mail order, or from any firm that does not have computers as its main business, you may have to look further for help. If it seems that the hardware is not working properly, and you do not have a maintenance contract, you should certainly ring the supplier. Most equipment has a guarantee of at least a year, though you may have to return it to the supplier for this. In any case, the firm would like to do more business with you and your friends, so will try to be helpful. The first problem is that they may have no one who knows enough to be able to help much. The second is that if you bought parts of the system from different suppliers, it may be hard to tell which is at fault.

When you have trouble with software, in most cases you should ring the software company or its UK agent rather than your supplier. Software, unlike hardware, always has minor faults. The producers will know of most of them, and should want to know of the others. Often they can give you a solution over the telephone. They may send you a disk with a corrected version of the program. Many software companies print a 'helpline' telephone number in their manual. If not, your supplier should be able to put you in touch. Some software companies state that they provide support for only three months, or only for the latest version, and perhaps that they will charge for support after that time. While this is valid if you are just asking for help which you should have found in the manual, it is not so if you have reason to suspect that there is a fault in the program. Most software firms will willingly help in this case. If you find them unhelpful, complain to the supplier. If you bought after reading an advertisement, complain to the advertising manager of the journal concerned. All these parties have a reputation to keep up, so will usually try to assist. If you get no co-operation at all, you may get help from one of the other sources mentioned below; but you will obviously shop elsewhere in future. It is usually best to make the first approach by telephone, but if you do have difficulty a formal letter at least gives you a record of what you have done.

If suppliers fail you, the best place to turn is to a user group. Indeed, if your question is not linked to a particular item, this may be where you go first. Most of these groups have experts ready to answer your telephone queries. If your question is a common one, you will get an instant answer. Otherwise they may need longer, but they will usually find some sort of solution in the end. If the problem is complex they may ask you to put it in writing, and perhaps send them copies of the files concerned, but it is usually best to ring first. This goes for both kinds of user group, though those that specialise will obviously know their own product in greater depth. For a beginner, the subscription to a general user group (typically £30 to £50) is well worth while for the advice service alone, unless you can count on a dealer. As you get more experience, you will have fewer questions to ask, and those you do ask may be more abstruse. So an answer is less certain. If your user group has local contacts, one of them may be able to help. They may be less experienced than the staff, but at least the telephone call will cost less.

Many PC magazines have a 'Help' section. Readers can send in their problems, though in this case they must be in writing, to be answered by the experts. There are two snags. Firstly, only a selection of the questions will be answered – those which are of interest to most readers. Secondly you will never get a direct reply. You will have to wait and see whether one is printed in the magazine, and this will take at least a month.

You can, obviously, ask friends and business contacts for help. It would not be fair to demand much of their time, and you will have to judge their competence for yourself. If you are a beginner, this is worth trying. If you have more advanced problems it may not be.

If all else fails, you may have to call in a consultant to sort you out. This will be expensive. Make sure you know what the fee will be before you start, and whether it will depend on a successful outcome. If you don't know of a good consultant, your trade association or a local enterprise agency may be able to help. Microsystems centres often do this sort of work, and a local college or training organisation may have staff who could help.

Enhancing your system

You chose a system that would do all the tasks you had in mind, and perhaps allowed a bit extra for future developments. But sooner or later you may want to do more tasks, or you may be invited to upgrade by a mail shot from one of your suppliers.

Should you? Software upgrades are a different matter from hardware upgrades, so we shall look at the two separately.

Software upgrades

Most software companies upgrade their products regularly, often every year. These upgrades should be distinguished from revisions which are made just to clear faults. Often these are described as 'minor revisions' and are issued free of charge, or at a nominal fee, to those who complain of the particular fault. Others may never hear of them. An upgrade, on the other hand, adds new features to the program, although it may cure some faults as well. There will be a charge for it. This is usually much less than the price of the program as a whole. Most software companies will send a mail shot to all their customers telling them that the upgrade is available, though a few rely on advertisements in the press.

Should you take up the offer of an upgrade? The first question is whether any of the new features would be of real use to you. Adding features often makes the program more difficult to use. The new program will invariably take up more space on your disk. It is likely to take up more memory too, although in a few cases the coding has been improved so that it actually needs less. If it does need more, and you have only 640 kbytes or 1 Mbyte of memory, you may find that the new version does not run on your machine. If it does run, it may be slower than the old one. Consider all these things before you upgrade. The mail shot may be very tempting, but think about what it doesn't say. I have to admit that I don't always practice what I preach – I'm a sucker for upgrades!

The process of upgrading is usually easy, and should take only a few minutes. There should be no need to make any changes to your data, although there are occasional exceptions. If you have configured the old version in any way, make sure that your settings will be carried forward to the new version, or at least make a note of them. The instructions often forget to tell you how to preserve your configuration, so you may have to ring and ask. It is a wise precaution to install the new version in a different directory, so that you can go back to the old if you have problems. You may be able to copy the file which records your configuration into the new directory.

A change of application software

You may decide that you want to change to a different software package of the same type. Perhaps the first one you bought was difficult to use, or didn't do all that you needed. Or perhaps you weren't sure what you wanted so you bought a simple, cheap package to try out. Now you want something more powerful.

There is no problem at all about installing the new package. Nothing stops you having two different word processors, for example – or three or four, if you want. However, the question you may ask is whether the data you have already entered will work with the new package. This may or may not matter. For example, once you have written a letter it is finished with, so it does not matter too much if your new word processor cannot handle it. But if you were halfway through writing a book, you might have a problem.

There is no general answer to the question, it depends on the two packages concerned. If you are going to want to carry data forward, find out before you buy the new program. In most cases it is possible, though it may take a bit of fiddling. Keep the old program on your hard disk for the time being, as you may need it for some of the fiddling.

Word processors are usually easy. Each stores its files in a different way, but most can also store them in the ways used by the most popular word processors such as 'Word Perfect' and 'Wordstar'. In this case, you can probably use either the old or the new word processor to change the files to suit the new one. However, if you have used some of the more elaborate features of the old program to control, say, the layout of the text on the page, you may find that some of this is lost. There is one very simple way of storing files, ASCII. Nearly every word processor can convert its own files into this form. In fact a few of them, and most text editors, only use this form. Likewise every word processor can read this form, so you can be sure of transferring your files this way. The snag is that ASCII does not recognise features such as underlining, or bold or italic typefaces, so this information will be lost. The text itself, however, will be preserved.

There is no standard method of coding for spreadsheets. However, some of them can store data in a way which is acceptable to other spreadsheet programs. In particular, low-cost programs often use the coding methods of the market leaders. In this case you may find the change is easy.

Much the same applies to databases. There is one format that is quite widely used. Conversion from one program to another that uses this format is easy, though there may still be a bit of fiddling before you get it right.

Some graphics programs use common formats, and some can produce files in formats that suit other programs. There are more discrepancies here than with text, however, and sometimes what seems to be a standard format actually has several versions – this applies particularly to the 'PCX' format. So if you want to transfer graphics files from one program to another, see it demonstrated before you buy.

Apart from facilities built into application software to let it exchange files with other packages, there are utility programs which can often do the job. Some are supplied with the relevant programs, others are separately written and sold. They are particularly useful in the graphics field.

Even if there is no obvious way to transfer data from one program to another, it is always possible to write a program specially for the job. You do need to know a little about programming, but you do not need to be an expert programmer. You will only use the program once, so it does not matter if it is slow and perhaps a little difficult to use. I have a very rudimentary knowledge of programming, but I have been able to convert data in this way. The biggest task is to find what format each program uses. Sometimes the manuals for the two application programs will tell you, but more often you have to find out for yourself. The approach is to write a dummy file with each program, and look at them in detail. The format is unlikely to be as simple as ASCII, so you will probably need a 'disk sector editor' to let you see the file format in detail; you can use the 'Debug' utility which forms part of MS-DOS. Always use this on a duplicate copy (on floppy disk) of the data file, not the original, in case you inadvertently alter something.

Although you can convert data this way, it may take you a long time to write the program. If you want to teach yourself a little about programming, as I did, it's a useful exercise. Otherwise you may find it quicker to key all the data in again. You could pay a programmer to write the program for you, but this would be expensive and would rarely be worth while for a one-person business.

Enhancing the operating system

Operating systems are upgraded from time to time, though not as often as many application programs. There are two reasons why you may want to upgrade. Firstly, the enhancement may offer features which you would find useful. Secondly, if you enhance an application program, or buy a new one, it may only work with the latest version of the operating system. The latter case is unusual, and most users do not upgrade their operating system until they replace the whole PC.

If you do want to upgrade, there are two things you should check. Firstly, is the upgrade compatible with your machine? Most PCs use the 'generic' or standard version of the operating system, in which case there is no problem. A few use versions that are especially adapted to suit the hardware. In that case you should consult the PC manufacturer to see whether the upgrade will work correctly. You may have to buy the upgrade from the PC manufacturer to get the correct version. Failing this, if you upgrade with a generic version the system will work, but you may lose some special features added by the PC manufacturer. The second point to check is the amount of memory needed by the operating system. Unlike application programs, operating systems often take less memory when they are upgraded. This is because one of the aims of an operating system designer is to leave as much memory as possible free for the application program. However, sometimes there is an increase. Check before you buy.

If you want more features from your operating system, you do not necessarily have to upgrade it. You can instead buy a 'shell' or an improved command processor, from another company. You can also add 'Windows'. Both of these were discussed in Chapter 3.

You should find that all your software works as normal with the upgraded operating system, or with 'Windows'. There have been a very few exceptions. These are a consequence of poor programming in the application packages. Their suppliers should be willing to provide a corrected version free, or at a nominal price. Failing this, you will have to keep both operating systems on your hard disk and use the one that suits each application best.

Enhancing your hardware

If you find your machine will not run some new piece of software, or runs some programs more slowly than you would like, then you may need to enhance your hardware. We saw in the last chapter that there are three main factors that affect performance. These are processor type, memory capacity and hard disk speed. You may be able to work out for yourself which of these is your problem. If not, and if you cannot readily get expert advice, you will have to resort to trial and error. The first thing you should try is adding more memory. Memory shortage is the only thing that will prevent a program running at all. It is also the most likely cause of an unidentified speed problem. Even if it is not the prime cause, adding more memory will improve the performance of most PCs unless your machine was very well provided from the start. You can add memory to a 386 or later machine quite cheaply. Several firms which specialise in memory enhancements advertise in the press. They will send instructions with the parts, though you may have to ask for them. You will have to open the case of the PC's system unit to fit the extra memory. The task is not difficult, but if you prefer not to do it, ask your dealer. If you have a maintenance contract, the company concerned will do the job but will charge for it. An 8086 or 286 machine can have memory added as an expansion card, which is more expensive but easier to do. But note the warning in earlier chapters that not all software will benefit from this sort of memory upgrade. In any case, you may have to change the operating system configuration to take advantage of the extra memory – see the manual or Gookin's book.

You may have decided that it is your processor that is too slow. What you can do about it depends on the particular PC you have. It may have an 'upgradable processor' (which means that you can throw away your processor and fit a faster one in its place). It may have a socket for a co-processor instead, or as well. Either of these changes will be expensive. Co-processors can be bought from many mail order companies. A faster processor may have to be bought complete with other components on a small board, in which case you can probably only get it from the supplier of the original PC. You will have to open the case of the machine to fit either. Again it is not difficult, and you should get instructions with the part, but your dealer or maintenance firm will do it if you prefer. A faster processor will speed up many programs, though the extent of the improvement varies from one program to another. A co-processor will only help those programs which are designed to use it.

If your machine does not have a co-processor socket or provision for a processor change, any upgrade will be more expensive. The simplest way is to replace the system unit of your PC with one using a faster processor. You can retain the keyboard, screen, mouse and any expansion cards (whether you' fitted them or they were supplied as part of the system). However, you should get in touch with your original supplier, or a good dealer, to make sure the new system unit will be compatible with everything else. Apart from this, the change is not difficult and does not require you to open the system unit, except to get at the expansion cards. This upgrade will probably cost you half to two-thirds the cost of a complete system. You can cut this down by retaining the hard disk from the old system, and this has the advantage that you will not need to reload most of your data and software. This will be a bit more difficult than moving expansion cards. It is also possible to replace just the 'mother board', the part of the system unit that does most of the work. This needs some expertise, and will save less than a hundred pounds. If you have to ask a dealer to do it, it may cost more than replacing the whole system unit.

Fitting a faster hard disk is more expensive. It is also less simple, though still not beyond anyone who is reasonably handy. However, the improvement in performance will not be so marked unless the original disk was unsuitable for the type of machine. You are more likely to fit a new disk because you need more capacity than to improve performance, but you may as well choose a fast one if performance has been a problem. You will have to transfer all your hardware and software from the old disk to the new one. You can do this by copying everything to floppy disks before you change the hard disk, though this may take a lot of disks. Alternatively you can temporarily re-install your old hard disk as disk 'D', assuming the new one becomes 'C'. You may need to move a jumper on the old disk or its controller to assign the new letter, and you will probably have to make a change to the CONFIG.SYS file. If the instructions with the new drive do not explain this, ask the supplier for advice. Once the two disks are installed together, you can copy directly from one to the other. You can, of course, retain both hard disks permanently if you wish. In that case the faster disk should be 'C'.

Adding peripherals

Your system probably started with no peripherals other than a printer. You may decide to enhance it by replacing the original printer or adding another, or by adding some other device such as a modem or scanner. This is straightforward, and you should be able to do it without help.

Most printers have a 'parallel' interface and you simply plug the printer cable into the parallel port (socket) on the rear of the PC's system unit. Sometimes this is labelled 'printer' port. Sometimes it is not labelled at all, and you will have to consult the handbook. Once this is done the printer should work straight away. You may have to set switches hidden inside the printer to get all the details right, such as correct printing of the '£' sign and of some other symbols. Most printers have some method by which you can test them without using the PC, so try this first if you have any problem. The printer manual will tell you what to do.

A few printers have a 'serial' interface, and some give you the choice of both. The parallel interface should be used if possible, but if you have two printers you may find it convenient to use the serial interface for the slower one. Connect the printer to the serial interface socket with a suitable cable; you may have to order one specially to suit the particular printer and PC. Or if you are handy with a soldering iron, you could make your own. You should get some response from the printer straight away, but in this case there will be more switches to set because the serial interface has many options, and the PC and printer must be set to options that match. The PC options are set by a 'MODE' command, which you can add to the AUTOEXEC.BAT file once you are sure it is right. You should find guidance in the PC and printer manuals, but don't be surprised if it takes some trial and error to get good results. If you get it wrong, you may get error messages on the PC screen or the printer may indicate an error, or it may just print gibberish. You may also find that stretches of the text sent to the printer get lost. Keep trying; once you find the right settings you should have no further trouble.

If the new printer is of a different type to the old, you may have to tell the software about it. Usually you will have to tell each application program separately, except those which depend on 'Windows'. This is usually done with the application's 'configure' or 'install' facility, but you will need to read the manuals to find just how to do it. Occasionally you will have to install a new 'printer driver' which is a simple program that links with the operating system. In this case the driver will probably come with the printer, together with instructions. You would be wise to find out about this before you buy.

If you want more than one printer and you do not want to use the serial port, you have two options. One is to add another parallel port to the PC, which will take up one of your expansion slots. The other is to use an external printer switch. Both are fairly cheap. You do have to remember to set the switch manually, but it does not take an expansion slot.

Other peripherals, with rare exceptions, either connect to the serial port or else have their own controllers (or 'interface boards') which plug into expansion slots in your system unit. They should be easy to install, and come with full instructions. As with printers there may be switches to be set, and you may have to add drivers or otherwise tell the software that they are there. The instructions that come with the peripheral should tell you how to do this.

Upgrading portable PCs

Portable PCs give you much less scope for hardware enhancement. There is rarely any space for expansion cards, and the disk drives are not easily changed. In some cases you may be able to increase the memory size, and in a few you can add a co-processor. Beyond this it is usually a case of replacing the whole machine.

Most portables do have parallel and serial ports, so you can attach printers and modems. Both of these are available in very compact sizes, so they too can be portable. You may, however, prefer to leave the printer on your desk and use it only when you return to the office. You may also like to connect a CRT-type display when at your desk. Many portables allow this. For some you can buy a 'docking station', which remains on your desk and carries all the connections to display, printer, battery charger or mains, and possibly other peripherals. You can connect the portable to this in a single action, instead of fiddling with several separate plugs.

A case study

To round the book off, we shall have a look at a real one-man business – my own – to show how I set about choosing and installing a computer system, and what I have used it for. I don't claim that this is a typical business, if there is any such thing. But describing it should add a touch of realism to what may have seemed a rather abstract discussion of computers and their place in the one-person business.

I became a one-man business quite late in life, after the company I worked for decided that 55 was the right age to retire many of its staff. This company was concerned with computer hardware, and my corner of it with peripherals. Most of these were for large machines rather than PCs. Strangely enough, my group had no computer for its own use until a year or two before I left, when we installed a machine which was not a PC. So I retired from that company knowing a lot about computers, a little about computing, but nothing about IBM-compatible PCs.

As I had expertise in a particular type of peripheral, my first idea was to become a technical consultant. For various reasons, this has evolved into technical writing, first on my specialist subject and later on more general subjects such as this one. So my main requirements have been a database manager, to organise all the data about my subject, and a word processor. I also use a simple accounting program, and a drawing program to help with illustrations. I have a number of other applications on the machine which I use occasionally, as much to get to know what they are like as to produce any practical output. These include a spreadsheet, desktop publishing, and a paint program. I don't play computer games (though I have one or two to amuse young visitors), but for my spare-time interests I use the database manager and a genealogy program.

Hardware

I started in business in late 1986 and at that time IBM-compatible PCs were priced out of my reach. I considered buying an Amstrad PCW, a machine which is not IBM compatible, but which has a good word processor program and is very cheap – it is still available. But before I had made up my mind, Amstrad announced their PC1512. This is an IBM compatible machine, and it caused an upheaval in the market because its price was about half that of existing PCs. Besides this, while software had been expensive in the past, a few suppliers slashed their prices drastically in line with that of the hardware.

So I bought this machine. It was the only IBM-compatible I could afford, at £975, and in fact it met my needs so well that I used it for five and a half years. It is an 8086 (or 'XT') machine with 512 kbytes of memory. It was available with mono or colour display, and with one or two floppy disks or one floppy and a hard disk of 10 or 20 Mbytes. I chose the 10 Mbyte hard disk, because I knew this would be much more convenient than a machine with only floppies, and I didn't think I could ever use that much disk space. I also chose a colour monitor. This is a bit of an extravagance really, though it does make some programs easier to use. It is a CGA monitor – the only one available then, though a year later Amstrad brought out a machine with the higher-definition EGA screen.

The only peripheral I needed was a printer. It would have been logical to have bought an impact matrix printer, though at that time the only cheap ones were 9-pin and this does not give a good impression in correspondence with clients. However, through my old firm I was able to buy a good daisywheel printer (a Ricoh 1200N) at a quarter of the normal price. This has all the disadvantages I described in an earlier chapter, but it uses one-time ribbons and the print quality is superb. I still use it for correspondence. This machine happens to have a serial interface. It can handle only single sheets, not fanfold, but this is all I need for correspondence. I have several daisywheels including some for proportional spacing. After nearly six years use this printer shows no sign of wear, though the daisywheels do wear out.

I also bought, again at a reduced price, a thermal matrix printer – an Okimate. This is a type I have not described, as it is no longer available (except in a very high price range for colour work). It works in a similar way to the impact matrix but has tiny heaters in place of pins, and uses special paper which blackens when heated. The printer would be almost silent, if there was not a loud clank at each carriage return. It is also a good deal faster than the daisywheel, and has a parallel interface. But thermal paper is expensive, and tends to fade. The printer can also use plain (but very smooth) paper and a wax one-time ribbon, but this too is expensive because of the short ribbon life. And the printer is only designed for light duty. It served me well for a year or two, but when I started printing drafts of books I needed something faster and cheaper to run, and able to stand up to heavier work.

By this time 24-pin impact matrix printers had become cheaper, so I bought one – a Star LC 24-10. This handles both cut sheet and fanfold, and has a choice of four typefaces. They can be selected either by software, or manually at the printer. It can print at various character spacings – 10, 12 and 15 to the inch – and can also handle proportional spacing, although I rarely use this. It will print graphics, like nearly all matrix printers, and has other features which I do not use. The ribbons are fabric, and for top quality work need to be replaced often although I keep them much longer for draft work. This printer has worked hard and behaved well, although I did have to replace some parts of the ribbon drive mechanism recently.

An automatic sheet feeder is available as an optional extra for this printer, and after a year or so I bought one. The main advantage is that cut sheet (I use ordinary copier paper) is about half the price of fanfold. Also it saves the trouble of separating fanfold sheets and removing the side strips. Against this, it does take a little longer to feed each sheet, and occasionally it misfeeds – probably not more than once a month, once it has been adjusted correctly. Most programs work satisfactorily with it, though some have to be given a figure for paper length which is found by trial and error. A few cannot use it, and also I sometimes want charts which are several pages long. In this case I remove the sheet feeder and use fanfold. On this particular printer the change is easy and takes less than a minute.

The only other peripheral I have is a hand-held scanner. This is not a great success on the Amstrad; it really needs more memory, a faster machine, and a higher definition screen.

The PC itself has had three upgrades. Firstly, as I upgraded the software I found that 512 kbytes of memory was too little so I increased it to 640 kbytes, the maximum internal memory that can be fitted to an XT. On this particular machine it can be done by removing the covers and inserting extra 'chips', although had I not been an engineer I should have been reluctant to do this myself. Secondly, after a couple of years I found the 10 Mbyte disk very limiting. More and more often I had to go through all my software and decide what I could do without. Note that it was software that caused the congestion, not data. The average person is unlikely to key in as much as a megabyte a year (this book is about half a megabyte), but one new application program can easily take up a megabyte, often more. So I fitted a 32 megabyte 'Hard card'. This is a hard disk which, with its controller, simply plugs into an expansion slot. As well as the extra capacity, it is a lot faster than the old hard disk. This improves performance in several of my applications, especially the database. I could have kept kept the old hard disk as well, but I removed it to make room for the third upgrade. This is a 3.5 inch floppy disk drive. I fitted it because I wanted to exchange data with other PCs which I was working with on a client's site. However, it has the advantage of doubling the amount of data which I can put on a backup disk. This size of disk is also more robust, and so better for sending through the post.

This system was adequate for several years, which included the writing of three books. After this time it was still serviceable, although the screen was getting a bit dim and one or two unexplained error messages came up occasionally. However, as I enhanced my software some operations became very slow because of lack of memory, and the latest upgrade to my word processor was impossible because it needed 1 megabyte. Also I was making a little more use of graphics programs, and these ran very slowly. On top of that, although I had lived with a CGA display for so many years, I was aware that it was not very easy on the eyes and was not really suitable for graphics work. So recently, after much thought about my bank balance, I decided on a new machine.

The new machine is a 386SX. I bought it from a UK direct mail company, Dan Technology, since their price was competitive and their products had a number of favourable reviews in the PC magazines. The machine cost me £1000; substantially less, allowing for inflation, than my original machine. Had I not become reasonably familiar with PCs by this time I might have preferred a dealer, though Dan do have a telephone helpline which sorted out one or two minor problems for me.

The new machine has a 25 megabyte 386SX processor, 2 megabytes of memory, and a 100 megabyte hard disk. This has 15 milliseconds access time, which is two or three times better than the hard card I had fitted to the Amstrad, and about four times as fast as the original Amstrad disk. It has an interleave factor of 1, compared with 6 and 3 respectively for the disks on the old machine, and so the transfer rate is increased at least in proportion – I have not been given the actual figures. There is a single 3.5 inch floppy disk drive, and a 'super VGA' colour monitor. The operating system, MS-DOS version 5, was included in the price and so was Windows version 3.1. Both MS-DOS and Windows were installed on the hard disk for me by the supplier. This saved me a good deal of time, not so much in actually installing them but in deciding what options I needed to choose during installation. On the other hand, of course, some of these options are a matter of personal preference rather than matching the system, and some of these I altered later.

The new machine is considerably faster than the old one. Of course I do not notice this when entering text, because my own typing speed is the limiting factor. But the difference is very marked when loading programs or moving from one function to another within a program, and when moving through files. I put this down mostly to the extra memory and to the high data rate of the hard disk. Processor speed will have little influence on the sort of applications I use, but the short disk access time helps with database work. It took me about three days to get up and running with the new system, but this was partly because I chose to make some alterations to my batch files.

A very short acquaintance with Windows persuaded me that 2 Mbytes of memory was not enough, so I upgraded it to 4 Mbytes. This was a simple operation that cost me about £70. I also added a 5.25 inch floppy disk drive to give me access to old data and software. I had at first done this by using the old machine to copy from 5.25 inch to 3.5 inch floppy disks, but that machine developed a fault – probably a broken heart!

When I bought the first machine I took out a maintenance contract. I called on this once, after two or three years, when the hard disk became erratic and had to be replaced (in hindsight, using 'Spinrite' to re-format the disk might have avoided the need for a replacement). Later I let the contract lapse, since the cost went up as the machine became older; I decided that if there was another major failure I should replace the machine. I have taken out a fresh contract for the new machine, although this is less expensive because the manufacturer offers a 'lifetime guarantee'.

System software

The Amstrad PC1512 came with the MS-DOS operating system, in version 3.2 – this was a very satisfactory version for its time, and I never upgraded from it. It would have been difficult to do so, since it had been modified specially to suit the Amstrad. Much later I added '4 DOS', a replacement command processor which gives me a number of extra commands, and some other useful features. Of these, the one that sold the program to me was the ability to add a 40-character description to each file name.

I did have one problem with the operating system. I happened to come across a utility which tested the interleave factor of the hard disk (discussed in Chapter 8), and this showed me that the factor was set wrong. I bought a program, 'Spinrite', which corrected this for me (only suitable for older types of disk) and this tripled the transfer rate of the disk. The effect on machine performance was quite dramatic.

The new machine, as I said above, has MS-DOS version 5.0 and also Windows version 3.1. The new version of the operating system is not very different from the old, but it does include a few features for which I previously had to use separate utilities. One of these is a 'command line editor' which lets me step back through the last few commands I have entered, so I can repeat any of them without retyping the whole command. Another is a 'shell' which gives a diagrammatic display of directories and files and makes it easy to operate on them. Both these replace separate utilities which did these tasks on the old machine. There are a few extra commands, especially for batch files, which are useful. There is also the ability to 'task switch'; that is, to keep more than one application loaded (though not running) so that I can switch between them without having to close one down and start the other from scratch each time. However, as I have retained my own menu system I don't have much direct contact with MS-DOS. I have upgraded one of my application packages, the 'Timeworks' desktop publisher, to the Windows version since this gives me access to a wider range of type sizes. Otherwise I have not yet had much occasion to use Windows since the rest of my existing applications run better without it. If I did feel the need to transfer data directly from one application to another, Windows would make this easier. In future I may update other applications to Windows versions, especially those which are graphics-based. In the meantime I have used 'Windows Paintbrush' (which came free with Windows) to capture screen shots to illustrate this book.

Application software

I decided at the beginning to get the three classic applications – word processor, database and spreadsheet – largely because this was the usual thing to do, or so my reading of magazines told me. Along with their low-price hardware, Amstrad had arranged with some software manufacturers to introduce very low priced versions of their application programs. I bought two of these; a word processor, WordStar 1512, and a spreadsheet, Supercalc 3.1. I did not buy the corresponding database manager, because I had clear ideas about the sort of database I needed, and that package did not fit. Instead I bought a shareware database manager, PC-File. These were all the applications I used for some time, although there were a couple of others supplied with the machine – a simple 'paint' program and an interpreter for the BASIC programming language.

The word processor, WordStar 1512, was a simplified version of WordStar which at that time was the most popular PC word processor. Unlike its big sister, WordStar 1512 was easy to learn because it did not depend on remembering a lot of key combinations. Instead, every operation could be selected from a series of menus. As its low price suggested, it lacked some of the more advanced functions but had everything that was needed for straightforward work. This included a simple spell checker, although this sometimes came up with very odd suggestions to replace misspelled words. I used this program for a couple of years, and wrote my first book with it. But eventually I became disillusioned. This was partly because as my typing speed improved I found the all-menu approach was slowing me down, and partly because I wanted rather more facilities including a better spell checker. After a couple of false starts I found myself with 'Protext', a mid-priced word processor written in the UK. I have used this happily ever since, and have no plans to change. It gives me all the facilities I need, although possibly not all those that a secretary might want. It is fast, and has the choice of key combinations or menus for every function. It also has good support for accented letters and special symbols, not that I use them much. It supports proportional spacing, and can use all the facilities of my printer. All in all, I find it ideal for technical writing. Support from the publishers is reasonable but not spectacular – they answer telephone calls but do not always reply to letters. But the publishers say they will only support the latest version, and I could not upgrade to this while using the Amstrad PC because it needed more memory than I had.

I make little use of the spreadsheet, but nevertheless changed from SuperCcalc after a year or two. That was largely because it was not very good at drawing graphs and bar charts – I believe current versions are much better. It was also not very easy to use. I bought 'Logistix', which is still available for the PC although it has not been revised for some years. That does better at graphs, and adds a number of facilities which I don't actually use. It is no easier to drive than SuperCalc, but I still use it.

My first database manager was 'PC-File' and in fact I still use that, though it has changed a lot through a series of upgrades. It is sold mainly as shareware. The latest version is not available until you register. It does not try to compete with the real heavyweight programs, but I find it flexible and well provided with features. It is partly relational, handling one-to-many relations but not (as far as I can tell) many-to-many. It is reasonably easy to use, though as it is a complex program I have to refer to the manual quite a lot. In its earlier versions it was not entirely reliable, but seems better now. I have no plans to change.

For several years I kept my accounts on a database within PC-File. Eventually I decided this meant too much work, especially at year-end and in preparing VAT statements. Now I use a simple accounting package called 'Money Manager PC'. It takes the 'cash book' rather than the 'ledger' approach – no double-entry work. This fits in well with my simple requirements, averaging perhaps a dozen purchases and one or two sales a month, and no credit. A firm which was more active financially would need a more sophisticated package. I had to make one or two minor changes in my accounting practice to fit Money Manager but now find it easy to use. It produces all the VAT statements, end-of-year accounts and analyses that I need. The package has a brief but adequate manual. It is stable – no upgrades in the two or three years that I have used it. I shall stay with it.

One of my hobbies is family history, so I have a genealogy program called 'Pedigree'. I find it very flexible but difficult to use. This is partly because of a poor manual, which I understand is being rewritten. Before that I had 'Trees', which is easy to use but rather limited in what it will do.

Since writing is my business, I have a couple of style checking programs: 'Readability' and 'Stylewriter'. These go through my text (generated with the word processor) and do two things. Firstly they produce statistics on my writing, such as sentence length, distribution of long words, number of passive verbs and so forth. Secondly they point out weaknesses of various kinds as they occur in the text. I find the first function useful, though I don't take the results too seriously (except when they tell me that my style is good, of course). The second I find less useful. In any case, one has to avoid writing just to get a good score from the style checkers – the result can be very stilted. These are specialised programs and most businesses will not want them, though they do claim to improve your business correspondence.

Those are the programs I use regularly. I have tried many others over the years. Some I have discarded; others are still on my hard disk and I use them occasionally, sometimes just for the experience. They include several shareware drawing programs, some general-purpose and some more specialised. There is also a desktop publisher: I bought 'Timeworks', which seemed excellent value for money, and upgraded to its big brother 'Deskpress' only because I won that free in a draw at an exhibition. It does have some extra facilities, but is slow on an XT machine like the Amstrad. The Dan is much more suitable; but because Windows does offer advantages – such as better typeface management – to DTP programs, I now have the Windows version of 'Timeworks' on the Dan.

At one time I decided to teach myself a bit about programming. I had no plans to be a professional programmer, but I felt I ought to know how it was done. The easiest language to learn would have been BASIC, but I thought it was too limited for the exercise I wanted to try, so I chose 'C'. I bought two low-priced compilers, 'Zorland C' and 'Power C', with the auxiliary programs (editors and debuggers) that went with them. I did in fact learn enough to write a program to transfer my data from one genealogy package to another, so the exercise served its purpose. However I wouldn't recommend this lonely way of learning programming, especially in a difficult language like 'C'. The biggest problem is having no one to help you find why things didn't work. One reason for having two compilers was to help distinguish between my own errors and faults in the compilers.

Besides these application programs I have tried a number of simpler utilities, and I still use some of them. These do things like displaying an on-screen calculator or calendar, and finding a file when I've forgotten which directory it is in. A useful pair is 'Mark' and 'Release' which, between them, allow me to discard memory-resident programs without resetting the computer. Others are functions which I use only within batch files. Many of these utilities came on the 'free' disks published with magazines, others as shareware. Since these utilities are very cheap or free, it's worth trying any that look useful. I go through my hard disk every few months, and discard those utilities which I never use. In general I look for simple utilities which do just the job I want and nothing more, so are easy to use. Programmers like to write complex utilities which aim to do everything that anyone could ever want. I try to avoid these.

More extensive utilities are a defragmentation program, although I use this from a floppy disk rather than the hard disk, and a virus detector. I have this not so much because I am exposed to viruses, but so that when I do have problems I can eliminate one possible cause. Then it has to be either finger trouble, machine trouble, or a bug in the software. Finally, one essential utility on the Amstrad is the program which parks the hard disk. This ensures that data will not be lost if the disk is jolted, through moving the PC when not in use. Some modern hard disks park themselves automatically, including that on the Dan.

The change of hardware has not prompted me to change any of my application programs, apart from upgrading to the Windows version of my DTP package, Timeworks. I can also now upgrade to the latest version of my word processor, Protext, which needs more memory than I had on the old machine. I shall not look for a Windows word processor, because for my purposes a character-mode program is suitable and is faster. If I need a wider range of type sizes and typestyles than Protext gives me I can use Windows Write which is included in the Windows 3.1 package. I may go for Windows versions of some more of my graphics-based applications.

Batch programs

I mentioned earlier how useful batch programs can be in making it easier to use your system. I have a number of such programs on my own hard disk. I transferred them with only minor changes from the Amstrad machine to the Dan. One group of these forms a menu system, such as I have already described. When my PC is switched on and has done its self-checking, instead of a DOS prompt I see a menu from which I can choose the programs I use a lot – word processor, database, accounts, spreadsheet, genealogy program. I can also go to further menus with lesser-used applications and utilities, or to the DOS prompt if I want it, or to Windows. These menus do not actually call applications, they call batch programs from a second group. Each of these does any necessary setting up, calls the application, and then attends to backup of data when the application finishes. I have described how these work in a previous chapter. A few more batch programs do various odd jobs. One, called from the menu when I finish work, checks that there are no floppy disks in the drives. It then parks the hard disk, and tells me that I can switch off.

And that seems an appropriate place to finish this book!

Appendix 1

Useful addresses

User groups

There are several general user groups. I have found this one useful:

PC Independent User Group, 87 High Street, Tonbridge, Kent, TN9 1RX

A larger group, which in spite of its name is interested in all IBM-compatible PCs:

The IBM PC User Group, PO box 360, Harrow, HA1 4LQ

Shareware suppliers

Many of these advertise in the press, and in addition most of the user groups will supply shareware. One dealer with a particularly informative catalogue is:

Shareware Marketing, 3A Queen Street, Seaton, Devon, EX12 2NY

Computer bookshops

Many good bookshops have a small selection of computer books. In large cities there may be specialists, such as

The Computer Bookshop, 21 Sicilian Avenue, Southampton Row, London WC1A 2QH

There is also a good selection on bookseller's stands at computer exhibitions. Otherwise you can try mail order. One firm with a comprehensive list is

Computer Manuals, 50 James Road, Tyseley, Birmingham B11 2BA

Publishers issue more detailed catalogues of their own books. Amongst the UK publishers is of course

Sigma Press, 1 South Oak Lane, Wilmslow, Cheshire SK9 6AR

General business advice

For this you should enquire locally, perhaps using the Yellow Pages. 'Enterprise agencies' will give general business advice, 'Microsystems centres' will undertake consultancy, as may the computer departments of colleges and universities. If you cannot find a local address try

Department of Industry small firms service, Ashdown House, 123 Victoria Street, London SW1E 6RB.

The operating system

Since this is such a vital part of your system, it may be useful to know where you can get technical advice and other information about MS-DOS and Windows:

Microsoft Ltd., Microsoft Place, Wharfedale Road, Winnersh Triangle, Wokingham RG11 5TP.

Appendix 2

Further reading

A large industry has grown up around computer books, and in particular you will find several dealing with almost any application package that you can think of. For these see bookshops or booksellers' catalogues. I shall mention here just a few books that may be useful to beginners. They are mostly from the Sigma list, but many other publishers have equivalents.

Computing under Protest: the New User's PC Book. Phil Croucher; Sigma Press, 1993.

This aims to show you how to get to grips quickly with application software.

The New User's Mac Book. Kim Wilson, Sigma Press, 1992.

If you do think that a Macintosh rather than an IBM-compatible PC might suit your business, this will give you an introduction to what it can do.

Communications and Networks. Phil Croucher, Sigma Press, 1989.

Covers a subject which I have deliberately avoided in this book.

MS-DOS 5 File and Program Control. Ian Sinclair, Sigma Press, 1991.

Gives more information than I have done about the use of batch files and the other facilities of the operating system.

Managing Memory with DOS 5. Dan Gookin, Microsoft Press, 1991.

A very clear and practical account of how to make the best use of your PC's memory, at a modest price.

Windows 3.1: a user's guide. Ian Sinclair, Sigma Press, 1992.

One of many books on this subject. Choose from the selection at your bookshop or library, but make sure the book covers version 3.1 (if that is what you have) since it differs significantly from earlier versions.

Music and New Technology. Jacobs and Georghiades, Sigma Press, 1991.

This explains how computers can be used to compose, arrange and produce music.

The PC Games Bible. Matthews and Rigby, Sigma Press, 1992.

This covers rather more than the title suggests: it includes educational and board games and simulations.

Inside the IBM PC and PS/2. Peter Norton, Prentice-Hall: 4th edition 1992.

I have tried to avoid technical details. If you want them, this book tells you in detail what goes on inside your PC.

Electronic Computers. Hollingdale and Toothill, Penguin Books, 1965.

This is of course very out of date, but is much the clearest introduction that I know to the fundamentals of computers. Long out of print, but your library may have it.

Peripherals for Computer Systems. Alan Bradley, Macmillan, 1991.

A blatant plug; but if you want to know more about how peripherals work and what they can do for you, this book tells you.

Appendix 3

Special offer to readers

Shareware Bundle and User Group membership

Now that you've read the book, you're ready to buy a PC and start work! Maybe you've already decided what software packages would suit you best. If not, a good way to start is with shareware. Initially this will cost you only a few pounds, the price of the disks. It will let you get the feel of each type of application, and decide which features will be useful in your business and what is missing that you would like to have. If a shareware package meets your needs, you can register it and keep on using it. If not, you will have a better idea of what to look for – and what to avoid.

To make it as easy as possible for you to get started, we have put together a special bundle of shareware which is selected to meet the needs of readers of this book – effective but easy to use. The bundle includes the basic packages that most one-person businesses need; word processor, spreadsheet, and database manager. It also includes a simple drawing package to give you a feel for graphic applications, a menu generator to help organise your system, and a few utilities. We have added an 'install' program which will install the utilities, together with a suitable menu and help with backing-up data, on your hard disk at the touch of a few keys, and also instructions for installing each of the applications. Do this, and you are ready for work without any further complications.

When you first start using a PC, the 'helpline' support provided by a user group can be a great comfort. So we have arranged an initial six months or one year business membership of the PC Independent User Group at a reduction of 10% on the normal rate.

To take up either or both of these offers, copy the form at the end of this book and send it to the PC Independent User Group at 87 High Street, Tonbridge, Kent TN9 1RX, with your cheque or credit card number. Alternatively, telephone the PCIUG on

0732-771512 (or fax on 0732-771513), and have your credit card number ready. If the form is missing, you can still take up these offers; just telephone, fax or write to the PCIUG, and remember to say whether you want 5.25" or 3.5" disks (the latter will be sent by default). The disk set costs £14 including VAT and delivery. Six months membership of the group costs £21.50 plus VAT at half the current rate (i.e. £23.38 at the 17.5% rate), and one year membership costs £39 plus VAT (£42.41 at the 17.5% rate).

These prices are valid until the end of 1993. After that date, please write to the PCIUG asking for the current prices.

What the PCIUG can do for you

The PC Independent User Group exists to help all users of IBM-compatible PCs. It provides a telephone advice service; a substantial bi-monthly journal with hints, advice, solutions to members' problems and reviews of shareware and other software; and informal local meetings in many areas. It sells shareware disks, at a special price to members, and can register the most popular shareware programs (including the applications on our special offer disks) at a substantial discount to members. It does not sell commercial hardware and software, but discounts on some items are offered by their suppliers through the pages of the journal. The group is a non-profit limited company owned by its members, whose liability is limited to £1 in the event of the winding-up of the company.

The shareware disks

The disks include the following applications:

❏ Galaxy Lite – word processor (registration £63 – members £54); the registered version is 'Galaxy ProLite'

❏ As Easy As – spreadsheet (registration £58 – members £50)

❏ PC File 5 – database manager (registration £121 – members £104)

❏ Draft Choice – drawing package (registration £58 – members £50)

❏ BGMenu – menu generator (fee under review; about £20);

They also include the following utilities, which do not need to be registered:

RE – to display text files quickly and conveniently
CHOOSE – essential if you write your own batch files
MARK and RELEASE – useful if you need to remove TSRs from memory; (registration not required, but authors welcome donations)
COLTEST – displays a colour chart to help adjust your monitor

Finally it includes an installation program which will install the utilities on your hard disk and set up an appropriate menu, and instructions for installing the applications, so that you are ready to start work. It will not interfere with anything that you or your supplier has already installed on the hard disk. The whole bundle will take up about 3 megabytes of your hard disk.

All these packages run under DOS, so you can use them whether or not you have Windows on your machine. All can also be run from within Windows if you wish, although there is little advantage in doing so. Some Windows-based shareware is available, and if you are interested in this you should consult any shareware supplier or the PCIUG.

Remember that the principle of shareware is that you can evaluate each package without charge, but if you continue to use it you should pay the registration fee. This often brings you an updated version of the program or a printed version of the manual or both – see the documentation on the disks for details. You can register all these packages through the PCIUG; the fee for each is shown in the list above. VAT must be added at the current rate and the fees may vary with the exchange rate, so you should ring the PCIUG on 0732-771512 for the current figure.

How to use your shareware disks

The bundle occupies 7 disks, either 3.5" or 5.25". As with any software, the first thing to do is to make sure that each disk is write protected. On 3.5" disks the black tab in one corner should be moved towards the edge of the disk so that the hole adjacent to it is open. On 5.25" disks the small square notch on one edge of the disk casing should be covered. If you have bought any blank disks you will find some tabs supplied with them for this purpose, but any small self-adhesive label will do.

It is wise, though not essential, to make a copy of each disk, and then put the original disk away in a safe place and use the copy instead. It is easy to make a copy if you have two disk drives (use the XCOPY /S command), or if you have some blank disks of the same density as the disks in the bundle (i.e. 'Double density', 360 kbyte or 720 kbyte, not 'High density', 1.2 or 1.44 mbyte: use the DISKCOPY command). See your DOS manual for instructions on the use of these commands. If you do not copy the disks, check again that they are write-protected before you continue.

Having prepared your disks in this way, make sure that the DOS prompt is shown on the screen. It is usually something like 'C:\>'; it may have been altered on your machine, but will nearly always include a letter, usually A or C, and end with the '>' symbol. Normally the prompt will appear a few seconds after you switch on, when the machine has finished its automatic self-testing. However, your supplier may have installed 'Windows' or some other software so that this appears automatically when you switch on, and if so you will have to exit from it to get the DOS prompt. To leave Windows you move the screen pointer to the box containing a minus sign in the top left corner of the screen, and then click on it with the mouse. You will then see a menu from which you can select 'close', or a message asking you to confirm that this is what you want. To leave a Windows-based application you proceed in the same way. For any other application you can usually exit by pressing the 'Esc' key once or twice and following any instructions that appear; if that doesn't work, and there is no advice on the screen, I'm afraid you'll have to read the manual.

Now take the disk marked 'Alone with a PC Master Disk', or your copy of it, and insert it in whichever disk drive it fits (use drive A if you have the choice). Type 'A:' (without the quotes, but including the colon) if the disk is in drive A, otherwise 'B:', and press the 'Enter' key (which may be marked only with a bent arrow). The letter in the prompt should change to A or B as appropriate.

Now type RE READ.ME and press the 'Enter' key. Instructions for installing and using the software will appear on the screen; you can move forwards or backwards through them by using the 'Page up' and 'Page down' keys, or the 'Home' and 'End' keys to get to the beginning or end. To remove the instructions from the screen press the 'Esc' key; the prompt should re-appear. To print out the instructions (they will take up less than 10 pages), make sure your printer is switched on and ready to print and then type PRINT READ.ME, and press the 'Enter' key. If you are asked a question about printer ports, just press the 'Enter' key. The instructions should then be printed. (Read the 'PRINT' section in the DOS manual and the instructions for your printer if you have any difficulty; if this fails, and you have joined the PCIUG, now is the time to ring them). Now just follow the instructions.

Your shareware bundle is now installed on your PC and the menu gives you access to each application. You can go straight into any of them and experiment; there should be enough information on the screen, and in the 'Help screens' which you can call up, to get you started (though note that the 'As Easy As' screen does not make it obvious that pressing the stroke key, '/', gives access to a further menu which includes 'Exit'). But sooner or later you will need to refer to the instructions for each application. These are contained in a file which has been installed in the same directory as the application, and can be read or printed out. You will find instructions for doing this in the 'READ.ME' file that you consulted when installing the bundle.

ORDER FORM

Alone with a PC - special offer

Copy this order form, and when completed send it to:

PC Independent User Group
87 High Street
Tonbridge
Kent TN9 1RX

or telephone the Group on 0732 771512 (or fax 0732 771513) with your credit card number, mentioning this book to obtain the special terms.

Tick the following as appropriate

❑ Please send me the Shareware Bundle on 3.5" disks
(price £14 including VAT and postage to UK or Europe)

❑ Please send me the Shareware Bundle on 5.25" disks
(price £14 including VAT and postage to UK or Europe)

❑ Please enrol me as a business member of PCIUG for six months
(Price £21.50 **plus VAT** at half the current rate)

❑ Please enrol me as a business member of PCIUG for 12 months
(price £39.00 **plus VAT** at half the current rate)

❑ Additional postage outside Europe; £2

And also tick one of the following:

❑ I enclose cheque/PO for £............ made out to PC Independent User Group

❑ Please charge to my credit card
Card number _____ expiry date _____
signature_____
Name on card, if not that given below _____

Please note that payment must be either in sterling or by credit card. If you wish to pay in any other way please contact PCIUG first; there may be an additional charge.

This offer is valid until the end of 1993. After this date, please ask PCIUG for the current prices.

Name and address for delivery:

Index

Entries refer to the subject described by the words indexed, not necessarily to the exact words.
Only significant entries are indexed; passing references are not – this applies particularly to
the terms 'Personal computer' and 'Windows', which are widely used throughout the book.

Words for the wise - from
Sigma Press

Sigma publish what is probably the widest range of computer books from any independent UK publisher. And that's not just for the PC, but for many other popular micros – Atari, Amiga and Archimedes – and for software packages that are widely-used in the UK and Europe, including Timeworks, Deskpress, Sage, Money Manager and many more. We also publish a whole range of professional-level books for topics as far apart as IBM mainframes, UNIX, computer translation, manufacturing technology and networking.

A complete catalogue is available, but here are some of the highlights:

Amstrad PCW
The Complete Guide to LocoScript and Amstrad PCW Computers – Hughes – £12.95
LocoScripting People – Clayton and Clayton – £12.95
The PCW LOGO Manual – Robert Grant – £12.95
Picture Processing on the Amstrad PCW – Gilmore – £12.95
See also Programming section for *Mini Office*

Archimedes
A Beginner's Guide to WIMP Programming – Fox – £12.95
See also: *Desktop Publishing on the Archimedes* and *Archimedes Game Maker's Manual*

Artificial Intelligence
Build Your Own Expert System – Naylor – £11.95
Computational Linguistics – McEnery – £14.95
Introducing Neural Networks – Carling – £14.95

Beginners' Guides
The New User's PC Book – Croucher – £12.95
Alone with a PC – Bradley – £12.95
The New User's Mac Book – Wilson – £12.95
PC Computing for Absolute Beginners – Edwards – £12.95

DTP and Graphics
Designworks Companion – Whale – £14.95
Ventura to Quark XPress for the PC – Wilmore – £19.95
Timeworks Publisher Companion – Morrissey – £12.95
Timeworks for Windows Companion – Sinclair – £14.95
PagePlus Publisher Companion – Sinclair – £12.95
Express Publisher DTP Companion – Sinclair – £14.95
Amiga Real-Time 3D Graphics – Tyler – £14.95
Atari Real-Time 3D Graphics – Tyler – £12.95

European and US Software Packages
Mastering Money Manager PC – Sinclair – £12.95
Using Sage Sterling in Business – Woodford – £12.95
Mastering Masterfile PC – Sinclair – £12.95
All-in-One Business Computing (Mini Office Professional) – Hughes – £12.95

Game Making and Playing
PC Games Bible – Matthews and Rigby – £12.95
Archimedes Game Maker's Manual – Blunt – £14.95
Atari Game Maker's Manual – Hill – £14.95
Amiga Game Maker's Manual – Hill – £16.95
Adventure Gamer's Manual – Redrup – £12.95

General

Music and New Technology – Georghiades and Jacobs – £12.95
Getting the Best from your Amstrad Notepad – Wilson – £12.95
Computers and Chaos (Atari and Amiga editions) – Bessant – £12.95
Computers in Genealogy – Isaac – £12.95
Multimedia, CD-ROM and Compact Disc – Botto – £14.95
Advanced Manufacturing Technology – Zairi – £14.95

Networks

$25 Network User Guide – Sinclair – £12.95
Integrated Digital Networks – Lawton – £24.95
Novell Netware Companion – Croucher – £16.95

PC Operating Systems and Architecture

Working with Windows 3.1 – Sinclair – £16.95
Servicing and Supporting IBM PCs and Compatibles – Moss – £16.95
The DR DOS Book – Croucher – £16.95
MS-DOS Revealed – Last – £12.95
PC Architecture and Assembly Language – Kauler – £16.95
Programmer's Technical Reference – Williams – £19.95
MS-DOS File and Program Control – Sinclair – £12.95
Mastering DesqView – Sinclair – £12.95

Programming

C Applications Library – Pugh – £16.95
Starting MS-DOS Assembler – Sinclair – £12.95
Understanding Occam and the transputer – Ellison – £12.95
Programming in ANSI Standard C – Horsington – £14.95
Programming in Microsoft Visual Basic – Penfold – £16.95
For **LOGO**, *see Amstrad PCW*

UNIX and mainframes

UNIX – The Book – Banahan and Rutter – £11.95
UNIX – The Complete Guide – Manger – £19.95
RPG on the IBM AS/400 – Tomlinson – £24.95

HOW TO ORDER

Order these books from your usual bookshop, or direct from:

SIGMA PRESS,
1 SOUTH OAK LANE,
WILMSLOW, CHESHIRE, SK9 6AR

PHONE: 0625 – 531035; FAX: 0625 – 536800

PLEASE ADD £1 TOWARDS POST AND PACKING FOR ONE BOOK.
POSTAGE IS FREE FOR TWO OR MORE BOOKS.

CHEQUES SHOULD BE MADE PAYABLE TO **SIGMA PRESS**.

ACCESS AND VISA WELCOME – 24 HOUR ANSWERPHONE SERVICE.